ASSIGNMENT IN
ISRAEL

ASSIGNMENT IN ISRAEL

Edited by

BERNARD MANDELBAUM

PUBLISHED BY

THE SEMINARY ISRAEL INSTITUTE

OF

THE JEWISH THEOLOGICAL SEMINARY OF AMERICA

DISTRIBUTED BY

HARPER & BROTHERS

NEW YORK

CONTENTS

INTRODUCTION

"For out of Zion shall go forth the Law; and the word of the Lord from Jerusalem" (Isaiah 2:3). The prophetic vision of justice and peace in a brotherhood of nations is projected for the end of days. The road to the idyllic heights follows a slow, tortuous route. At each new plateau of achievement, however, Zion and Jerusalem stand as signposts, pointing to a more just and peaceful future.

In today's world, a house divided between nations of "haves" and "have-nots," developed and backward, free and enslaved, justice demands that the under-privileged and oppressed be given opportunities for self-determination. Zion—modern Israel—has demonstrated what can be achieved by people who have the will for freedom and the courage to build a land and a nation. It is a dramatic story that has been written large in the headlines of our times. The real achievement, however, is the story behind the headlines. It is being written in smaller print by dedicated, hard-working, patient men and women in and out of the new State. *Assignment in Israel* reports a part of this story.

Israel's promise for the future and the drama of its past have captured the imagination of creative minds throughout the world. Many pioneers have contributed their energy and knowledge to the enterprise of building a state. Others have come to Israel's shores to learn from the living history unfolding before their eyes.

The reestablishment of the land of the Bible by the people of the Book has had special meaning for America, in whose founding the Bible played a central role. Many of the problems of a democratic society, which are faced by Americans, have their counterparts in Israel. In addition to their common tradition of freedom, Israel and America have the two most significant Jewish communities of the world.

The relationships between Israel and America place the new State in a unique historical and geographical position to serve as a bridge of understanding between East and West. In order to advance this goal, The Seminary Israel Institute of The Jewish Theological Seminary of America, was established on February 21, 1952, and was co-sponsored by the Jewish Agency for Israel and an invited group of institutions of learning and national organizations. The program of the Institute was formulated by Dr. Louis Finkelstein, Seminary Chancellor, as follows:

The purpose of The Seminary Israel Institute is to strengthen the spiritual and cultural bonds between the State of Israel and America; to offer Americans an interpretation of the spiritual and cultural values of the State of Israel; to foster an understanding of the potential role of the State of Israel as intermediary between the Orient and the Occident; and to help develop a recognition of the State of Israel as a spiritual center for Jewry everywhere.

The Seminary Israel Institute has sought to fulfill this fourfold purpose through the courses and lectures which it has conducted during the past nine years.

The theme of this volume was the lecture series delivered at the Institute's sessions in the Spring of 1959. All of its chapters reflect the personal association of fifteen Americans and one European with the ideas and events that created the modern State of Israel. Nonetheless, the essays merely suggest a small part of the remarkable story written in deeds by people from many nations, who have given of their life, insight, and energy in the fashioning of a new democracy. From the partial report recorded in this book, it is clear that many frontiers of achievement in the State of Israel remain to be conquered by creative talents. Each chapter has its implicit appeal that trained personnel in every specialty has endless opportunities for service to a thriving, growing community.

There is still another theme which all the chapters have in common. It is a theme that has proven to be of significance to many areas of the world: how to overcome the economic and social neglect of many centuries. The example of Israel's leap from a primitive, neglected land to a modern nation demonstrates what can be achieved. The chapters in this volume indicate what free people everywhere are prepared to do in service to their fellow man's quest for progress. Indeed, the activities of the authors of these chapters portray a new and affirmative world citizen, the American who labors to turn alien land to fruitful and constructive purpose.

We are grateful to the writers for what they did in Israel for the cause of freedom, as well as for their additional efforts in recording their experiences for inclusion in this volume. Their stories may inspire other Americans to emulate them. They have already inspired the Israelis to follow their example. For the most remarkable development in this record of international service through personal involvement is the role that Israelis are playing in giving of their own newly acquired knowledge and experience to other states faced by problems similar to their own.

The addresses of Dr. Greenberg, Mr. Klutznick, Dr. Mead, and Bishop Pike now appear in print for the first time. The other chapters were written especially for this book, with the exception of General Marshall's, which first appeared in Harper's magazine (October 1958).

Dr. Greenberg's opening chapter charts avenues of communication between the Jewish communities of America and Israel. In a later chapter, Governor McKeldin describes the interest of Americans of all faiths in such communication. Robert St. John and Waldo Frank demonstrate the special role of the literary figure in paving a highway of exchange of ideas and ideals.

The chapters of Bishop Pike, Dr. Davis and Dr. Mead describe areas of religious, historical and sociological interest, which are of mutual concern to America and Israel.

That the culture of a nation demands the inspiration of the creative soul is demonstrated by the chapters on the arts by Zino Francescatti, Anna Sokolow and Mitchell Fields.

The chapters by Leon J. Keyserling, James Plaut, Philip Klutznick and Walter C. Lowdermilk deal with the nation's breadbasket. The final chapter by Dore Schary serves as a kind of epilogue which captures the spirit of the people who carry out the tasks described in the earlier chapters.

One of the contributors to this volume is responsible for much more than a single chapter. Dr. Moshe Davis, one of the guiding spirits of The Seminary Israel Institute from its inception, conceived of the lecture series which resulted in this publication. I am deeply grateful to him for the invitation to serve as editor, and feel deeply indebted to him for his encouragement and guidance along the way.

Many friends and associates were generous with their time and suggestions in reading the chapters. Rabbi Jules Harlow was especially helpful in the editorial work. Miss Ida E. Westerman was tireless in her many administrative and editorial efforts. I am particularly grateful to Miss Ann Sprayregen for her compilation of the index, as well as her constructive comments in reviewing the manuscript.

The way to advance the prophetic goal, and to achieve world brotherhood is set forth by the men and women who record their experience here. They demonstrate that all men, despite differences of national loyalty and racial origin, have a responsibility to one another as brothers made in the image of One God. The Jewish communities of America and Israel, despite difference of national allegiance, embody this higher brotherhood in their relationship to one another. It is a pattern which can have many variations in uniting all the families of men in a world dedicated to human advancement.

BERNARD MANDELBAUM

New York City
September, 1960
Elul, 5720

I

CONTINUING ASSIGNMENT—BUILDING SPIRITUAL BRIDGES

SIMON GREENBERG

Among man's many endowments, none gives him a greater sense of fulfillment than does his power to communicate with his fellow man. It transforms an animal herd into a human society, and bestows upon human kinship its unique capacity to emancipate itself from bondage to blood and physical proximity. But it is this very power that all too often transforms individuals bound to one another by ties of heredity, history, geography, and destiny, into implacable enemies. For men can communicate not only their agreements but their differences as well. America's great folk philosopher Will Rogers once remarked that international conferences, convened with the hope of arriving at some common points of agreement, usually end with a greater clarification of the irreconcilable differences among the participants.

Because of this power of communication, and our pride in our own opinions, the threat of inner dissension hovers ominously over every people. Four score and seven years of common glorious historic experience, a common government and language, could not avert the tragedy of the American civil war. Lincoln's hope that "the mystic cords of memory stretching from every battlefield and patriot grave . . . will yet swell the chorus of the union when again touched . . . by the better angels of our nature," was not realized. For five blood-drenched years the existence of the nation hung precariously in the balance.

1

The constant nurturing of "the mystic chords of memory," those intangible spiritual bonds which bind one section of a nation to another, is of primary importance even to a people that lives upon a contiguous territory and under a common political government. How can we possibly overestimate its importance to the Jewish people, whose dispersed segments live under such vastly varying political, economic, and social conditions?

If I believed, as some do, that Jewish existence and unity depended upon anti-semitism in the past and will continue to be dependent upon it in the future, I would have little respect for our past, and even less interest in our future. It is my firm faith that we have succeeded, not merely in surviving, but in maintaining a considerable degree of unity amongst ourselves, despite the many obstacles that faced us, because each Jewish community, wittingly or unwittingly, was constantly building spiritual bridges between itself and all other Jewish communities.

What is a spiritual bridge? It is that which links two human beings in devotion to one another because they share a loyalty to something which they acknowledge to be greater and more precious than either of them, something which each one can claim wholly as his own without feeling that his ownership infringes upon the ownership of the other. A spiritual bridge is one on which human souls, venturing forth in search of understanding, love, and purpose, meet one another, recognize one another and forever after remain loyal companions. A spiritual bridge is that over which we travel without leaving our physical habitats.

The task of building such bridges was never an easy one, nor was it always performed with complete success. The sad truth that we dare never forget is that the fathers of the Jewish people repeatedly failed, and that we have paid dearly for their failure. The United Kingdom which David established 3000 years ago was hopelessly divided less than one hundred years after its establishment. Shortly after the triumphant re-establishment of the Jewish state by the Maccabees, sectarian movements developed within the Jewish community, dividing the people into irreconcilably hostile camps. The Karaite movement in the eighth century split our people into two vindictively antagonistic groups that never found the way back to mutual understanding.

The failures of our forefathers would have been far greater and more serious than they were during the centuries following the destruction of the Temple by the Romans had they not possessed one great advantage. There was widespread agreement among them regarding the nature of the spiritual bridge that they were called upon to erect, and regarding the pillars upon which that bridge was to rest. For let us bear this truth ever in mind: while spiritual bridges are in essence intangible, they require tangible moorings. During the seventeen centuries that elapsed between the destruction of the Temple and the opening of the modern era in Jewish history, it was universally acknowledged that the tangible moorings of the spiritual bridges that united the scattered Jewish communities were the synagogues. Each community planted such a mooring firmly in its midst. The tenuous but powerful over-arching spiritual structure connecting the widely scattered communities was thus provided with a tangible pier to which it could attach itself. The Synagogue was a living organism which spun out the fine threads of faith, emotion, aspiration, and memory, forming the substance of the spiritual bridge between Jew and Jew.

The opening of the modern era in Jewish history removed none of the old threats to the existence and the unity of the Jewish people. It added new ones. The blessings of political freedom, which enabled Jewish communities to integrate themselves more fully than ever into the larger cultural environment of which they were a part, tended to diminish the specifically Jewish element in their lives and to envelop that element with many and substantial cultural layers that were not the common property of all other Jewish communities. These outer cultural layers had to be penetrated before Jew could reach out to Jew. We in America discovered how great an impediment they are to Jewish mutual understanding—even when geographic distances are removed—when German Jew met Polish or Russian Jew on American soil. We are discovering it anew in the State of Israel where Jews coming from a vast variety of non-Jewish cultural backgrounds are seeking to rediscover the eternal bonds that unite them. Moreover, the revolutionary changes in the political, economic, social and intellectual life that swept over the Jewish communities of Europe during the past two centuries, violently shook and undermined the Synagogue, threatening with utter collapse the spiritual bridge which rested upon it. For a while it appeared as if the spiritual fabric of Jewish life would disintegrate, never to be rewoven.

Fortunately, long before the cataclysmic debacles that befell our people between 1914 and 1945, its most loyal and sensitive sons and daughters became aware of the danger. They heard the ominous echoes of the crumbling bridges. They saw the deep breeches in the old supporting towers. Some set themselves to the task of mending the towers of the bridges. Others abandoned them and determined to build new spiritual bridges, resting upon new supports. But of what were these to be made? Many answers were offered. The one that concerns us now consisted of two words—"territory" and "language." There were those who said "Any territory." There were others who said, "A modern European language." But the most creative and determined among them said, "The land of Israel and the Hebrew language." It was they who, in the last quarter of the 19th century, initiated the chain of events that a decade ago led to a Jewish community in Palestine capable of proclaiming itself a politically independent state.

This community differs from all contemporary Jewish communities in two basic aspects: 1) It exercises political sovereignty over a geographic area within whose boundaries it constitutes the majority population, and 2) the Hebrew language is the official language of its state, the vernacular of its citizens, and the vehicle through which the dynamic culture being fashioned by it finds literary expression.

While the Jewish community of the State of Israel was coming into being, the American Jewish community was also taking shape. It is unique in the annals of our history. Never before was there a Jewish community in the diaspora numerically so large, politically so free, and economically so soundly established. It is now self-evident to even the most casual observer that, insofar as it is given man to determine his future, the future of the Jewish people and the destiny of the State of Israel depend upon close and faithful cooperation between the Jewish community in Israel and the American Jewish community. Hence, every thoughtful observer of the Jewish scene should be profoundly disturbed by even the slightest indication that a chasm of misunderstanding or estrangement may be developing between them. Only the willfully blind will deny the evidence pointing to the possibility of such a development and even to its existence. No matter, therefore, how urgent any political or economic task may be, there can be no doubt that, from the long range point of view, no task is more important than that of building spiritual bridges between these two communities. How shall this be done? Let us start by defining our task negatively by pointing to a number of things that we should not do, or which we at least should transfer from the center to the distant periphery of our thought and action.

Chief among the things to be avoided is the passionate elaboration of the differences between us. We dwell upon them with a wellnigh pathological compulsion, broadening and deepening them in the process. Thus, for example, there is legitimate room for differences of opinion on the future role of the diaspora in Jewish history. But nothing significantly new has been said in this discussion for many a decade. The only thing added has been heat, without light. If we must continue this fruitless debate let us at least speak with the utmost possible awareness of the ultimate meaning of what we say. Let us not speak as if we actually hoped for the rapid liquidation of the American Jewish community or as if we believed that Jewish emigration from America to Israel is an act of treason either to America or to the American Jewish community. The truth of the matter is that no one of us, either in Israel or America wants to see the American Jewish community disappear either through inner disintegration or persecution. Nor does any one really believe that all or even half of the Jews of America can or will emigrate to the State of Israel within the next twenty-five years. No one is more outspoken than Premier David Ben-Gurion in this insistence upon the duty of every Jew who would describe himself

as a Zionist to settle or to plan to settle in the State of Israel. Yet
even he does not expect, and certainly does not hope for the early
or even the eventual dissolution of the Jewish diaspora, least of all,
of the Jewish community in America. Speaking in Jerusalem at the
historic occasion in May 1952 when Dr. Louis Finkelstein, in behalf
of the Jewish Theological Seminary, bestowed upon him the degree
of Doctor of Hebrew Letters Honoris Causa, Mr. Ben-Gurion said:
"The State of Israel is not intended merely for its residents, but for
the whole of the Jewish people, even for those who do not intend
to settle within its borders." Hence, regardless of how anxious
we may be for American Jewish immigration to the State of Israel,
or how sincerely concerned some may be about the future of the
Jew in America, let us agree that no debate is more barren of good
than the one which is based on the assumption that American Jewry
is doomed to a rapid disintegration.

On the other hand, no matter how sanguine we may be about the
future of Judaism and the Jews in America, let us not talk as if we
believed that the Jewish community in America can contribute as
much to the development of a distinctly Hebraic civilization in the
world as can the Jews in the State of Israel. On the occasion
previously referred to, Dr. Louis Finkelstein said, "It is our view
that Judaism does not have two centers in the world, but only one,
and that is the place in which the Lord delighted to dwell . . . It
is our fervent desire to be your partners in the common enterprise
whose center is located here in Jerusalem, and whose interests en-
compass the world." Above all, let us desist from name-calling and
from attributing mean motives to one another.

Nor does it help to create a true sense of brotherhood and equality
if we think of the State of Israel as a place chiefly for the persecuted
who have no other place to go, and of ourselves as their benefactors.
No one likes to be cast in the role of either the poor, inept relative
or the spiritually insensitive, materialistic rich uncle.

There can be no real spiritual bridges erected between communities whose best sons and daughters do not honestly and deeply
respect one another's integrity, and who do not view one another
as equally worthy members of the people whose spiritual treasures

are their common possession and to which both of them can make unique and indispensable contributions.

These "Thou-Shalt-Nots" are important, yet they are but the clearing of the approaches to the spiritual bridge and the preparation of the ground upon which its pillars are to be erected. The bridge itself will not rise unless we focus our attention upon the great need we have for it and unless we muster our resources for a long and incessant effort to build it.

I have pointed out that spiritual bridges, though tenuous and intangible, must rest upon substantial and tangible pillars. How are we to define these pillars? Firstly, they must be independent of the particularities of time and place. Secondly, they must embody the innermost spiritual essence that animates the life of both the American and the Israeli Jewish community. It is only as each of these communities plants firmly within its midst such visible pillars that we can hope for the rise of spiritual bridges that will bind us to one another with bonds that are lighter than air but stronger than steel.

What is the most tangible evidence of the unique quality of the spiritual life of our brethren in Israel? The political institutions of the State of Israel, its knesset, its courts, and its political party structure are tangible embodiments of spiritual qualities, but we can neither transplant nor effectively imitate them, for they derive from the privileges and powers inherent in political sovereignty.

The economic institutions and patterns of a society also embody spiritual qualities, but it seems obvious that the American Jewish community will not look to Israel for models for its own economic life. The *kibbutz* is the most inspiring economic expression of the spiritual ideals animating a very large segment of the Israeli Jewish community. However, it is far from being universally representative of it, and infinitely farther from being a possible form of expression for the economic life of any substantial portion of American Jewry.

I have frequently heard the opinion that personal involvement of American Jews in the economic life of the State of Israel should become the significant pillar upon which to erect the bridge between them. Every American Jew who has the means, should, to be sure, own State of Israel bonds, and should invest in some specific economic enterprise in Israel. But, in my opinion, looking to stocks and bonds as the chief building blocks for the bridge between American and Israeli Jewry borders upon the sacrilegious. It will be a sad day when American Jewry's concern for the welfare of the State of Israel will be motivated primarily by concern for the capital it has invested in Israel's economy.

There is only one factor in the life of the Israeli Jewish community which, more than any other, embodies its innermost spiritual quality and which can be appropriated by the Jews of America: the Hebrew language. The revival of Hebrew in Israel concretizes more dramatically than any other single phenomenon the spiritual vitality that was at the core of the Zionist movement, and epitomizes in unmistakable terms the essential quality of this vitality.

Language is always more than a means for intelligent communication. In the case of the Jewish people, during the last century, the renaissance of Hebrew symbolized the final and irrefutable vindication of the proposition that Judaism is as broad as the life of the mind and the soul, and that it welcomes all truth, all beauty, and all goodness. In Israel the language of Scripture has become the language of the market place as well, exemplifying the essential unity of the two which was intended and which should prevail.

But while the Hebrew language is the key that opens the door to the innermost soul of the Jewish community being fashioned in the State of Israel, and is at the center of cultural and spiritual life there, it belongs to United States Jewry as much as it belongs to the Israelis. We have an inescapable duty to claim it and to make it a most treasured possession. For Hebrew is one of the pillars upon which any spiritual bridge to be built between us and our Israeli brethren must firmly rest. It is a tower which the Israel community has lovingly and self-sacrificingly erected. If we fail to erect a sturdy tower of living Hebrew in our midst, then the spiritual bridge which our Israeli brethren project towards us will never be completed, for there will be no tower amongst us to which it might be moored. It will remain suspended in mid air.

Obviously, Hebrew cannot play the same all-pervasive role in the life of the American Jew that it plays in the life of the Israeli Jew. But our community life can be so structured, our educational system can be so directed, and our personal lives can be so fashioned that the place of high priority which Hebrew occupies within them would be easily recognizable. The Hebrew spice must be readily distinguishable by any one who tastes any aspect of Jewish life in America so that an Israeli Jew may at once sense a spiritual kinship between himself and his American Jewish brother. Every American Jew should know Hebrew well enough to feel at home amidst the Hebrew signs and sounds of the streets of Tel-Aviv and Jerusalem even though he may never be in a position to visit them. Some people have the attitude that the Hebrew language's one natural and possible habitat is the State of Israel. If this should become the dominant attitude in American Jewish life, we would abdicate our rights to the heritage which is equally the possession of Jews everywhere, namely the vast spiritual treasures of Hebrew literature from the days of the Bible to our own day. By doing this, we would reject the conception of Judaism as an all-embodying intellectual and spiritual experience. To our brethren in Israel, this will mean more than merely a rejection of a language. They will intuitively and correctly sense in it a rejection of them as well.

It is no simple or easy matter to give to Hebrew a center place in our lives in this country. It will require of us a quality of devotion and of spiritual, if not physical heroism bordering on the devotion and heroism of the men and women who revived the Hebrew language, who built the Emek,[1] and who are now pouring their heart's substance into the Negev.[2] This effort will identify us more intimately with the travail of the hundreds of thousands who, in Israel today, are struggling to acquire a mastery of Hebrew. Let us not imagine that the acquisition of Hebrew by the new immigrants in Israel is a simple process. We know the difficulties of our own fathers and mothers in their struggles with the English language. We are living in the generation of the great return. Not all of us can return physically to the land of Israel. But we can all

---

[1] Hebrew for "valley"—refers to northern Israel, region of the valley of Jezreel.
[2] The southern region of Israel.

return to the language of Israel. Not all of us can be *ḥalutzim* in Sdeh Boker.[3] But we can all be *ḥalutzim* in an Ulpan.[4] It will be striking evidence of our determination to maintain a rich Jewish life here, and of our willingness to give not only of our funds, but of ourselves, even as they do, for our common spiritual heritage.

If we mean to give to Hebrew a high place of priority on the American Jewish scene, we will have to reverse the current trend in Jewish elementary and secondary education, and increase rather than diminish the amount of time we expect our children to devote to their Hebrew studies. This will require an intensification of our efforts to introduce Hebrew as the second language in the Jewish home, and of the establishment of Hebrew Foundation Schools and elementary and secondary all-day schools, in which Hebrew has a fair opportunity to be studied under favorable conditions. With the renewed interest in language studies in our high schools and universities, we should do far more than what has been done to encourage the introduction of courses in Hebrew in the high schools and universities and to persuade our children to attend these courses.

Nor should any effort be spared to enable boys and girls of high school and college age to spend a year of study in the schools of the State of Israel so that they may acquire a basic knowledge of the language in its most natural setting. Above all, we must increase the number of Hebrew summer camps such as Massad and Ramah. There should be a hundred such camps in the United States and Canada. Such summer camps crystallize the Hebrew educational program of our congregational and communal schools. They will prepare the student for our institutions of higher Jewish learning. These camps furnish the most natural setting for the introduction into American Jewish life of the literature, the dance, the drama, the music, and the arts and crafts being developed in Israel, upon the folk level as well as on a more sophisticated level. Through the camps, these creative forces can reach into hundreds of Jewish

[3] Kibbutz in the Negev, the frontier of the growing State of Israel.
[4] A type of school in Israel offering an intensive course in the Hebrew language for non-Hebrew-speaking youths and adults.

communities and into the personal lives of hundreds of thousands of Jews. Only thus can we give a final answer to the question of whether or not Jewish life on this continent has the possibility of acquiring a significant Hebrew coloration. Only thus can we erect in our midst that pillar which embodies the innermost spiritual essence of the new Jewish life arising in the State of Israel.

Is there anything in the life of the American Jewish community which parallels the role of Hebrew in the life of Israeli Jewry? I believe there is. I believe that in America the Synagogue is the chief tangible vehicle of the uniquely Jewish and the essentially spiritual component of the life of the Jewish community. The conditions of political freedom, legal equality, and economic opportunity under which we in America live have inevitably and benignly resulted in our integration into American life. Our non-Jewish fellow citizens think of us as a community founded upon a religious principle and associate all of us with the Synagogue, whether we are individually affiliated with it or not. An increasing number amongst us are affiliated with the Synagogue, and identify it with the principle that gives meaning and significance to our Jewish identity. Hence even as our Israeli brethren project their spiritual life towards us via the Hebrew language, we project our spiritual life towards them via the Synagogue.

If our brethren in Israel, therefore, are to contribute towards the maintenance of the spiritual bridges between us, they must keep in good repair the pillar of the Synagogue at their terminal of the bridge. Israeli Jews should not speak of the Synagogue in terms that are carbon copies of the opinions expressed by many American Jews about the Hebrew language. Israeli Jews in all stations of life have told me repeatedly that while we in America need the Synagogue to identify ourselves as Jews, they in Israel do not require such self-identification. Hence they do not need the Synagogue.

The role of the Synagogue, thus interpreted, declares it to be essentially a diaspora institution, and as such it carries a stigma for many an Israeli. However, though the Synagogue may have had its origin among the exiles in Babylon, it developed its full stature in the land of Israel during the Second Commonwealth when the

Jews there enjoyed either political independence or at least spiritual autonomy. Even as the Hebrew language is more than a means of communication, so the Synagogue is more than a means of group identification. If the Hebrew language in Israel today symbolizes Judaism's universality of cultural interest, the Synagogue symbolizes Judaism's message to mankind, its rootedness in a world outlook associated with a conception of God, unique in the annals of human history, and its message of hope and faith, of courage and purpose to the individual human soul. The Synagogue is no more the exclusive possession of diaspora Jewry than Hebrew is of Israeli Jewry. Hence it is to be regretted beyond words that the renascent Hebrew civilization in the State of Israel, so creative in many aspects of Jewish life, has thus far been virtually barren in the realm of the Synagogue, and all that it represents in the history and the aspirations of our people.

It would serve little purpose to apportion blame for this situation or to justify it. But it should be a matter of great concern to all of us that the Synagogue, which to the American Jew is the chief institution for Jewish self-expression, is presented to him in Israel as an item on a tourist's itinerary to which he pays a hurried visit in order to observe what to him may appear as bizarre customs brought from distant lands. The institution through which the American Jew visiting Israel should make contacts with his Israeli brethren on the deepest spiritual levels and in a manner that would most effectively carry over into his life when he returns to the States, is not equipped to fulfill its most significant function. The Synagogue in all Jewish communities must eventually take the place it holds in the life of the American Jewish community. For the Synagogue, despite its obvious and well-advertised shortcomings, continues to embody the spiritual essence of the *raison d'être* of Jewish communities throughout the world. No Jewish community has ever succeeded in creating a long-term meaningful existence for itself centered in an institution other than the Synagogue.

The most heralded large scale attempt to organize such a Jewish community has been made in our time in Soviet Russia. The failure, and the causes and the consequences of that failure, constitute a chapter in Jewish history second only to the one written by the Nazis, in the scope and depth of its tragedy. Despite four decades of barbarous and unrelenting persecution of the Synagogue, the only evidences of Jewish group life still found among the Jews of Soviet Russia are associated with it. It is the only place where a visitor in Russia can find some semblance of a living Jewish community. It was therefore tragic indeed to read the report of the experiences of young Israelis who on their recent visit to Russia could not make full use of the one opportunity they had to reach out to their Jewish brethren there, because these youth were strangers to the one institution in which the Russian Jews could as a community receive them—namely, the Synagogue. The inside of a Synagogue and its ritual were as strange to those Israelis as the inside of a Hebrew book is to most American Jewish youths.

In my opinion, the failure of the Synagogue and what it represents to find its proper place in the education of the entire youth of Israel is largely responsible for the wide-spread phenomenon which is disturbing Israeli educators so deeply—the lack in so many of the best Israeli youth of identification with the totality of the Jewish people of the past and of the present. The geographical and chronological parochialism which is all too prevalent among them, was poignantly summarized by the Yiddish poet and essayist H. Leivick in a report of his conversation with a young *sabra* who had participated in the Sinai campaign. With deep emotion, the young man poured forth his innermost convictions. "The members of the old generation (of Israelis), though they are citizens of Israel, belong emotionally with you. Like you, they are history-conscious or religion-conscious Jews. Like you, they are still either *Kiddush Hashem* [5] or *Kiddush Haam* Jews.[6] But I, and those like me, are simply Jews and nothing more. We, who were born here, pride ourselves in the one great merit which we possess; we were born here. It is a merit bestowed upon us by nature. We require no other. Because of it, I participated in the Sinai campaign

[5] Sanctification of God's name through personal action.
[6] Sanctification of the Jewish people through personal action.

and if necessary I will be ready to participate in other campaigns to defend and save my homeland. For it I am ready to give my life. For it and not for anything else. . . . I know you will accuse me of trying to identify myself with the pre-Israelite Canaanites. But I tell you it is not so. I am not, nor do I want to be, a Canaanite. I need neither idols nor gods. I need not exist by virtue of my pedigree. My own personal reputation is enough for me. I need not skip generations nor leap into the bosom of any previous generation, be it that of Isaiah or Joshua. What I am is enough for me. Let all the gods leave us alone."

Israeli educators propose to correct this unfortunate development by introducing into the curriculum an area of studies to be known as "Jewish consciousness" or "Jewish self-identification." It would include courses in the history and the institutions of the diaspora, in which a course on the customs of this Synagogue would be included. All of this should undoubtedly be most helpful. But the classroom itself cannot achieve the hoped for transformation. There must be an institution with which an individual can be identified all his life, one which would concretize and embody within itself this sense of unity in space and time, not only with the Jewish people but with the highest ideals of all mankind. The Synagogue is the only institution that can fulfill this function, for at its core is a message of eternal and universal import, responding to the needs of the individual human soul.

The Synagogue in Israel is far from fulfilling the purposes we envision for it. Our brethren there will have to exercise at least as much courage and creativity in restoring the Synagogue to a place of centrality in their spiritual life as they exercised when they transformed Hebrew into their language of daily discourse and as we will have to exercise if we are to Hebraize our own lives. In this task we may perhaps be more helpful to them than we were in their herculean efforts to revive Hebrew. But it is a task which will have to be done by them primarily, even as the Hebraization of American Jewish life is a task that will have to be done by us primarily.

If these gigantic tasks are to be pursued with any hope of success and with any degree of intelligence, there must be constant and intensive contacts between those in both communities who are most aware of the need and who mean to devote themselves most persistently to the meeting of that need. It is with that in mind that the Jewish Theological Seminary, the United Synagogue, and the Rabbinical Assembly of America have decided to erect in Jerusalem a center that would vividly testify to the spiritual ties that exist between the land of Israel and the entire people of Israel. We hope that every one preparing himself for the American rabbinate or for leadership in American Jewish education will live at least for one year at this center and attend either the Hebrew University or other schools of higher Jewish learning in Jerusalem. It is our hope that students from Israel or from other Jewish communities, who are also preparing for educational or religious leadership would share quarters with our students in our center. The future leaders of the Jewish people throughout the world should be given the opportunity to live together during their formative years in the shadow of the prophets and the sages of old, so that in friendship and in an atmosphere of utter honesty and devotion, they may probe one another's deepest levels and together forge the bonds of spiritual understanding and conviction.

I do not delude myself into believing that there is anything which can guarantee any people absolute protection against disintegration from within. Every people faces that danger constantly, the Jewish people perhaps more so than others. Nor do I imagine that, if all Jews spoke Hebrew and all Jews were loyal members of the Synagogue, peace, tranquility, and idyllic mutual understanding would follow. I can easily envision most acrimonious controversy carried on in perfect Hebrew by Jews adorned with *tallit* [7] and *tefillin*.[8] But, to return to the metaphor which is the title of this chapter—spiritual bridges, moored to Hebrew and the Synagogue, can, I believe, stand up under the most violent storms of controversy. Nor do I believe that any other moorings can replace these. If these moorings should disappear, the bridge would

[7] Prayer shawl.
[8] See glossary.

collapse completely and the winds of controversy would cease blowing for there would be nothing to stir them into motion; the silence of death would descend upon the scene.

It is that silence which above everything else our people has dreaded and successfully has held at bay for thousands of years. More than two millenia ago they sang—"We shall not die but live and proclaim God's glory." [9] To proclaim a message to mankind requires a language; to proclaim God's glory implies that we make Him a sanctuary.[10] Hebrew is the language of our proclamation. God is the theme. The Synagogue is the sanctuary. Wherever and whenever Jews in the sanctuaries proclaim God's message in Hebrew, they not only bring benediction to man, but simultaneously do they build for themselves spiritual bridges which storms cannot destroy nor time corrode.

[9] Psalms 118:17.
[10] Let them make Me a sanctuary, that I may dwell in their midst . . . Exodus 25:8.

2

RELIGIONS IN ISRAEL

JAMES A. PIKE

For almost 1900 years—since the year 70—the Jewish people have existed as a minority group in most of the world's countries. This fact emphasizes one of the unique qualities of the Jews of present day Israel: they constitute a majority group.

In Christianity, there is a doctrine called "original sin," symbolized by the Adam and Eve story, and there are certain strains of this same thought in Jewish theology. It means that there is a tendency toward the abuse of power. As Lord Acton put it, power corrupts, and absolute power corrupts absolutely. Minority groups are often better about matters like religious freedom than the majority groups are. It is just due to the nature of the human animal. It is not because of being Jewish or being European or being American. It is just the way we tend to be.

In the Ottoman Empire, there was clear evidence of an attempt to maintain a pluralistic society, i.e., to allow each group to have its own community organization and peculiar customs, religious or otherwise. Whether this was due to some generosity on the part of the Turks or whether it was the only way they could manage this large, loose area (which was not well administered anyway), is difficult to establish. But in the thinking of the Islamic Turk, in the thinking of early Judaism itself, and in the thinking of Christianity until recent centuries, the idea of the *individual's* religious freedom never occurred to anybody. People were to be treated in groups. In the Middle East there was the "millet" concept—you live where you were born, with your family and your relatives. Occasionally someone might go away, like the Prodigal Son, but it was expected that he would return. The group is to be treated as a group. Hence, if the group is Moslem-Arabic in background, that is all it ever will be. If it is Jewish in background, it will remain so.

When this kind of thought developed, there was not the great variety in types of Judaism that we see in this country. True, there were small sects and groups with different liturgical emphases, but in general, if you were talking about Jews, you were talking about Orthodox Jews—at least, in that part of the world.

A modern American Jew might happen upon a book of Mary Baker Eddy and decide after serious reflection that he wanted to be a Christian Scientist. This possibility would not have been understood in the Ottoman Empire. Without regard to what he thought, a Jew remained a Jew. Therefore, he would worship as a Jew, and his family affairs, matters of inheritance, adoption, divorce and custody of children would be worked out in the same framework.

This point of view was a reflection of reality. In the decades preceding the foundation of the State of Israel, very few individual Jews made independent religious decisions. Therefore it created no real deflection, either in the cultural pattern or in the legal structure.

The British mandate inherited this system from the Ottoman Empire and continued it. To be more specific, it meant that everything in relationship to worship, family law, wills and estates were governed within the religious group. The state law had nothing to say about any of this, except where occasionally collateral enforcement was needed, in which case the civil courts or the civil administrators would play their part.

It is important to realize this because some people who do not like the peculiar system which exists in Israel today have blamed Israel. Actually, Israel made no innovations. The system is derived from British mandate and Ottoman Empire policy.

If you are Greek Orthodox and you want to remarry after a divorce, that is the business of the Greek Orthodox Bishop's ecclesiastical court. The State could not care less. If you are a Roman Catholic, then the law governing your affairs in that realm which I have defined is settled through the Roman Catholic Church. If you are a Jew, it is through the rabbinical courts.

Difficulties exist today because, first, there are a good many people who make religious switches, and second, there are those who are unaffiliated. The latter is especially true of the ethnically Jewish group in Israel. There are many of the population who are not religious Jews. I must qualify that right away. I have come to learn that almost every Jew in Israel is more religious than he himself realizes. I refer to the degree to which the Bible and the whole tradition are not only in the blood on account of inheritance, but in the air—an important part of conversation and a kind of basis of almost everything military and political. This is not only because of the very thorough education on these subjects in the state schools, but it penetrates the whole culture.

Some young intellectual Jews in Tel Aviv once told me, "With us it's just a culture." I believed them. But since then, as I have thought more deeply and at greater length, I have come to realize that it is more than that. Such Jews are really more Jewish, even religiously speaking, than they admit to be.

Difficulties arise under the legal system in Israel for a man who does not classify himself as a Jew religiously. If he wants to follow some course in life which is not in accord with Jewish law, he is rather resentful when he suddenly finds himself in a *rabbinical* court, especially if the decision reached is not in his favor.

Mr. Justice Olshan, the Chief Justice of the Supreme Court of Israel, was kind enough to send me the full text of a most interesting court decision that highlights this point. I know this court quite well. I have met at least four of the justices in Jerusalem and I must say it is one of the most remarkable courts in existence, made up of distinguished legal scholars from all parts of the world. Israeli Arabs have told me that regardless of their unhappiness with certain phases of the policy of the government, particularly that of the military government in Galilee, they would trust their lives to the

Supreme Court of Israel. The court has justified that trust. A number of times it has decided against the government in favor of Arab citizens.

This decision has to do with a gentleman named Cohen who was not religious. However, because his name was Cohen, there was a presumption that he was of priestly descent (the Hebrew word for "priest" is *ḳohen*), and therefore, under rabbinical law, had to be regarded as a priest. This could not be proven but, unfortunately, it was very difficult for him to prove that he was not. Therefore the rabbinical authorities decided that the presumption was against him. As a result of this, he was not able to marry a divorcee, because according to Jewish law, a priest may not marry such a woman.

Mr. Cohen was very fond of the lady and after some time, they appeared before a town clerk to announce, "We're married." The clerk, oblivious of any future complications, recorded the event. Thus they were able to say, "We have declared before a civil official that we are married." How would the court work out this problem? Since the couple were Jews, though not religiously, there was no other place for them within the pluralistic arrangement. They were not Roman Catholics, they were not Greek Orthodox, and they were not Moslems. There seemed to be no place for them at all.

Forty long pages record the court's attempt to find a way out. They found that the couple was married. It has been suggested that the way to solve future problems is to provide the opportunity for civil marriage. Politically this is not feasible. In order to maintain a government coalition of the present type, it has been essential that the two Jewish Orthodox parties be represented. Otherwise, other parties would have had to be taken in which would create other problems, such as one or two of the Communist-oriented groups (splinter groups which have now very little effect in orienting the nation toward either the East or the West, but, which, if they were represented in the government would be influential) or the Herut party.

If orthodoxy *today* would propose to the government that a

system be inaugurated whereby the rabbinical courts controlled as much of the lives of all of Israel's ethnic Jews as it already does, I doubt that it would be accepted. Actually, the orthodox are simply holding out against changing a very old system—one that they did not inaugurate. By analogy it is very much like the peculiar problem about contraception in Connecticut and in Massachusetts. If the Roman Catholic Church today tried to pass legislation making contraception illegal in the New England states, it would not have a chance in the world of passing. But unfortunately, the Puritans put in a law that later was able to be interpreted against the use of contraceptive devices for planning of parenthood. Now in the attempt to change it, one faces a very strong, very well-organized minority, and one cannot get it changed.

I will say one good word, too, for the "millet" concept. I am the last person to deny the importance of an individual's right to change his religious allegiance. I was raised as a Roman Catholic, became an agnostic, and now I am an Anglican. I hope to remain in that faith until I die. However, though I believe in that individual right, any responsible view of biblical theology in any of the traditions I have mentioned does see us as *corporately involved*. Religion is not merely a matter of an individual's reading his books and saying his prayers. It is a family. In the New Testament we call the Church the Body of Christ, with many members, arms, legs, fingers, and eyes. In the Old Testament, understanding of the people of the Covenant is like this too. This is very deeply ingrained in biblical religion.

I do not oppose the ancient theological concept which has brought about the difficulty, but I have explained the more recent historical background as well as the current political factors so we may sensitively and sympathetically look at some of the difficulties.

The first has been already suggested—the problem of those whose own religious choices have led them outside of the Jewish religious community but who still find themselves involved in its legal and canonical machinery.

Second, the type of Orthodox Judaism which has expressed itself in Israel has often taken an obscurantist turn of mind which has often put off many thoughtful people of this generation and some of the last. In other words, with only one Jewish religious alternative of any significance, the choice is unfortunately either Orthodox Judaism or nothing. Possibly Jews could study the interesting Druse religion; maybe they could become Christians, and a few do; but in practice, there really is no option. Thus, there is only *one* way of expressing religious feeling or religious ideas, belief in God, or other fundamental matters of the Bible and of the whole Jewish religion. This has resulted in a widespread negative reaction to Judaism. However, it is not really a reaction against Judaism; it is a negative reaction to certain aspects of the only kind of Judaism generally available in Israel.

This is, I believe, unfortunate for the religious future of the country. I state this not as an attack against Orthodox Judaism, for I would be very unhappy if it were not represented in Israel. However, I do believe that a variety of real options should be available.

Let me say that in our Christian world we work hard for Church unity. We have all kinds of conferences and we try—a lot of us do, at least—to be ecumenical. We say, "It is against the will of God that the Church is disunited." But, sometimes I consider it fortunate that we are not completely united for, if we were, I would be afraid of the resulting institution. I pray for unity and I fear its possible result!

I do believe, that on the whole, man being what he is with the temptations to power, a set of choices is probably more wholesome. It is good for the individual so that he won't throw out the baby with the bath water, as he often does when he rejects a particular form of religion. A variety of groups also benefits the dominant group—because nothing is so healthy as other groups in a somewhat competitive and critical position.

The solution of Israel's problem is not for me to offer. It should come from within the Jewish tradition. It is quite obvious that American Reform and Conservative "Jewish missionaries" cannot as such be sent to Israel. Judaism does not work that way. Also it would look a little bit like American imperialism. Yet, I wish

Conservative and Reform Judaism were there. For this reason, I am very glad about the recent plans of the Jewish Theological Seminary and the Hebrew Union College for centers of studies there. Their own students will be going over, so that at least there will be serious religious students there, talking to those who have chosen alternative ways. Of course they are not alternatives in the sense of a complete split: there is great common ground in teaching, in loyalties, and in worship. Conservative and Reform Judaism present alternatives to the Israeli Jew who has rejected the Orthodox synagogue.

The development of this possibility is very important for two reasons. First, the tremendous enthusiasm, pioneer spirit, courage and perseverance that you find in Israel makes a visitor feel that he is back in the days of early America. It reminds me too of the great confidence that problems can be met that I felt when I was an attorney with the early New Deal. I had no religion at that time; that almost was my religion. We felt we were knights on white horses. We were going to get everything done. I was with the Securities and Exchange Commission; by next Tuesday we were going to have the market all straightened out. We did not; but the point is that you do not need a formally professed religion to have that kind of enthusiasm. The fruitage of a deep religious rootage continues to bloom for quite a while after the flower has been cut off from the roots. But eventually, the flower will wither and die. If you give me a nice carnation today, I may be able to salvage it and use it again tomorrow. But by the day after tomorrow it will be looking rather poorly. Three days from now I will throw it out. Religious roots are needed for Israel's continued flowering.

Second, the individuals themselves need the transcendent level of religious influence. They need to be conscious of the things they believe and stand for, in addition to the unconscious reception and expression of it which undoubtedly exists. This will make for their salvation as persons, and will nourish the ideals of the young people.

I do not at all mean this as a negative estimate. I know of the real religious devotion of at least 20 or 25 per cent of the population, plus a wide range of real religious influence that cannot be measured. There are beginnings of certain religious options, along the lines I have suggested. However, I think that friends of Israel concerned also with the future of Judaism must think of this problem.

Non-Jewish religious groups—Christian, Moslem, or Druse—enjoy complete freedom as far as the official position of the state is concerned. But there are two factors which seem to delimit the place and role of these groups. One of these factors stems from human nature and the other results from a fault of the religious groups themselves.

As an example of the latter, I shall draw from the experiences of my particular group. There are about ten Anglican parishes in Israel. (In the United States our group is generally called Episcopal, since the word "Anglican" did not sound very well here after the Revolutionary War.) Some of our parishes are English-speaking, but most of them are Arabic-speaking. One, in Jerusalem, is a combination of English and Hebrew-speaking. This is not due to the presence of many Hebrew Anglicans. Rather it arose because many of the Jerusalem parish's visitors are scholars who are familiar with Hebrew and who want at least part of the service to be in the language of Jerusalem.

These Churches are under the jurisdiction of the Archbishop of Jerusalem, whose seat is in Jordan, at St. George's Cathedral. Due to lack of adequate support from the home base in England, and due to a slow adaptation to the change of the governmental lines after 1948, I am afraid that we are not equipped with an adequate ministry there.

Until recently, we had only two priests to serve all of Israel's Anglican Arabs, and now we have only one. We have no candidates from Israel in seminaries; we have not raised men for a future ministry there. I have corresponded with the Archbishop and his predecessor, stating, "I will find the money in America to place one or two of these Arab Israelis in any seminary which you designate, if you will find them." But none with adequate academic background has yet been found.

I mention this not because I want to castigate my own Church. But when some of our members state—"Well, we're practically dying out in Israel," I have had to reply, "Whose fault is it?" Nobody stopped us. There is no official blockage from Israel's point of view. A prominent Arab in America recently charged that Israel has refused to return Anglican properties to the Church. I checked both with the Israel Ministry for Religious Affairs (through Dr. Chaim Wardi, its official for Christian matters) and with the Archbishop in Jordan, and I found that Israel has been ready to transfer the property. However, our Church has not designated to whom the property should be transferred, and in the meantime Israel is paying the income to the Archbishop for the work of the Church. I suspect that if one looked at a number of situations where it would seem as though Christian bodies are suffering from the 1948 arrangements, it might turn out to be, in part at least, the given Church's fault.

On the other hand, it is true that it has been rather difficult for a Jew to become an Anglican or other kind of Christian. Any majority group, when strongly entrenched, finds it difficult to accept the fact of conversion away from it. This is true not only in Israel. It is true in Boston as well. For example, a Roman Catholic in Boston politics who decided to become an Episcopalian would not be in politics very long. This is, again, the human nature factor. I do not endorse it; I do not like it anywhere; but it is a fact.

There is in Israel a wonderful system for judicial protection of civil rights. The Supreme Court is also the High Court of Justice, with primary jurisdiction in civil rights, on which cases it must decide within fifteen days after they are presented. In this country, one might wait months or even years before seeing a case through the courts, and during that time social progress has been held up in one particular realm or another. The fifteen day ruling is one of the most admirable aspects of the Israeli judicial system.

A few years ago in Israel, a young Jewish lady became a Roman Catholic. She was fired from her civil service job. She took it to court. The Supreme Court said in effect: "Reinstate her with all back pay. She can become anything she wants to become." Thus the official government position clearly allows religious liberty in Israel, with freedom to change religious allegiance.

The communities who are still somewhat in the true "millet" situation present no problems to the state whatsoever, nor does the state present problems for them. In other words, Israel is in transition, with the old Ottoman Empire plan really working in some places. But with the increased mobility of society, and with the growth of secular thought, we see the old system not working as well as it did when everybody was really in his place, unable and unlikely to change his position.

An example of where the old system works is found in the Druse communities on Mount Carmel, which I had the privilege of visiting. This is an almost completely self-contained community. They are an esoteric group, in the sense that nobody can see their services of worship or observe their liturgy. As religion it is a mixture of Jewish, Christian and Moslem facets. But strangely enough, it claims to have "apostolic succession" (to use an Anglican term), all the way back to Jethro, Moses' father-in-law. I did not press the chief priest there about the details of that succession and would be very surprised if it turned out to be historically true. In fact, it is a medieval movement that has been somewhat eclectic about various Middle East religions. It resembles a New England Puritan community near the time of the origins of our country, where church, state, ethics, social life, marriage and law came under one heading.

Many of the religious communities in Israel would not raise the questions that we are asking. It is important to realize that. I taught in the field of church-state relations for six years at Columbia Law School, and some of the foreign students could not even understand the questions we were discussing. The questions are obvious to Americans only because we are used to a pluralistic society in which civil decision is one thing and religious choice is another.

We had an Iranian graduate student in our Church-State Seminar several years ago. After two or three class sessions he finally said, "I do not understand what you mean by church-state relations."

The hyphen troubled him. In his country, the Islamic arrangement is determined by the Shah. His decree is dogmatically the will of God. There is no leverage by which to judge whether he said the right thing or not. Religion does not serve the prophetic function to which we are accustomed, saying for example, that a governmental decision against the will of God is a bad thing.

Israel must evolve its system of church-state relations in an area of the world with traditions which are strange to the West. Thus our criticism should be tempered with an understanding of the area's long and involved background. In addition, a new nation seeking national unity and beset with many problems, both external and internal, is not entirely free to settle the problem of religious liberty in an ideal way.

Despite these problems, the general atmosphere is that of a free country. There is free discussion of religion among people of different faiths. Problems that sometimes appear to be the results of religious divisions often result from other factors. One such issue is the treatment of the Arabs in Galilee (which, happily, has been much improved). It is not a problem of the *religion* of the Arabs. It is not that they are Moslems and Christians, while the majority are Jews. I realize that unconscious prejudices do exist (as everywhere); but there is nothing of this on the surface of things.

The problem does not derive from any sense of ethnic, educational or economic superiority over the Arab on the part of the Jew. I saw nothing of that. What I did sense was a nervousness about the fact that people living near the border look very much like those living across the border. We are all like that. All Japanese tend to look alike to westerners, and so during the Second World War we put all West Coast Japanese in concentration camps, regardless of their loyalty or disloyalty. To the Jewish people, an Arab is an Arab (they nearly all dress in the same standard fashion), and it is very hard to know in a given situation whether the enemy has arrived or whether these are citizens just having a frolic. Sometimes the State of Israel has been overly cautious in limiting the internal freedom of its Arab citizens. I am not hesitant in this criticism of Israel, because many Jews within the State of Israel are of this same opinion (and it should be noted that they are free to state it in print). Good reforms often have come because of this internal urge for reform.

The final solution, of course, will come when there can be real peace and real borders. I have no fear myself for the future of the Arab in Israel once there is a permanent context where this over-cautiousness will no longer be necessary. The fact is that during the Sinai campaign, the Israeli Arabs did not show any signs of disloyalty to their nation. I do think, too, that the resentments of the Arabs will slowly abate as they see they have more freedom and more opportunity for work and more chance to move about in Israel.

It is fair to say that while there are still inequities, the Arab in Israel, by and large, is better off than the Arab almost anywhere else in the Middle East, in terms of opportunities for education and health and opportunities to become part of a nation that has a real future. The large-scale planning in Israel will benefit the Arab as well as his Jewish neighbor.

We can anticipate a continuing religious life for all faiths in Israel. The various religious groups will continue to thrive, if they can provide the right kind of leadership themselves, and continue to do what the State very happily allows them to do and, in many a practical way, helps them to do.

The largest single Christian group is the Roman Catholic of what we call the Uniate type. They are like Greek Orthodox in worship and customs, but they are part of the Roman Catholic Church.

The next largest group is the Greek Orthodox. They have their own leadership problems with the Arabs because of a set-up which requires that the Bishops be Greek. It would be wrong for any church to say that a Bishop must be of a particular nationality, and they do not say that. But to be an Orthodox Bishop in the Middle East, you do have to be a member of a particular Brotherhood, and only Greeks can join it.

There is freedom of movement across the borders for the officials of these various groups. If one particular group has its Archbishop or Bishop in Jordan-held Jerusalem, he can enter Israel to take care of his parishes. This is true even if the Jordanian prelate is an Arab. When a Coptic Bishop died in Israel several years ago, Coptic Bishops came in from Egypt, Jordan and Syria. There was no problem, and Israel was cooperative in every way.

Islam has every opportunity to thrive. The top Islamic executives are paid by the State, as are the two Chief Rabbis. There are many democracies which have similar systems. For example, Scotland is certainly a democracy; and yet the government gives equal support to Presbyterian schools, Episcopal schools, Roman Catholic schools, and secular schools. One's feeling about such a policy should not color the fact that democracy and some measure of non-preferential relationship between church and state are not necessarily incompatible. What is desirable is another question.

It is clear that Israel is destined to have a pluralistic religious pattern. It will result in a variety of wholesome cultural influences and contacts in various areas of the community. With more freedom of movement within the State and, ultimately, between Israel and Arab states, a greater number of Arab students of different religious backgrounds will attend school with persons of Jewish background. It will result in greater contact between the future leaders of the churches, both lay and clergy. The future will see an influx of scholars of various denominations as visitors, long-term guests and citizens. Because of their presence, such persons will attract students from surrounding Middle East countries and from this country. All of this will enrich Israel, in no way detracting from its central Jewish heritage.

A Christian visiting Israel, if he is at all thoughtful about his own religious heritage and the Bible, cannot help but sense a renewal of his faith in God's Providence, and His working in history. That certainly happened to me when I visited Israel. I felt much more a Christian for the experience of having been to Israel. Why? Because I felt much more a Jew. This could really start me on a new chapter, so I shall simply file this by title; I am convinced you cannot be a Christian without being a Jew. Every heresy in Christendom has been the result of getting away from its Jewishness, and in reforming ourselves we always have to get back to our Jewish heritage. I do not mean this lightly, merely in a sense of what we call "brotherhood" these days. Not at all. I mean it very seriously, in theological terms.

Therefore, as there is more and more understanding, more and more kindness, more and more diminution of those personal factors that always arise in any society to create unpleasantness, we will find a religious harmony developing in Israel. It will be pluralistic, with a strong basic Hebrew foundation. This will benefit all who live there, not only those who are connected with the Synagogue.

In short, in Israel there is religious diversity and a religious vacuum. There are serious problems connected with this condition. The problems are understandable. One can criticize, but one should criticize with understanding and try to discern the evolution of a a new and healthier pattern. At the same time, one should glory in the situation that makes for these problems.

Most of our problems in this country that involve church-state inter-group relations derive from a *good* thing, namely that we do have the diversity. If we did not have the diversity, there would be no problems. Along with these problems, diversity brings a blessing—the contact with personalities and ideas of great traditions. The authentic quality of each tradition need not be compromised in a pluralistic society, but one can share the best insights of all for the enrichment of the nation—whether it be the United States or Israel.

3

TEACHING AMERICAN JEWISH HISTORY
IN ISRAEL *

MOSHE DAVIS

Teaching American Jewish history begins with America. For the first time in all of Jewish history, continuous and pervasive interaction governs the life of Jews and the people among whom they dwell. In this country, established by men whose faith was influenced by Hebrew Scriptures, one might say that many basic Jewish concepts had taken root before the Jews arrived. In that sense, the ideas of Judaism welcomed the Jews to America.

If teaching American Jewish history is to teach America, the task is facilitated by America's position in world affairs. In Israel, America is being taught all the time. She is represented first and foremost by what she is and does in the world. For the Israeli, America is part of the day's news. The radio and newspapers report her affairs and her policies, and the national ideals which they embody are subject to continuing discussion and deep interest. Moreover, the ideas of America are available to Israelis through literature and periodicals. The English language is the leading second language in the country. (In the early decades of the century, German and Russian were the dominant foreign languages. For the contemporary generation, English and American literature are

* Extension of a lecture originally delivered under the auspices of The American Jewish Historical Society and the Jewish Museum of The Jewish Theological Seminary of America (March 11, 1959).

more widely read.) The State Department arranged several years ago to export to Israel books and magazines from this country on a free-exchange basis. The result is that the book stores, as numerous in Israel as drug stores in the States, are full of the latest American books and papers. In this way, American thought finds its way into the heart of Israel, and the individual Israeli measures the quality of the American idea by his own insights and background. Furthermore, American public officials, civic leaders, artists, intellectuals, business men and tourists create a human bond with Isreal. A list of the eminent American visitors who have worked in the country in its formative years reads like a sampling of *Who's Who in America*. Many of these people correspond with Israeli friends and colleagues in the institutions they served. Many return again and again. Thus, Israelis understand America through her deeds, through her creative thought, and through personal contact with excellent representatives of American life.

Israel's best path to understanding America, however, lies through American Jewry. In the experience of Jewish life in America— as in the experience of other religious and ethnic groups—American democracy was transformed from an abstract ideal into the daily opportunity to develop in freedom. The waves of immigration, the attainment of full political rights, the place of Jewish enterprise in the ever-broadening economy, the opportunities in professions and arts—these elements are details in the larger growth of the American nation. At the same time, the inner life of American Jewry, its growth in education and culture, the elevation of the Synagogue to the central place in communal life, the formidable development of the Zionist movement, fraternal orders and mutual aid societies—all these internal concerns were also shaped by the national culture. When Israelis understand the American Jewish saga, they come to know the unique quality of America.

Yet it is commonplace that Israelis know far too little of the history, institutions and aspirations of the American Jewish community. The realities of American Jewish life today are only dimly perceived in the Jewish State. The Israeli student knows more about the Jews in medieval Spain and East-European Jews of the nineteenth century than he does about his contemporaries in America. Even men and women high in government and intellectual life have only the vaguest knowledge of the social and institutional structure of American Jewry. In a lecture at the Hebrew University in 1954, on "American Jewry in the Light of Historical Research," I developed the idea that modern Jewish history cannot be understood without the knowledge of American Jewish history. This was an elementary thesis, and yet the demonstration of the thesis, as I had anticipated, opened a new avenue of thought to the students at the Hebrew University.

In the United States, my academic vocation is to study and teach American Jewish history at The Jewish Theological Seminary. Since my graduate studies at the Hebrew University in 1937, I have also been privileged to teach and lecture on this subject both formally and informally in Israel. During the academic years of 1959–1961 my assignment in Israel is to help establish the Institute of Contemporary Jewry at the Hebrew University, in which American Jewish studies is, for the first time, an integral part of the curriculum. Teaching American Jewish life to Israelis has therefore been for me a continuing assignment, and my impressions and observations are cumulative, covering two decades of experience. In this report, I want to describe the insights not so much from what I taught but from what I learned as a student, lecturer, and teacher.

What does this assignment teach? What are the exciting discoveries of Israel about American Jewish life? What are the questions, the misconceptions, the insights learned over these years?

My first discovery was the excitement of Israelis at the importance attached to Hebrew culture in America, and the growing interest in it. Invariably, the story of Hebrew in the American public school system caught the imagination of Israelis. The introduction of the Hebrew language into public secondary education is, to be sure, without precedent in modern education anywhere in the world. Started experimentally in 1923 in New York City, Hebrew is now taught in more than 200 colleges, graduate and professional schools, and in 85 secondary schools in 16 cities; and the movement for instruction in Hebrew as a modern language is increasing steadily. Israelis were struck by the correspondence between the growth of Jewish settlement in Israel and the growth of Hebrew culture in America. Furthermore, they found striking the recognition of Hebrew in American official circles. For example, Lawrence Marwick, Chief of the Hebraic section of the Library of Congress, published in 1957 a *Handbook of Diplomatic Hebrew,* to meet the need for such a text among government agencies, translators, and abstractors. All this was totally foreign to the Jewish experience in Europe and in Arab countries from which most Israelis derive their knowledge of the world. As Europeans, they knew that Hebrew and Bible were studied under Christian auspices, but always as ancient, classical language and text, never as a living tongue of a living culture. Furthermore, Hebrew was always classified under "Semitics" or "Oriental Languages," and it remained the concern of a limited and particular academic group. In America, they learn, Hebrew is taught in tax-supported institutions, to transmit the Hebraic heritage in Western culture and to include it in the formation of the American intellect. Thus it happens that many Jewish children meet Hebrew first in public high school. Furthermore, the part of Hebrew culture in Western tradition, pointed up by Edmund Wilson in an essay in *A Piece of My Mind,** seems to be emphasized more and more in American universities. Wilson proposed a two year curriculum in classic Hebrew culture for students in his ideal university. The growing acceptance of these ideas was indicated, among many ways, by Millicent Taylor's article in the *Christian Science Monitor,* "The Study of Classical Hebrew Is Very Much Alive in Schools" (May 10, 1958). This phenomenon of Hebrew's new rooting on American soil, limited though it still is, provided Israelis with a new insight into America and its open-minded civilization.

A second never-ending source of surprise to Israelis is the relation of Christians and Jews in America. Israelis are, of course, deeply impressed and grateful for the many generous acts of Christians to the State of Israel. The deep-rooted love that these Christians have for the sovereign State delighted them and yet

* Farrar, Shaus and Cudahy, New York, 1956.

puzzled them, too. They would not have been puzzled had they simply seen themselves in perspective. Israelis know only too well that they live in the land of the Bible, but they find it difficult to understand that the western world—and the Jews who live in that world—look upon Israelis as a people dwelling in *The Holy Land*. Most Israelis are not mindful of the fact, even if they know it, that American Christians regard themselves as "children of the Bible," and that their special relationship to Israel flows from their faith.

In a touching memoir about Shalom Aleichem's first visit to the United States in 1914, B. Z. Goldberg recalls his own student days at the University of Iowa several years before:

There were but three Jewish students—one was preparing for law, the second for medicine, and I was the third, a freshman at the college. Not only was there no sign of anti-Semitism there, but they carried the three of us aloft—we were their darlings—as the children of a people who had given them, these Iowa farmers, the Bible.

In this light, Israelis have come to understand President Truman's insistence, for example, that he is "the modern Cyrus," and the revealing autobiographical statement of Secretary of Agriculture, Ezra Taft Benson:

My particular interest in Israel goes back a long way—back, in fact, to the days of my youth . . . I have long known of God's covenant with Abraham, Isaac and Jacob that their lands could be for them and their seed an everlasting inheritance . . . And so the development of the new nation of Israel was of no real surprise to me . . .

The Bible as a solid foundation for Christian-Israeli understanding is now well-known in Israel. What the Israelis do not know and have yet to learn is that the relationship of Christian and Jew in America has been translated into a pattern of religious equality amid religious diversity. To explain this idea, which is quite novel to people who grew up in European traditions, I often used Thomas Jefferson's extraordinary statement in response to a Discourse delivered by Dr. de la Motta at the Consecration of the Synagogue at Savannah:

"Monticello, Sept. 1, 1820

Thomas Jefferson returns his thanks to Dr. de la Motta, for the eloquent discourse on the consecration of the synagogue of Savannah which he has been so kind as to send him. It excites in him the gratifying reflection that his own country has been the first to prove to the world two truths, the most salutary to human society, that man can govern himself, and that religious freedom is the most effective anodyne against religious dissension: the maxim of civil government being reversed in that of religion where its true form is 'Divided we stand, united we fall' . . ."

From such a text, I could begin to explain the equality freely given to Judaism to build an indigenous Jewish life in the American social structure.

I also developed the theme of American Jewry as "the spiritual third of the nation," citing the fact that even in the early 1800's, when Jews were a tiny fraction of the population, they were valued as heirs of an ancient *People-Tradition* and not only in accordance with their numbers. This surprised my students. They came to understand, however, that Jews are indeed a "spiritual third" of the American nation, that they are judged by the quality of their ideas rather than the quantity of their adherents and that together with the Protestant and Catholic faiths, they are an organic part of the spiritual life of the country.

A recent example of the Christian love for the Holy Land which illustrated my discussions on the subject in the summer of 1958, was the extraordinary correspondence of Governor Theodore Mc-Keldin of Maryland, and a citizen of Baltimore. This correspondence was published in Israel and elicited widespread response. Governor McKeldin had received the following question:

"Dear Governor McKeldin:

As long as I can remember, I have been taught by my family, by the Maryland public school system . . . that we are Americans. Since this is so, our allegiance is always to our own country—America. We cannot then, it seems, call any other land 'Ours,' and be loyal to the United States. We do not refer to another nation's army as 'our army,' its soldiers as 'our boys' nor the nation itself as 'us.' The officers of the sovereign states of the United States are dedicated to the support of the constitutions of said states and to that of the union . . .

I could not understand from your remarks whether you were an American or an Israelite, a Jew or a Gentile, a Hebrew or a Christian. Which are you, I would like to know?" . . .

Governor McKeldin replied as follows:

"You ask if I am an 'American or an Israelite' (and I shall assume that you meant Israeli).

"You know, of course, that I am an American, because you know that I was the Mayor of an American City and am the Governor of an American State.

"You ask if I am Jew or Gentile, Hebrew or Christian. To the Jew, of course, I am a Gentile. In my faith, I am a Christian.

"Because I am an American, and because of the freedom which is rightfully mine, I can call any man my brother, and when I feel a kinship for his land because it, too, defends the dignity and the liberty of man, I can call it mine—or, in the form to which you specifically object, 'ours.'

"Because I am a Christian, I dare to extend the hand of brotherhood in the full measure, and to identify myself as closely as possible, with a great people who are fighting a gallant fight for that which is right.

"I thus reply to your letter because I, too, was reared in a family with a great and abiding love for America and for the opportunities of America, and I am most grateful for the fruits of the opportunities which I have been permitted to harvest.

"I hope that my gratitude always will be strong enough to keep me from hoarding these fruits to decay in a dark and narrow cellar.

"I hope that its light will be always so bright as to permit me to see the good in other lands and in other peoples, to glory in their struggles for liberty as I glory in ours, and, indeed, even to speak of theirs as 'ours' —because man's fight for freedom is not a thing of isolation. It is a universal and unending battle . . ."

Many Israelis discovered America when they came to understand the foundations upon which so representative an American as Governor McKeldin could say these things.

There were several discoveries about America that dismayed Israelis. One of them is America's passion for change. Invariably, they would question this change and mobility of the American people. When I described America as a land of "inner vibration," they would ask, "Are you not confusing change with growth?" Change for its own sake troubled Israelis, who themselves live in the most fluid of societies.

A second such "negative" discovery is the way the immigrants were absorbed into the American culture. For Israelis, the continuous integration of various groups into the life of the country is a pressing problem. They would like not to learn from America her mistaken idea of a "melting pot." America actually had in its country all of civilization. By the first decade of this century, the whole world was there. Americans felt then that "Americanization" meant to eliminate all differences. In the process of eliminating all differences, children were taught in the schools to repudiate the cultures from which their parents came. Now Americans have to undo the whole process. We will have to train our children to study Italian, Spanish, German, Japanese. We have to undo the long and costly work of "assimilation." Israelis see this and want to learn from our mistakes. In the great process of acculturation in Israel, Israelis are hoping to be able to *preserve* as much as is possible of these cultures.

What are some of the conceptions and misconceptions of the Israelis about the internal structure of American Jewish life? And what do they have to learn about us?

When it comes to the sheer size and intricate network of American Jewish organizations, Israelis are completely baffled. In 1958, the mission of the Council of Jewish Federations and Welfare Funds talked to a cross-section of forty leaders of the Knesset, Jewish Agency, Army and other institutions and held another session with the editors of over twenty leading daily newspapers. The mission reported that even this high-placed and highly responsible group did not know the elementary facts about American Jewish communal life. How, then, could they be expected to grasp the social forces which create our multiple organizations and the variety of cultural forms of American Jewry? One has therefore to explain that the phenomenon of "a nation of joiners" derives from our being a citizen-led nation. Nor do Israelis readily understand the role of laymen in the direction of American religious life. Europeans, generally, do not understand voluntarism in public life as a dynamic of democracy. In a book of mine, translated into Hebrew, I had used the phrase, "the rabbis and the lay leaders." When I got back the proofs, I found that the translator had said: "rabbis and secularists." The idea of a voluntaristic and nonprofessional society is therefore a real discovery. When one explains this background to the Israelis, they then understand why we do not have in American Jewry a centralized form of *Gemeinde,* similar to the communal pattern in Europe. They see why free enterprise in Jewish organizational life was established for the first time in Jewish history in America: it comes as a direct result of voluntarism in American life.

As one continues to describe the internal life of the Jewish community in America, one revelation follows upon another for the Israeli. For example, the re-emergence of the Synagogue as the central unit of Jewish communal life surprises them. The character of the Synagogue as a family institution, filling cultural and social needs, as well as individual religious needs, is almost totally unknown to the Israeli. For Israelis, the choice in religion is between orthodoxy and secularism. They are slowly coming to learn the great strength inherent in American Jewish religious life, in which both adaptation and modification may mean an enlargement of the Tradition.

Another discovery is the nature of the Jewish involvement in *Klal Yisrael,* in the needs and concerns of fellow-Jews. Israelis know this because Americans have taken on themselves a great part of the burden of helping their brethren overseas to rehabilitate themselves in Israel. It surprises Israelis, however, to learn that this was, in fact, a part of American Jewish life from the very beginning. To cite but one example which has contemporary overtones—the Jewish situation in the '70's, of the past century. The following few lines come from a report in the *Cleveland Leader* of May 21, 1877, describing an address of Benjamin F. Peixotto, former consul to Roumania.

"Yesterday afternoon, the Honorable B. F. Peixotto delivered an interesting lecture in the Eagle Street Synagogue on ROUMANIA AND

THE ROUMANIAN JEWS. The speaker had lived for 6 years in one of those dark lands where the Son of Israel had suffered so much and had been looked upon as no better than a dog. He took great interest in the terrible massacre of the Jews, which occurred in Roumania in June of 1870, and about that time resolved to do what he could to lighten the burdens of these oppressed people. He then went to Bucharest as the consul of this country to Roumania, and on arriving there found that the Israelites were much alarmed and oppressed in spirit. But as soon as they learned who he was they looked upon him as a new Moses and took courage. They came to him and he assured them that he would do all in his power to protect them. The speaker said, further, that when he first located in Bucharest he advised the Jews to protect themselves and fight in self defense whenever necessary . . .

"Many of the outrages, which have been perpetrated in the East, the speaker thought, were due to Russian influence—a country which he thought has long been striving to bring about the present state of affairs. . . ."

These discoveries of America through American Jewry have given the Israeli a new respect for the values of the democratic order. It makes him want to come here to study, and to absorb and to apply what he learns here to his own life and institutions. It makes the Israelis feel that in the fraternity of nations, they want to be close to America as, indeed, America wants to be close to them.

No finer summary of the respect that has grown up over the years for the American Jewish community can be given than the remarks of Premier Ben-Gurion at the ceremony of the cornerstone laying of the American Student Center of the Jewish Theological Seminary in Jerusalem in the summer of 1958.

"This new step is of particularly great importance in that it comes from the United States. Three momentous events have taken place in the history of our people during the first half of the twentieth century: the loss of two thirds of European Jewry, which in recent centuries was the mother of the Jewish people; the growth of the greatest Jewish center that has ever existed in the Diaspora; and the rise of the State of Israel. These three events may determine our future and the future of the Jewish people all over the world for many decades and even centuries.

"American Jewry, which enjoys full equality of rights and consists of immigrants or the descendants of immigrants like the rest of the Americans (except for the Indian minority), gives outstanding expression to the Jewish individuality, Jewish creativeness and attachment to the Jewish people. There are numerous differences within American Jewry on matters of religion, faith and outlook . . . Yet there is a wonderful unity in American Jewry, in their concern for the fate of Jewry in many countries, and especially in their love and spiritual attachment to Israel.

"This is perhaps one of the most extraordinary phenomena in the life of any people, though it is only one of the expressions of the extraordinary uniqueness that has characterized the Jewish people ever since it came into being . . ."

While the Israelis have indeed come to respect the American Jewish community, as Premier Ben-Gurion's statement reflects, they do put straightforward questions about the character of the community and its future. Can Jews create in America an indigenous Jewish creative community to take its place beside the past diasporic centers of Babylonia, Spain, Russia and Poland? Can America produce a Jewish laity who will practice the *mitzvah* of study and learning so that there may be created in America a distinctive American Jewish culture? Can American Jews join the Israeli Jewish community in shaping a creative Judaism in the modern world? Is the dream of a *Jewish* group future in America dream or mirage?

One question is asked so often in Israel that it is almost a slogan: Can American Jewry be a modern Babylonia? Or, in its literal translation from the Hebrew, the question goes: "Can you produce a Talmud Bavli?"

Addressing the Conference of Historians convened by the American Jewish Historical Society on the occasion of the 7th Tercentenary of the first Jewish settlement on this continent, Professor Ben Zion Dinur put the question in the form of an historical generalization:

". . . Wherever you find a Jewish community which exerts great influence on other communities in other countries, you can assume that the history of the Jews in that country gave rise to new elements of Jewish culture which are of vital importance to all Jewish communities of that

generation. The place of that Jewish community is determined by the
extent to which these principles (taking the heavenly yoke upon themselves jointly, with the will and readiness to work together for the
knowledge of Scripture, the service of God, the keeping of the Law and
the work of charity and of brotherly assistance) influenced the total community. Only to that extent can we determine whether a community is
native and whether it will make its own contribution beside the great
contributions of the communities of the past."

From this one question flow many other questions. What is the
nature of American Jewish youth? Do the young have a spiritual
quality? Do they want to build a Jewish future? And what about
the Jewish family? Does it have the solidarity and cohesion of
which past generations were so rightfully proud? Where are the
real *ideals* of the American Jewish community? Do the synagogues produce people of piety or attendance figures? Do the
Jewish schools produce Jewish scholars? Does the Jewish home
train character, the love of fellowman?

Out of these questions and the historical generalization comes a
valid insight into American Jewry. It is, in a sense, a perception
which is the heart of what I learned out of my assignment in
Israel. The Israelis recognize and accept the fact that *Jews* can
survive in freedom. They know that Jews as a people will continue
to live and flourish in America. What they want to know is whether
Judaism can survive in freedom. Despite the bitterness and horror
of the ghetto, Jews and Judaism did survive. They ask whether
the faith and heritage of the Jewish people in the Diaspora can
endure without the compactness of Jewish group life and its intellectual and spiritual walls. Israelis express sincere doubts. For
themselves, they have chosen to live in a majority Jewish culture.
They do not believe that American Jews are superhuman. They
do not think, on the whole, that American Jews will be able to
create a Babylonian Talmud.

Without entering into the realm of "prophecy" or trying to
guess what the nature of American Judaism will be in the next
generations, it is nevertheless important to indicate that in part,
but not entirely, the doubts of the Israelis are based on miscon-

ceptions and on a misreading of actual events. Israelis tend to view all diasporic communities from one point of view. They refuse to recognize the differences between them. They generalize on the Jews of South America, of North America, Europe, the Anglo-Saxon countries. This is a profound error. The problems of living in Latin America or in Europe are altogether different from the problems Jews face in America.

Another Israeli misconception is to identify all anti-Jewish acts with racial anti-Semitism. There is virtually not a single major critic of American Jewry in Israel who has not lived through the great sorrows of our times. It is therefore very difficult to explain to them that in America, there are hostilities between various groups, region and region, area and area, Negro and white, industry and labor and so forth. All of this is part of America—problems which Americans are trying to work out. But such conflict, even when Jews are hurt by it, is not to be equated with racial anti-Semitism as Israelis knew it in Europe.

A third misunderstanding is based on the interpretation of American Jewish assimilation. They are aware of the changes that have transformed the Jewish people in America. They know the civilization of Eastern Europe; many of them were born there, many more know the kind of Jews who lived there. They know, too, that American Jews are not identifiably Jewish in ways that they can discern. They see the Jewish community undergoing great inner corrosion. They not only see this, but their press features this process. They are only beginning to learn, however, about the return to Judaism and to the Jewish community of vast numbers of Jews. They do not know about the phenomenon of the third generation. They do not perceive the great positive changes for good in Jewish life here.

Finally, Israelis have yet to explore the potentialities of the State of Israel itself for Jewish life in America. They have been busy building their own State. They do not realize how much American Jewry expects from them and needs of them. They do not know how desperately many American Jews want Torah to come forth from Zion rebuilt. In truth, there has been a great revival of the Jewish spirit in modern Israel and it has transformed

Israelis. But the spiritual impact has not yet been felt by American Jewry. Before Israelis can bring religious and cultural assistance to American Jewry, they must come to know and believe in American Jewry in its own terms. The only action that will be successful is inter-action. The more we know about each other, the better the chance to evolve specific ways whereby we can be helpful to one another. To get Israeli Jews to know and believe in American Jewry is my assignment in Israel and, in truth, the assignment of all American Jews, for in that way, we are also building our own community in America.

What are some of the ways in which the cultural bonds between the two communities are being established and strengthened?

The first bridge is human. Until American Jewry is adequately represented in Israel by its spiritual and cultural leaders, Israelis will never fully understand us. Two American Jews who played singular roles in this bridge of human interpretation were Judah Magnes and Henrietta Szold, both of whom, as Americans, already are part of the modern Eretz Yisrael legend. There are important American figures in Israel today who are helping to shape the present generation. The contribution of such men as Reuben Avinoam, Alexander Dushkin, Israel Efros, Simon Halkin and a group of younger American scholars, artists and intellectuals to Israeli education today is unique. These men come to Israel with a love of American life and they are deeply rooted in Hebrew culture and literature. In a sense, they are the best ambassadors of American culture to Israel. For they come as creative forces to a new country in the process of creation. Relating the American and Jewish traditions, they create in the contemporary Hebrew idiom. Thus they add a new dimension to the Israeli amalgam. To cite three examples out of their rich contributions: a recent work of Professor Halkin is an exemplary translation into Hebrew of Walt Whitman's *Leaves of Grass* with an admirable introduction and notes, which, in English, would be a major contribution to American literary criticism; Reuben Avinoam's volume, *Anthology of American Poetry* introduces a new point of view into current Israeli literature; and Professor Dushkin is responsible for the reorganization of the undergraduate division at the Hebrew University, in a way which effectively integrated the University into the educational life of the community.

The profoundest achievement of such men is their presence on the day-to-day scene. Their very personalities exert influence on decisions with regard to standards of study and materials for the curricula of Israeli cultural life outside the formal educational structure. These men serve as consultants to publishing houses, newspaper editors and cultural departments of national organizations. Their counsel is sought and their advice carries a good deal of weight. The Israeli hopes that other individuals of such calibre and background will identify themselves with the cultural enterprises in the new State.

Second, American studies must take a greater part in the training of Israeli scholars. American Jewish history must find its rightful place in all teaching about world Jewry and Judaism. I am gratified to report a developing alertness to this lacuna in historical studies and curricula. Lectures in American Civilization are given from time to time and distinguished American historians like Allan Nevins and Henry Steele Commager have lectured at the Hebrew University and to scholarly gatherings in other institutions. Recently, a documentary history with interesting selections from American Jewish history, was published as a high school text. It was good to see the announcement of the American Jewish Tercentenary theme, in 1954—300 years of American Jewry—posted on the billboards of Tel Aviv, Haifa, Tiberias and Beer Sheba. The comparatively large audience which attended the various lectures given in Israel on this theme was a further indication of awakened interest in American Jewish life. A good deal of the future development of this interest rests with American Jewish scholars and educators.

 As I reflect on the overwhelming changes in understanding between these two great Jewish communities which have taken place in a short span of time, I am struck by the significant opportunities that await all of us. These promises for the future are symbolized in the story of a flower described in *Mount Carmel Flowers* published in Israel recently. The flower is the famous *shoshan* (lily), called "the rose" in the Song of Songs, whose white petaled bells open in the spring between Passover and Shavuot. The *shoshan* disappeared from the Land of Israel when the woods in whose shade it had flourished were cut down. It no longer grew wild in the land. For centuries, however, it had been uprooted and exported to other countries because of its religious associations, and it became a garden plant in the West. It was even re-exported to modern Israel and cultivated in gardens there. In our own day, this *shoshan* is once more blossoming, between the rocks of Mount Carmel and in the woods of Galilee. Thus the *shoshan,* born in the soil of the Land of Israel, had to be nurtured abroad and sent back to its native country. Like the *shoshan,* many of the ideas of Judaism, which had been nurtured in the Land of Israel, were sustained in foreign soil, even in America and among its Jewish community. Some of these ideas will be brought back to Israel by way of the American Jew. This return is welcomed by Israelis. In the process of return, American Jewry, too, will gain a greater vision of its own destiny.

4

THREE ASSIGNMENTS IN ISRAEL

ROBERT ST. JOHN

It happened in 1941 during the German occupation of Rumania. King Carol had been forced to abdicate and flee. The British had finally broken off diplomatic relations and had left the country. But two pro-Nazi leaders, Horia Sima and "Red Dog" Antonescu, the *Conducator,* as he liked to be called, were wrestling for control. There had already been some street fighting, and then—

One night Alex Coler, the Jewish editor of a Bucharest morning newspaper (until the Nazis suppressed it) came to the villa in which I was living on Strada Vasile Alexandri and asked me to hide his wife and daughter. He had been forewarned that there was to be a pogrom that night and that his name was on the list. Because Coler was one of the best friends I had ever made, I locked the three of them in my own bedroom and sat up all night with a revolver in my lap.

The next morning, after I unlocked the bedroom door and liberated my guests, Coler made a telephone call. When he came to the breakfast table his face was white.

During the night the Fascist Iron Guard had rounded up several hundred (the exact total was never determined) leaders of the Jewish community, their wives and children, had taken them to an abattoir on the edge of Bucharest where, treating them as if they were animals, they had forced them to get down on all fours and thus mount the ramp leading into the slaughter house.

"Someone who escaped has told me the details of what happened after that," Coler reported. "Would you care to hear?"

I listened. There is no advantage now to repeating what he told me. It was the worst example of man's inhumanity to man I have ever heard. And I have covered race riots, a number of revolutions, several wars, and a great deal of miscellaneous blood-letting in my time.

No one gave me my first assignment in Israel. I gave it to myself that morning in the villa on Strada Vasile Alexandri in Bucharest, Rumania, for as Alex Coler talked I swore an oath: as long as I lived I would try in every way possible to make some atonement, infinitesimal though it might be, for the twenty centuries of persecution that a group into which I had happened to be born had inflicted upon an innocent people. This persecution had culminated in the unspeakable events of 1939—1940—1941—

Thus it was that in 1948 I boarded a plane for Haifa, which was at that time the airport-city for a brand-new little country that the airline office in Paris still insisted on calling Palestine. I went there because a few Jews from Rumania who had survived all that had happened, along with a handful of other Jews from widely separated parts of the world, had decided to accept the United Nations' offer of a small piece of the Holy Land in which, God and the Arabs willing, they would be permitted to live out the rest of their lives as normal human beings.

The "education of a goy [1]" had begun in Bucharest. It continued, now, as soon as the plane was in the sky over France and I began to feel the excitement of my fellow passengers; the excitement of a people returning, finally, to a land which had been denied to them, on one pretext or another, for so many hundreds of years, until suddenly one day the world, its nerves raw from the experiences of a zymotic war, began to have pains in its conscience. This going-home was such a strong emotional experience for them that it set off a chain reaction. I felt it, especially, early the next morning. The plane was at 20,000 feet approaching the shore line of Israel. As the sun poked its way over the horizon of white clouds, an aged Orthodox Jew put his prayer shawl over his head and shoul-

---

[1] The Hebrew word "goy" in the Bible means "a nation." Colloquially, it has come to mean anyone not of the Jewish faith.

ders, girded on his phylacteries and began his morning prayers, standing in the aisle, the rising sun painting him with its reds, yellows, and golds.

My first visit to the Land of the Book led me into a *cul de sac* from which I had difficulty escaping. The armies of five or six Arab nations had attacked. Journalistically, the "story" was the miracle of how a handful of young Jewish men and girls, armed with inadequate weapons, were beating back the invaders, while older men, not fit for battle, were busy creating a new nationalism in this corner of the world which had seen so many other nations come and go.

Before this—long before this—I had put onto paper my belief that war and nationalism were the twin evils of the twentieth century and that they might well bring down the entire civilized world. The United Nations had been formed, but I believed in going much farther than that. I had been one of the founders of the United World Federalists and I had already done a great deal of public arguing for an end to narrow nationalism and the creation of a real world state. Also, participation in one world war and close observation of another had made a pacifist of me. What I had seen had convinced me that the man who lives by the sword runs a good chance of meeting his end by the sword; that he who drops atom bombs on others may well end up being atomized to death himself; that militarism in this day of nuclear fission means race suicide.

Yet here was this new country being created out of chaos and war, while on all sides there was the mumble-jumble of a new nationalism. Those who were not fighting were making a flag, singing a new-old national anthem, deciding what design of coins and stamps to have, discussing the cut of military uniforms for an army which had never even had a name before, arguing about whether there should be medals, whether streets should be named after local heroes, where Parliament ought to sit. Problems of nationalism.

A country was being born, and it would be a refuge for people who had been denied a home for almost two thousand years. It was heart-warming to see their happiness, even in the midst of so much danger as there was in Israel in 1948. Yet what about my principles?

I finally reconciled them with the reality that was all around me, and with my enthusiasm for that reality. I at least satisfied my own conscience and kept firm hold on my convictions by writing in the foreword to *Shalom Means Peace* * (an account of the birth-pains of the new state, Israel) these words:

The State of Israel is an experiment in nationalism and it survives today as a result of bravery in battle. But it needs to be often repeated that the Israelis were forced down the path they followed by moral corruption at the Great Power level. Had the Balfour Declaration been carried out, had the Jews not been made pawns in the game of power politics, imperialism and oil, had the United States not vacillated after November 29, 1947, had the U.N. created an instrumentality to enforce its Partition Plan, the evils of excessive nationalism and war could have been avoided.

My first "assignment in Israel" had an emotional background. The second was more intellectual in its motivation.

At a cocktail party on Park Avenue (sometime in late 1951) a friend of the Ben Yehuda family maneuvered me into a corner, and for half an hour I was compelled to listen to stories about the man who almost single-handed had revived a language which had been dead for so many centuries. Before the story-teller (now a dear friend) finished, I decided I wanted to be the biographer of this man, even though I knew only a few phrases in Hebrew myself and had so little grounding in Jewish history that I would have to work twice as diligently as any Jewish scholar might have had to do for the material of such a book.

My second self-assigned assignment led me first to the hospital bed in New York City of a kind and wise old lady, Hemda Ben Yehuda. She was dying, and her children were afraid that, when she went, she would take with her the story of her many decades of life with a man who had been first the husband of her older sister and whose child-bride she herself became after the sister's death. Propped up in bed, her dark eyes twinkling mischievously, she passed on to me many details of her husband's struggle to create a

---

* Doubleday and Co., New York, 1949.

modern Hebrew language fit not only for worship but for ordering groceries and swearing at the cattle. She talked day after day of their struggle together, of the strange quarters from which his opposition came, of the philological problems, of the Englishman who offered them a thousand pounds sterling if Eliezer would quickly create a word for "sporting event" and how he refused, because he was a scholar and "the word will not be ready for several more years."

The longer I worked on *Tongue of the Prophets* * the more I knew how pathetically unprepared I was to start writing. So I went to the study in Geneva, Switzerland, of a quiet-mannered little man who once had been Chief Rabbi to the hundreds of thousands of Jews in Rumania, and from him I borrowed, one book at a time, all twelve volumes of a Jewish encyclopedia. Eventually I became perhaps the first man in history to sit down and read every word of every page of a twelve-volume encyclopedia. For several weeks after I finished this chore, and until the vast store of new knowledge I had acquired commenced to slip, one fact at a time, from my mind, I felt I had the necessary factual orientation to start work. After research in various parts of the world, the book finally was finished.

In Berne, Switzerland, there is a great clock tower which, at noon each day, presents a theatrical performance of mechanical bears, soldiers and other figures moving with mathematical precision, as bells chime the hour. The story of Ben Yehuda proved again that history works with as fine a sense of timing as the makers of that clock tower. It almost seemed as if some nineteenth century manipulator of strings, looking into the future, had said:

"Before the next century is half over the world will be cursed by a great war during which acts of frightful barbarity will be committed against Jews. Many of the survivors will flock to the Holy Land, and there will be need of a common language. In order to have this language ready in time, someone must start working on it in the early years of this century. Therefore, Eliezer Ben Yehuda had better be born in a Lithuanian village in 1858."

Several years after *Tongue of the Prophets* was published I re-

* Doubleday and Co., Garden City, N.Y., 1952.

visited Israel for the first time. What I saw should have been made the subject matter of a long epilogue to the biography, and would have been, had there been a second edition. What I saw would have pleased Eliezer Ben Yehuda. The language he had loved so greatly and had modernized so painstakingly had become far more than a medium for conducting the moment-to-moment business of life. It was now the cement being used by wise men to bind together hundreds of thousands of immigrants who had little else in common but a long tradition of persecution and suffering.

I saw old people with wrinkled faces and white hair sitting in school rooms studying the language their ancestors had spoken. I saw people with skins almost black, who looked, dressed, ate, and even smelled like Arab nomads, because they had lived so many centuries in Arab lands, proudly exchanging words with men who had been learned doctors and university professors in Central and Eastern Europe. American Jews still might not be very well acquainted with the life and work of Eliezer Ben Yehuda, but these immigrants knew about him. They had been taught how much this one fanatical scholar had had to do with creating the freedom they were now beginning to enjoy: the freedom of communication.

On that first return trip to Israel I discovered something else, which made me less worried about the militarism that had been forced upon Israel by Great Power politics and Arab intransigence. For the first time in my life I saw an army being used for a really noble purpose. In military camps across the country young immigrants, girls and men alike, were being taught to think, dress, and behave as Israelis. This was not an attempt by conformist-loving autocrats to kill individuality. If it had been I would have been one of the first to condemn it. Rather, it was education: education in modern hygiene, personal cleanliness, respectable table manners, intelligent sleeping habits, twentieth century living. It was an attempt to raise the standards of primitive people, teach citizenship, cut the mortality rate, increase longevity, broaden horizons.

What I saw made me realize how foolish it is to generalize about such a thing as nationalism. I still believed (perhaps more strongly than ever) in one flag, no customs barriers, a free flow of money, goods, people and ideas from every corner of the world to every other corner; an end to stupid little loyalties and patriotic prating about the superiority of "us" and "ours" compared to the inferiority of "you" and "yours." But until this millennium approached, until at least the two Great Powers currently running most of the world could be persuaded to move in that general direction, it apparently required some form of nationalism to weld people together and make it possible for them to be creative, for their own good and that of humanity in general.

I had seen, in certain other not distant places, the sort of ugly nationalism that races through streets with smoking revolvers and is interested only in destroying, always with brutality and a certain fiendishness. While it is true that the past often has to be utterly wiped out before a bright new present can take its place, the test of nationalism is what happens after its enemies have been routed.

When I went back to Israel I found nationalism everywhere. Patriotic songs had been composed; political speakers talked with pride about Israel and her accomplishments; fear had been replaced by self-assurance; self-assurance had engendered a certain degree of boastfulness. But these group-conscious people were destroying nothing, harming no one. Theirs was a constructive nationalism. They were building rather than tearing down. They were creating useful articles, solid buildings, attractive villages, verdant mountain sides. They were conquering a desert, making ugly brown sand bloom with beauty, reversing the ravages of nature, raising the living standards of themselves and anyone else who was wise enough to remain in contact with them, offering help to their neighbors if their neighbors would only stop talking about a Holy War and join their nationalism with Israel's nationalism, for the greater benefit of the entire Middle East.

From a plane it was possible to demark the boundaries of this new Israel by noticing where the green stopped and the brown began.

One had only to listen to the frenetic words of radio broadcasters in certain Arab capitals to note the difference between a nationalism which was using hate as the fuel for its locomotion and a nationalism which knew that pride of accomplishment is a less dangerous and at the same time more powerful carburetant.

Frontiers were being guarded. The defensive forces were ever on the alert. Yet not a single speech was ever made—even by spokesmen for Israel's rabble-rousing extreme left or Israel's rabble-rousing extreme right—that breathed hatred for those millions in neighboring countries who were making the task of building a nation so much more difficult than it otherwise need have been for this conglomerate people called Jews.

During the several years immediately after the publication of *Tongue of the Prophets* I tried to pay installments on my debt by taking part in fund-raising activities and by lecturing on Israel, often to fundamentally antagonistic audiences and often with professional Arab hecklers scattered through the hall.

Then I gave myself another literary assignment, more exciting and intellectually stimulating than any I had ever had before. Once again it was not a task for a *goy*. Yet perhaps there would be some advantages to the life story of David Ben-Gurion being told by an "outsider" who actually felt more in tune with the heart-beat of Israel than many who were born with the twenty centuries of persecution bred into their bones.

Back in 1948, having little knowledge of the history of Zionism, I had never heard the name David Green. David Ben-Gurion was nothing more to me than a Zionist labor organizer and professional politician who had the habit of making interminably long speeches, had little use for the press, although he claimed to be a professional journalist himself, and somehow had been catapulted into leadership at the moment when statehood was inevitable.

Slowly during the next nine years I changed my opinion. Along with the rest of the world, I became impressed by the character, the courage, the ability at constructive leadership, the catholicity of interests, the unconventionality of this man who was beginning to be called "a modern Moses," a "prophet in a business suit."

I suppose the real reason I became the biographer of Israel's Prime Minister was that I became so interested in him I wanted to know more about him than I could find in magazine and newspaper articles; I wanted to read a book about him. Because there was none, I had to write one.

(Until publication of *Ben-Gurion, the Biography of an Extraordinary Man,** the only volume in English about him was a book written some years earlier by an Englishman which had since gone out of print.)

So, out of my interest in Ben-Gurion, the man, grew an agreement with a publishing house in New York to go to Israel and write a biography which would attempt to reveal to the book-reading world the genius of this man who seemed to represent something entirely new in the realm of statesmanship, and who had already had so much to do with leading hundreds of thousands of his own people back to the land from which they had sprung.

Here was a man in a hundred respects unlike Ben Yehuda. They had in common only that they had both dropped their real family names to take names with a Biblical sound (both were Ben, *son of*) and that they both had a love affair with Israel.

All the world, by 1958, knew David Ben-Gurion and most of the world respected him. They knew him for different reasons. The readers of certain popular pictorial magazines knew him because of a full page photograph printed in many countries showing the then 70-year-old Ben-Gurion in swimming trunks standing on his head on a sandy beach near Tel Aviv, doing certain self-control exercises he had learned from an instructor in yoga. An American weekly news magazine had used his portrait in colors on its cover twice within a single year. Average Americans liked him because of his informality, his insistence on an open-neck shirt when lesser figures were wearing striped trousers and cutaway coats, his brusque honesty, his unpretentious forthrightness.

But he is also an intellectual, and he had dared reveal himself as such at a moment in history when intellectuality of any sort was being shunned in some quarters as if it were sign of the plague. Here was a politician who had studied the Greek classics in the original during London's air-raids and who could discuss Oriental philosophy with men from the East and the search for truth with Albert Einstein.

* Doubleday and Co., Garden City, N.Y., 1959.

Here was a man who appealed to anyone with even a slight streak of bohemianism, because he dared to be different. He called shaking hands useless, now that men no longer had the need to prove that they were not carrying daggers. He could never understand anyone celebrating the anniversary of his own birth: "the one event in your life with which you had nothing to do and for which you can take no credit."

Most important of all, here was the head of government in a country with a population less than that of Philadelphia, giving the world lessons in statesmanship, despite the fact that he often had a goodly proportion of his own people against him, that Israel was surrounded on three sides by nations which insisted that a state of war still existed and refused even to discuss peace, and despite the fact that the friendship of each one of the Great Powers was dependent on circumstances entirely out of his control.

So I went back to Israel and found David Ben-Gurion in Jerusalem. He was not only Prime Minister but Minister of Defense, and there were innumerable departments and bureaus under his direct control. Besides, at this moment Parliament (the Knesset) was in session and there were problems pressing in on all sides. But his public relations advisor said certainly he would see me; in just a few days. Meanwhile, there were his friends, his wife, his son, his daughters, his old associates, and his present-day colleagues to talk with.

At this point, formidable obstacles started falling into my path.

A young fanatic threw a bomb from the gallery of the Knesset, and Ben-Gurion was one of those taken to Hadassah Hospital, wounded in one arm, one leg. Even if he eventually recovered his normal vigor, it would be weeks, perhaps months, before he could spare the time to answer a biographer's thousand questions.

So I turned to his wife. But the day before we were to have our first long interview, Paula Ben-Gurion was taken to Hadassah Hospital with a serious case of Asiatic influenza.

Number three on my list was Nehemiah Argov, who had the title of Military Secretary to the Prime Minister, but who was much more than that, for he was a living shadow of the white-

haired man whom he worshipped so intensely. They had told me
that Argov would be able to answer all questions and relate Ben-
Gurion stories without end. But one chilly day just before I was to
see him, Nehemiah Argov locked himself in his Tel Aviv apartment
and committed suicide.

There was another man who had been closely associated with
Ben-Gurion and from whom I expected to get rich material. The
day after our first short interview his son was killed in an auto-
mobile accident. He was unable to see me again.

There were other disasters, major and minor; other obstacles.

Yet Ben-Gurion and his wife both finally recovered sufficiently
before I left Israel to grant me interviews, and by the time I
finished my work, I had talked to more than fifty people who had
given me a composite insight into the character of this amazing
little man with the head like a gnome who reminded Richard
Crossman, the English writer, of a "Pickwickian cherub." When
I flew away from Israel, I took with me a dozen notebooks containing the transcripts of all these interviews, as well as several suitcases
of documents, principally copies of Ben-Gurion speeches dug out
for me by the efficient Government Press Office and its researchers.

In second-hand bookshops in New York and London I found
more than fifty volumes containing words written by or about
Israel's self-educated Prime Minister.

Then, in a small hotel room just off Piccadilly, surrounded by
this wealth of material, I sat down to read and think and make
an outline. During the first month I read nothing but words
written or spoken by Ben-Gurion; well over a million of them. At
first I decided that my subject was a rather wordy man, but the
more I read the more I realized that the most surgical editor in
New York would have a difficult time excising paragraphs, sen-
tences, phrases, or even superfluous words. An important Ben-
Gurion speech may go on for several hours and on occasion he
has spoken for five or six hours, non-stop, yet he rarely uses an
unnecessary word. Cut a paragraph, a sentence, or even a phrase
and you have eliminated something important he wanted to say.

Reading Ben-Gurion's speeches proved to be much more educational than studying the twelve-volume encyclopedia had been. It was worth a year at a university taking courses in ancient history, philosophy, logic, ethics, and the social sciences.

Here was the mind of an intellectually alert man who, even in his seventies, was constantly enlarging his interests, exploring new fields of the mind and spirit, while at the same time guiding a new-old nation besieged by problems. As soon as he had discovered some new bit of wisdom, acquired a slightly better understanding of life, gained a fresh historical perspective, he was eager to communicate it to others, especially his own people.

My investigations indicated that in his contacts with others, he seldom argues or holds Plato-like discussions. He is either seeking ideas and information from those he meets or is contributing ideas and information to them. That is why his speeches and writings are so educational. He is by nature a teacher. He has even conceived his role of Supreme Commander of the Israel Army not as that of a strategy-maker or a planner of brilliant maneuvers, but as an instructor in such thoroughly non-military matters as the philosophy of the Greeks, the wisdom of oriental teachers, and the history of the Jewish people.

Actually, writing the book was not easy. There is a special literary problem in writing on a Jewish subject which even a Jewish author encounters, although it is doubly a problem for anyone else. It grows out of what is at one and the same time the strength and the weakness of Jews as a group, namely Jewish individualism.

I knew about Jewish individualism. I had had certain troubles in writing *Shalom Means Peace* and *Tongue of the Prophets*. But in London in the summer of 1958 Jewish individualism caused more problems than ever before and added weeks to the writing chore.

My sources, all good, gave three different figures for the distance from Tel Aviv to Jerusalem.

"Chaim" is a very common Jewish first name and it is spelled that way by almost everyone named Chaim, except Haim Zohar, a government official in Jerusalem and a rugged individualist who likes his without the "c."

Two of the best known Israel military commanders are Yigael Yadin, the archeologist, and Yigal Allon, the *kibbutznik* and politician. Although their first names are identically pronounced, each has his own idea about how to spell it.

I spent hours, and days, weeks in the British Museum checking one source against another. I wrote beseeching letters to Jerusalem. I consulted authorities in London and in New York. I had an intense desire to write a book free of errors. I wanted to prove that even if I had no Jewish background, I could get my facts, my spellings, my dates, and my distances correct. But my desire for perfection proved my undoing. Truth, in cold print, often looked like blatant error. After *Ben-Gurion, the Biography of an Extraordinary Man* was published there were many readers and a few professional reviewers who were convinced that I had made errors. For example, in the spelling of young Mr. Zohar's first name. For example, in not spelling Yigael (Yigal) consistently.

The case of Allon was a good example of the predicament I faced. Almost everywhere that his name had ever appeared in print, even in Israel papers, it was spelled "Alon." One day during the last of a long series of conferences we had, he looked down at my notebook and observed that I had spelled his name with just one *l*.

With great feeling in his voice, he said:

"Do me a favor, St. John. No one ever spells my name correctly. It has two *l*'s, and—"

When he saw the expression of disbelief on my face he became a little annoyed.

"It's my name. I ought to know."

Then almost wistfully he added:

"Do me a favor. Please see that it is spelled correctly in your book. It would make me happy to see it spelled right just once!"

So I did him the favor, at the expense of being accused of careless reporting.

The word "Israeli" posed another problem. The manuscript was read, as fast as each chapter was written, by a friend in Jerusalem, at my request. Although I wrote occasionally in criticism of Ben-Gurion, I was not asked to eliminate anything. But one request did come back with the returned chapters.

"Please do not use 'Israeli' as an adjective. The adjective is 'Israel.' The word *Israeli* cannot properly be used except to designate a citizen of Israel, anymore than Spaniard can be used for anything but a citizen of Spain."

The note added that this was not just a bit of "Israel" obstinacy or "Israel" eccentricity, but that it was philologically correct.

Being already the biographer of Ben Yehuda, I was eager not to offend his philological successors, and so in *Ben-Gurion, the Biography of an Extraordinary Man,* the word Israeli never appears except in its pure and correct sense, although almost every daily, weekly, monthly, quarterly, and yearly publication printed in the United States uses it as an adjective.

The color of Ben-Gurion's eyes was another problem. Surely a biographer ought to know at least the color of his subject's eyes, especially if the subject is still alive.

Within a few months of each other a reporter for a New York newspaper, a diplomat-turned writer, and the author of a radio script all called them blue, while a celebrated literary figure who had just visited him described them as green, and a weekly news magazine made them brown in one of its cover portraits and blue in another.

During my own interview with him, the lights were turned low in the hospital room and it was impossible for me to tell.

I asked dozens of his close associates. Often they would look as startled and embarrassed as if I had asked them:

"How many steps are there leading from the sidewalk up to the front door of your house?"

Just as I was writing the chapter in which Ben-Gurion is physically described, his military secretary came on a visit to my temporary quarters in London.

"You see Ben-Gurion every day, don't you?" I asked.

"Certainly."

"You know him intimately, don't you?"

"Of course."

"You are a military man and therefore are very precise?"

"Yes."

"What is the color of Ben-Gurion's eyes?"

Colonel Chaim Ben-David blinked, gulped several times, and finally said: "I—I am not certain."

But he agreed to let me know as soon as he got back to Jerusalem. By that time I had left London and was in Switzerland on my way to Africa. I am sure the Swiss authorities thought I was receiving a coded message when a telegram arrived one day from the military secretary to a Prime Minister reading:

HIS EYES ARE BROWN

Three assignments in Israel.

How much they have helped to interpret Israel to America no one will ever be able to tell. At least a little, I hope.

Of course there will be other self-imposed assignments, for there was no time-limit on the promise I made to myself in Bucharest, Rumania, the day after what happened at the abattoir on the edge of the city.

5

A DIASPORA ASSIGNMENT

WALDO FRANK

As I told the Editor, when he invited me to contribute to this volume: I do not belong in it on the merits of any service of mine in the birth, the building or the defense of Israel's republic. But he insisted that he wanted my personal statement—and here it is, briefly.

Prior to 1927, when I first saw Palestine with my own eyes, my interest in the Jewish homeland was slight—as was my direct experience with the Zionist movement. Anti-Zionism certainly never appealed to me; if the Jews, principally of Eastern Europe, chose to make Judah's neglected valleys flower again with the milk and honey of their devotion, they had my respect, my admiration and my fervent wishes. But my own interests, cultural and even specifically Jewish, were elsewhere. I was not a child of Jewish culture; even its two great languages, Yiddish and Hebrew, were unknown to me. I was a Diaspora Jew; and I had even written that for me the greatest periods of Jewish culture were to be found, perhaps not in the era of the Prophets but in the Middle Ages. I was deeply aware of the major contribution of the Jews to the culture of the West, which was my culture. And I resisted the suggestion of so much Zionist thought, that the life of Judaism could not be at home in the West (which the Jews had done more than any other people—even the Greeks—to create) or that a modern Jewish experience could not integrally grow within the frame of Europe or the Americas.

This did not imply that I was unaware of the life-problems, the problems of survival for the Jews from the land of the *Affaire Drey-*

Jus to the land of the pogroms. But I felt that these problems had to be faced where they existed; and that to obviate them by escape into the uncharted problems of the Middle East was a romantic and utopian notion.

Late in 1926, Chaim Weizmann invited me to visit the Jewish homeland. I had met him in New York and he impressed me as a great citizen of the world. I was equally impressed, one day at lunch, by his friend, Schmarya Levin, whose voice, as he foretold new prophets rising on the ancient soil, rang with the intonation of the Prophets. Such men as Weizmann and Levin were products, I figured, of Diaspora Jewry. Their work had a national form, but— by paradox—the Jewish energy that inspired and gave them strength had long since transcended any nation.

My visit to Palestine, it was understood, was to be entirely personal. I was simply to come and see. Nothing was said about my writing of what I found. But it was, I am sure, tacitly assumed by Dr. Weizmann that I *would* write; and as to myself, I had every intention of writing. I spent over a month in Palestine in the spring of 1927, moving from Lebanon to the Red Sea. I visited several *kvutzoth;* I talked with labor men in Tel Aviv; I met such outstanding intellectual figures as Buber, Bialik, Bergmann; spent many hours with my old friend Judah Magnes (to whom I owed my first acquaintance with an orthodox synagogue in New York), and with the British military and Mandate officers. I also knew many Arabs—intellectuals and village sheikhs, discussing with them all the Arab-British-Jewish problems. I came back to New York. And (except for one insignificant little piece) I wrote nothing about my experiences in Palestine, or about my opinions and judgments. Such silence is extraordinary in any writer; and it had an extraordinary reason.

I had noted the growing animus toward the Jew, not of the humble Arabs but of the ambitious Arab leaders. And I feared these Arab leaders. I had noted the cold world-political motives of the British; their treacherous tricks to keep Arab and Jew apart, their cynical exploitation of the Zionist development of the land for their own purposes, imperialist and financial. And, much as I admired England, I feared the power aspect of the British. I had noted with love the luminous work of the *halutzim,* draining their swamps, hardening their soft intellectual hands to agricultural labor, striving to make a decent and open world for their children. But I was afraid for these gallant pioneers. I lacked faith in their success.

Before my journey, I had tried somewhat to prepare myself by visiting (for the first time) the post-World War ghettos of Poland, Galicia, Lithuania, Roumania. I had been overcome there with admiration and respect for that deep Jewish culture dwelling in the cellars, the misery, the mud, but rooted in God and flowering in human life. For the first time I had felt the great dignity of the Jew—to which I personally had no right and with which at home I had no living contact. I understood the yearning of these people for the opportunity of Zion. But I did not trust the Moslems. I did not trust the British. Short of miracle, I did not believe that the Zionist dream could prosper against these hostile forces. I trusted only *my reason,* which added the "pros and cons," and came up with a negative sum.

If I wrote of Palestine, I should have to be honest. That is: I should have to reveal my doubts, my discouragements, my lack of faith in miracles. I could not bring myself to speak a disheartening word before these pilgrims and humble prophets. Therefore, I did not write at all. The writer remained silent.

The Arab riots and finally the Arab war, the behavior of the British before they decamped, came as no surprise to me. My heart had foretold it all. What I had not foreseen was the miracle of Israeli resurgence, the miracle of Israeli strength over a twenty-times larger foe.

*   *   *   *

This is the first chapter of my "record." Hardly a proud one. I was simply too ignorant of Jewish *inwardness.* Yet I had seen its no-less miraculous survival in Warsaw, in Lemberg, in the Hassidic villages of the East. With more knowledge, I might have had more faith.

During the next decades, I did what little I could to strengthen my knowledge. In this sense, Palestine was already working in me, giving me "an assignment." I read Jewish literature, thought much on the meaning of the Jew, preparing for a book which I have not yet written (and may never write). But I did publish a few essays, enough to make a small volume entitled *The Jew in Our Day* [1] (1944). The book hardly referred to Palestine. It was about the Jew in the Diaspora, specifically in the United States. And it quietly suggested that if the American Jew submitted to the corruptions of American life, cultural and economic, he was a bad American and a bad Jew—even if he waxed emotional about the builders of Palestine and sent them money. The book was viciously attacked (one might say assaulted) by certain Zionists. I was called an anti-semite and a follower of Hitler! The reception of my message revealed, I believe, how urgently it was needed.

Thirty years after my first visit to Palestine, I was perhaps somewhat less ignorant—at least I knew my ignorance. Therefore, when I was invited to visit Israel and to write reports on what I found for a group of Latin American newspapers to which I was a regular contributor, I joyfully accepted. There were no more strings attached to this invitation than to the one long ago of Dr. Weizmann. But I knew that this time I would not be silent. The crisis of the Middle East was too urgent for such luxury. On previous journeys to the Near East I had come to know several of the great centers of Moslem culture. I had lived in the desert of Sahara, and I had been in Egypt. Now I spent another month in Israel. I wrote my reports and I re-fashioned them into a book titled *Bridgehead* [2] (*La Pasion de Israel,* in Spanish).

I was then asked to take my message personally to America Hispana. I began in Mexico. In talks with such outstanding liberal leaders as former President Lazaro Cardenas, I realized with surprise how cleverly the Arab propaganda had spread the conception and the fear of Israel as an aggressive military power! Even among those most fitted for a sympathetic understanding of Israel, the Arab refugee problem had ingested an insidious poison. Through a press conference, I got columns of honest information about Israel on

[1] Duell, Sloan and Pearce, N.Y., 1944.
[2] George Braziller, Inc., N.Y., 1957.

to the first pages of the metropolitan press. I gave a lecture on Israel in one of Mexico's largest theaters, which was crowded to capacity. Then I went on to Guatemala. Here I had long talks with President Castillo Arinas,[3] a devout and devoted Catholic, and with members of the Foreign Ministry. And again I found plenty of good will fumbling with erroneous information about Israel and its army, an army, I was told, before which the whole Arab world "trembled." The newspapers (covering all the Central American republics) were again open to me, and a long television interview, arranged by the President, spread my message beyond Guatemala's borders. I was supposed to continue south, but illness stopped my journey.

The method of my message to America was to reveal, by an objective, factual picture of the life of the Israelis, the common ground of all small nations; their mutual problems—and perils; and the deep spiritual relationship of the small peoples of Hispanic-Christian culture with the Jew. This was no new theme for me. As early as 1929, in lectures in Buenos Aires and Santiago de Chile, I had suggested the potential *at-homeness* of the good Jew, the observant Jew, in modern lands of Hispanic origin. Now, I did not lose sight of the voting strength of the Hispanic republics in the United Nations. My aim was to make a team of public opinion and the personal attitudes of public servants (diplomats, ministers, editors) which in any future Mid-East crisis could be counted on in the Assembly and the Security Council. For that crisis is permanently with us, and even deeper trial for Israel is bound to come.

Whatever good may have come of this mission, I feel that my best effort for Israel has been my unpopular criticism of the American Jew, my pointing out that American Jewish conduct is a dimension of the life of the Israelis—even as the face of Israel must be henceforth a dimension of all Diaspora Jewry. Our economic aid to Israel has of course been imperative, and must continue. Its danger is that it deem itself enough. The young republic, at this decennium of its birth, requires also sustenance of another nature; and the Diaspora Jew alone can give it.

[3] Assassinated a year later.

The American Jew who submits to the corrupt and false in American civilization betrays by his cowardice the heroes of the *kibbutz* close to the frontier of Jordan. Let him not delude himself about the effect of his dollars, the efficacy of the armored tanks which Israel buys with them—however needed these be. The life of man is more intricate than an accountant's columns. The very idea of a republic of social justice in Zion is a Diaspora contribution. The Prophets ploughed it into the loam of the West, and without the West it would not have achieved the social-economic form which has kept it alive. It is, moreover, a fertile vision in Israel because it is real wherever there are men. And all the Jews of the world are the custodians of this vision. If Brooklyn pollutes it, it is weaker in Tel Aviv.

But the converse is also true. When the vision of Israel as a realization of man's destiny is strong in a *kibbutz* on the waters of Jordan, it strengthens and supports the Jewish group on the waters of the Hudson. There is *reciprocity* of action. Israel cannot be alone; the Diaspora community cannot be alone.

In my book, *Bridgehead: The Drama of Israel,* I attempted to reveal how, implicitly and almost unconsciously, my first contact with Palestine had charged me with this sense of reciprocity. I sought to convey my sense of the religious values implicit in the pioneer work of Israeli youth, however remote their conscious articulation might be from set theological terms. It matters little, at the present formative phase, whether the *sabra* is aware of the relation between his work of survival and growth, and Diaspora survival and growth. The dynamic link is there. One of the new elements in present Jewish life, since the establishment of the Jewish Republic, is the direct circuit of vital interchange which now flows between Israeli and Diaspora Jew, between the land of Israel and all the lands of the earth where Jews are citizens of nations. No spiritual victory, no defeat in Israel, can fail henceforth to register in the Diaspora. No Diaspora deed of cultural creation or of cultural submission can fail to adumbrate in the small, intense Mediterranean republic. The idea that Israel, cut off from world Jewry, could shrink and harden into another ego-nation, is naive; and reckons without the enveloping dimensions which enclose Israel in the West and which enclose the Diaspora Jew, loyal citizen of many nations, within the specific destiny of Israel.

The Israeli today is busy with bare and bitter tasks of survival; with the manifold activities of growth in a perilous world: growth that must be joyous, for growth without gladness is stunted. The Israeli, in this sense, is a child of glory. What he needs most—and what is hardest to win—is perspective, not alone within the modern world and the Mid-East world, but even more within his own long history, which remains alive because every phase of it is still immediate. Such perspective is spirit; when it is lost, spirit sickens. Yet alone, in the constant crisis of its life, Israel—that glorious child—cannot possess perspective.

Here is a creative duty of the American Jew. It refers him ruthlessly to himself, to self-examination, and to intellectual self-aid. This is the weakest part of American Jewry. And the unclarities and ambiguities which issue from it threaten the organic health of Israel and could undermine with confusion the strength of Israel's armies.

6

MUSIC

ZINO FRANCESCATTI

as told to Jules Harlow

Ask a musician or a music lover to name the three B's of music, and you will most likely hear the answer: Beethoven, Brahms, and Bach. In October of 1958, I performed a program which featured compositions of the following three B's of music: Beethoven, Brahms, and Ben-Chaim. I was in Jerusalem, performing with the Israel Philharmonic in one of the concerts given to commemorate and to celebrate Israel's tenth anniversary. My assignment in Israel was essentially the same as my "assignment" anywhere: music.

During the course of my career I have had the opportunity to visit and to perform in many of our world's countries. As you might suspect, each country is different and, for the first time at least, presents one with new experiences. Yet, as an artist, it is quite a unique experience to have participated in the musical life of Israel. First in my mind is the fact that you never know what to expect. The schedule of a concert artist is usually a very conventional, fixed affair; some performance dates are often set years in advance. But in Israel, one is never sure of the number of concerts to be given or the amount of energy to be expended during any one visit. The many late improvisations—a kind of "save the situation" performance—which seem so natural for the committee of the Israel Philharmonic are a little confusing and harrassing for the performer accustomed to more conventional scheduling. Programming is also very elastic, and the artist must have a tremendous repertoire to be able to meet the demand for extra concerts. I was busier in Israel than in any other country. Aside from the matter of extra concerts, there is the matter of encores. Each concert is a serious and a tiring effort as well as a creative one and, in the midst of a busy schedule, faced with perhaps a concert on the following day to be preceded by early rising in order to make travel connections, one hesitates to perform and even comes to resent encore demands. Yet, what would be only catastrophe anywhere else always has a happy ending in Israel. They ask so much of an artist because they ask so much of themselves; you have to match them. Their great enthusiasm, their talent, and simply the great amount of hard work make the impossible possible in every area, and their contagious spirit infects the artist as well.

It is so exciting and exhilarating there because you surpass yourself, doing things you never expect to do in your life. Thus one evening I found myself giving an informal lecture on advice for the young artist. I spoke to two or three hundred people in the concert hall of a small conservatory in Tel Aviv. After my remarks, the audience participated in a discussion during which they asked very good questions. I remember that I spoke of the absolute revolution from playing for oneself to playing for other people, of transforming what one learns, of practice, of playing as a member of an orchestra, of balancing a recital and even of the artist's diet and dress. Usually there is a violin between an audience and myself. But that night I spoke directly to them. It was the only time that I have done so.

Everything is a challenge in Israel. Every one of the country's institutions had to be created anew, built up in the midst of war and other difficulties. The organizers of the Israel Philharmonic Orchestra were fortunate in that they had a great wealth of material to draw from in recruiting personnel. Many talented artists from the great orchestras of Europe came to Israel. Though Israel recently celebrated its twelfth anniversary, in many respects it is not at all a young nation; it is all of Europe. This is especially true of its musicians. They brought all the musical knowledge and heritage of Europe with them.

The composition of the Israel Philharmonic Orchestra is truly international. Communication between them and visiting soloists and conductors is never an insoluble problem, for these people speak practically anything. One among many outstanding characteristics of the musicians in this orchestra is the fact that they have worked well under such poor conditions and in such dangerous circumstances. During many months of 1948, Jerusalem could be reached only by means of a road winding through the hills of a narrow corridor which was within firing range of Arab military forces. Anyone travelling this road ran the risk of encountering the fire of snipers' rifles. Yet these musicians did travel to Jerusalem to give concerts. There are few musicians in the world who would undertake such risks.

One great hardship for orchestra personnel and visiting artists alike was the lack of a suitable concert hall. Concerts were performed in a building called *Ohel Shem*, a large white barn with terrible acoustics. For concert performances, eleven hundred people would be squeezed and crowded onto rows of backless benches and hard chairs. It was often so stiflingly hot that the large windows which covered one wall of the structure had to be opened, introducing a concert of horns and shouts of the street to the harmonies of Beethoven. But in spite of the hardships (or perhaps, because of them), musicians can be nostalgic about their performances in *Ohel Shem,* for there was an intimate quality in those performances which cannot be reproduced anywhere else. My memories of concerts there are cherished souvenirs.

To a musician performing in *Ohel Shem,* the idea of a modern concert hall in Israel seemed to be a miracle available only in a dream. In our travels, my wife and I have witnessed the construction of new concert halls, from the initial stages of planning to the completion of proud and modern structures. Even under ideal conditions, the process is always difficult and slow. Yet the miracle of a new and modern concert hall has happened in Israel. The

Mann Hall is a great hall, one which has the feeling of a Festival Hall. I must express my compliments and admiration to everyone connected with this hall, but especially to two who played vital roles: to Mr. Zvi Haftel, concert master of the orchestra, and to Mr. Frederick Mann of Philadelphia, whose name the hall bears. This hall permits three thousand subscribers to be seated together, which reduces the concert series from nine to four. People who are aware of the strain, fatigue, and monotony of playing the same program on nine successive days will appreciate the relief for the orchestra, conductor, and soloist, who now present the same program only four successive times.

The program of the Israel Philharmonic and the standard for guest conductors and soloists can hardly be matched by any of the world's great orchestras. The guest artists for the 1958–1959 season included conductors Mitropoulos, Munch, and Ormandy, and soloists Rubinstein, Peerce, Stern, Rabin, myself, and others.

How can Israel attract artists who normally are so difficult to obtain and who are so selective in their schedules? The answer is to be found in the Israeli public, in the great feeling of warm friendship and gratitude which the public and the orchestra give to the artists they admire and love. An incident which occurred during the Sinai Campaign illustrates this general feeling. Early in that campaign there was a special drive in the country to raise money for the *Magen David Adom,* the Israeli equivalent of the Red Cross. Each day the newspapers would publish the names of the contributors. I found myself reading this list every day in the English language daily paper. When one is in a foreign land, reading the daily newspaper in a familiar language becomes a ritual which is carried out in detail. Each day the donors' names were listed, followed by the amount donated and usually by a dedication, like "in memory of my mother," or "in honor of my brother." One day I was surprised to see my name among all the unfamiliar names of the list. An amount roughly equivalent to one dollar had been donated "To thank Mr. Francescatti for having played the Beethoven." I later found out that the donor was a nine year old boy.

The Israelis are one of the most hospitable people in the world. They give the artist everything that he needs. They themselves are gay, and they try to please you. Also, I believe that they work harder there than in any other country. Life there is quite hectic; there is a kind of electricity in the air of Tel Aviv which excites you and which urges you to participate in this great whirl of work and realization.

I remember a concert in Jerusalem, during the Sinai campaign. I believe that the performance took place on the first or second of November, 1956. Israel troops were fighting with Egyptian forces in the Sinai Peninsula, and the country was in a state of war. Jerusalem was under strict black-out conditions, and the streets were as dark as the catacombs. As we walked to the hall, a half hour before the concert, we could see only dark shadows, which we could guess to be the shapes of other people, also moving in the direction of the concert hall in an impressive silence. There were no buses or trucks and very few automobiles in the streets, for practically everything on wheels which could move had been requisitioned for military purposes. At the Jerusalem border, the Arabs, who probably knew of the concert, maintained military positions only a few hundred yards from the site of our performance. Yet the citizenry assembled for a concert without apparent fear, though the concert hall, with its concentration that night of two thousand people, must have been a good and a tempting target. More than three hundred people were turned away at the door. The house was filled to capacity. I shall never forget the warm, tense, musically religious feeling which was mine that night.

On the following morning, we had the honor of being received by President and Mrs. Ben-Zvi. I expressed the concern of my friends in America concerning Israel's situation. The country's relations with its neighbors had been tense, and while I spoke with President Ben-Zvi, Israel's troops were fighting a battle, the duration of which nobody knew. The President said to me, "Tell your American friends that we heard a great concert last night in Jerusalem. I doubt that they had one in Cairo."

This comment of the President's is, I believe, quite typical. The challenge of a conflict must be met, yet standards of cultural life must be maintained. My wife and I were in Israel in 1948, as well as during the Sinai campaign. For the state of Israel, these were times of emergency and armed conflict. Both of us were impressed with the quiet dignity of the people during those critical times.

I often have been asked to describe the effect which the Israel-Arab tensions have upon Israel's music. I do not believe that it has any effect, or at least not a detrimental one. If you speak with people who lived in London during the blitz of the second world war, you will note that many of them recall with pleasant warmth and deep feeling the concerts performed during black-outs and air raids. For example, those in blacked-out London who heard a Myra Hess concert cherish an unforgettable experience. One of music's most beautiful attributes often is emphasized in tense and critical moments: music is for the soul. Music can be a bulwark for defiance; it has heart; it is religious. In a sense, music can protect people in a time of crisis.

I have mentioned those members of the Israel Philharmonic who came to Israel from Europe's great orchestras. Let me speak now about another type of musician, the young Israeli, for the country's musical future naturally will depend upon him more and more as the years go by. There are many conservatories and music schools in Israel, staffed with excellent teachers. There are also a large number of students who study privately with instructors; perhaps there is a higher percentage of such students in Israel than in any other country. Israeli performers and teachers have been able to achieve great things artistically. This is due to the ever-necessary combination of talent and hard work.

I have heard more promising young talents in Israel than in any other country. I shall never forget one young man, who really typifies the music student of Israel. Nineteen or twenty years old, with thick and tousled hair, he plays the viola. He is tremendously gifted, and is possessed of a fantastic amount of energy and great determination. But this young man has no control; he is absolutely wild. This is his greatest handicap, and that of his contemporaries. "I have the talent," he told me. "I want to play at the first desk."

He is probably correct in his statement about his basic talent, but he wants to place himself at the first desk immediately, as if this were an automatic and natural process.

"Perseverance. Patience." These are the words which I used most often in my conversations with the young musicians and artists of Israel. This is the greatest lesson which an artist must learn, and it is very difficult. Israel is an eager country. Its people have accomplished a great deal in a few years, probably more than we can adequately appreciate, but there are some things which cannot be rushed. Artistic development is one of these things. Time is absolutely necessary for the violinist. He must exercise, he must memorize. You cannot improve upon human limitations. You can only recognize them, and work with them in mind. If you want to raise a tree, you must of course plant the seed yourself. You must maintain an active interest in it, and you must tend it; but seeds and saplings do have a standard rate of growth which cannot be rushed.

The great pianist, Arthur Rubinstein, has established a piano competition in Israel, awarding a prize which is similar to the Leventritt Prize which is awarded in New York City. I have established a similar competition for violinists in Israel. Each of us has established an endowment fund in a bank outside of Israel, by donating our fees received for performances in Israel and elsewhere. Mr. Rubinstein and myself hope to return to Israel approximately once every two years. For several weeks preceding each visit, local contests will be held throughout Israel. Then, during our visits (which probably will not be simultaneous), the selected finalists will meet in Tel Aviv, where one winner will be selected. In each instance the award will be one appropriate to the winner's point of artistic development. There is no fixed prize, other than an engagement with the Israel Philharmonic. Each award will entail granting the young musician aid in a program which we feel would best suit him. Thus, for example, if the winner should be a student in need of further training, we would send him to Europe or to the United States for study. If it is felt that the winner is ready for a concert career, we would arrange for concert performances and recitals in Europe and aid him otherwise in his early career.

The young student should be helped. We have a duty to our art and to the future in cultivating a new generation which could fill our places as we pass on. We cannot help the student to progress faster; development can only be normal. But we can help him materially. We must help the best students so that they may study abroad, develop their talent, and mature artistically.

7

THE DANCE

ANNA SOKOLOW

Looking back on my first two weeks in Israel, those two weeks with Jerome Robbins in the Winter of 1953, I realize that I have never been so swept off my feet. I do not recall that I ever slept, though, of course, I did. I do remember that I was excited, exhausted, and terribly moved. My emotional reactions to Israel were so strong that they have colored my entire relationship with the country. I have never seen so much work, so much unselfish dedication, such furious pride. The people, to a man, seemed to say, "We will survive. Nothing will prevent it." I think that I would have done anything to help them. One of the waiters in Tel Aviv's Armon Hotel, my stopping-ground, said to me when I asked him about the security of his country: "Where can we go from here? Only into the sea." After two short weeks in Israel, I knew that I would have to return soon.

In May of 1954 I did return, on a mission sponsored by the America-Israel Cultural Foundation. The Foundation had been actively engaged in encouraging several of Israel's outstanding groups in the performing arts. It had helped to sponsor an American tour of the Habimah Theater and was then in the process of introducing the Israel Philharmonic Orchestra to American audiences. In 1951, the Foundation had sent the choreographer Jerome Robbins to Israel, to survey the dance scene, in hopes of discovering a distinctively Israeli dance company for presentation in the United States. His recommendations led directly to the decision to assist the Inbal dance group.

The Foundation could support only one group, and Inbal was chosen for immediate help as the group which showed the greatest promise. My association with them is very close to this day.

I worked with many dancers in Israel, but my assignment was primarily with Inbal. Before speaking of them, let me refer to the physical working conditions of all dancers in Israel. It is very hot. Israelis, like all peoples in the Middle East, observe a siesta. The hardest work had to be concentrated in the early morning and in the late afternoon, with a good amount of time off for the midday meal. In 1954, there was a shortage of space and an acute shortage of wood. There was a housing problem in Tel Aviv and all the houses were of stone or concrete. The basement of an apartment house was secured for Inbal—a good thing because it was cooler. After considerable difficulty, we acquired enough ply wood to make a small floor over the cement. This was a portable floor, and it was often taken with the company for performances. The arrangements were sufficient, though far from ideal. For the large open classes, to which all the dancers were invited, I used the gymnasium of a high school on Ben Yehuda Road, complete with baskets and standard gym equipment. The hard fact is that the facilities for dance were poor.

However, despite these conditions, there was considerable dance activity in Israel. There was folk dance, more folk dance per square inch than there is rock-n-roll in the United States today. Nearly every hour of every day there were young people, and old, dancing the *Hora* or the *Debka* or the *Patch Tanz,* or any number of newer dances. Back of this was a delightful, energetic woman, Gurith Kadmon, who had come to Israel years before from Germany. She had taken a leading role in teaching and organizing dance until finally theatres full of people came to watch an evening of dance on stage. It was an amalgam of influences, complex as the people of Israel themselves: Greek, Rumanian, Polish, Russian, Arab (the *Debka* derives from the Arab dance), Persian, Druze, Circassian, and it included the oriental quality of the Yemenites. This activity reached its high point at the Festivals at Dahlia. There, in a huge outdoor amphitheatre, as many as six hundred dancers would perform for three days and nights.

There was modern dance too, especially in Tel Aviv, but also in Jerusalem and Haifa, and in the *kibbutzim*. It divided itself into schools, each under a different master, most of whom, like Gertrude Kraus—the outstanding exponent of the modern dance in Israel— had come from Europe, especially from Germany, and had studied under or been influenced by Mary Wigman. Their classes were full, and the dancers were proud of their particular schools. Each studio presented its work regularly in concert form, usually at the Ohel Theatre, and toured the *kibbutzim*. Many of the teachers undertook occasional jobs of choreography for the Habimah or the Chamber or the Ohel Theatre companies.

The few ballet teachers, like Mia Arbatova in Tel Aviv, Archipova in Haifa and Rina Nikova in Jerusalem, had come from Europe. Although their classes were quite successful, there was not as much interest in ballet as in modern dance, perhaps because the ballet was more traditional, more set in its technique, while modern was more open to new ideas and movements, thus closer to the temperament of a young, pioneering people.

There were also many ethnic dancers among groups like the Druze, the Bukharins, the Circassians, and the immigrants from Baghdad and Cochin. Among the Yemenites, under the direction of a tiny, fragile, Jerusalem-born Yemenite woman, Sara Levi-Tanai, was the group called Inbal (the tongue of the bell). Sara Levi-Tanai had been a kindergarten teacher and had also taught in *kibbutzim*. Intrigued with the young people from Yemen and their dance, she had set their talents to her own stories and songs which she took from the Bible, from Yemenite lore, and from her everyday experience.

The Inbal group had been organized in 1949. They had appeared in the cities, in *kibbutzim,* and in the military camps. The government or the *kibbutzim* paid them a small stipend when they performed, but the amount was insufficient for a living wage, so that their dancing was supplementary to their jobs. One of the men was an elephant keeper in the Tel Aviv Zoo. Another was a mechanic. Among the girls were domestics, a factory worker, and a teacher. They traveled in trucks supplied for the occasion by the Army or by a *kibbutz*. Such scenery, costumes, and lights as they used were carried by hand, as were their drums, their cymbals, and flutes. After the Foundation began its program, one of the first acquisitions was a second-hand bus complete with a driver who also doubled as light technician, carpenter, baggage and property man, and stage manager. He even served as a kind of sergeant, herding the dancers together after a performance to get them home. Eliezer Peri, and Judith Gottlieb, head of the Israel office of the Foundation, had been aware of the group's unique beauty from the beginning and served as their advocates in higher circles. And Sara Levi-Tanai! I hardly know how to account for this woman adequately. She is one of those rare, rare human beings who combine the imagination, the good taste, the zeal, the will, and the love to accomplish great things out of next to nothing. She had been working for many years before she received help, but she had always believed that the help would come. Curiously, the help came from outside her country. Her own countrymen tended to take herself and Inbal pretty much as they took their daily paper. Very few Israelis realized what Inbal was about. When I first set eyes on them, I knew they would be loved in Europe and America. They were that unique!

At the start of my work with them, I was, frankly, not quite sure how to go about it. Having seen them perform, I realized that their dancing represented a cultural expression I had never seen before and it presented a strange kind of problem to me. On the one hand I felt that I must not trample certain ground; I must not touch the flower, but rather try to find out how the flower could be nourished and made to grow larger. What seemed most important to me was to make the group realize its own potential. Actually, they were, and are, extremely innocent. (What more can one say about anybody in this day and age!) I felt the enormous responsibility on my part not to touch this innocence, but at the same time to give them a kind of strength and an understanding of what they were and to help them project this more effectively.

They were artists on the one hand; they were children on the other. Their temperaments were very unusual. The nearest I have ever seen were the Mexicans, who were also very innocent. But the Yemenites were extremely sensitive and highly refined, with a delicacy the extent of which completely overwhelmed me. They had an almost religious dedication to their work. At the same time they possessed the oriental quality of boundless talkativeness, yelling, and screaming. I used to think they were constantly angry with each other, until I realized it was just their manner of speaking. Working slowly, I began to feel my way with them and grew to love them very much. I must admit I did some screaming and yelling myself, because the more I loved them the more I wanted to make them good, to make other people proud of them.

They were one of the hardest-working groups I have ever met. They worked six days a week, from nine o'clock in the morning, when I would give them class in modern and ballet technique, through long hours that included voice lessons, lectures, rehearsals of course, and, many times, performances. Within one year, the year of my arrival, they gave two hundred performances. Often they would not reach home from a performance until the early hours of the morning, but they would show up for class at nine. I could not stop them. A group with such an attitude would make any teacher proud, and I was no exception.

Of course, I was not without criticism. "What style of work do you give Inbal?" I was asked. "Aren't you going to spoil their own style?" My answer was, and still is, that the body of a dancer must be that of a dancer. It must be a trained body, a controlled instrument. The prime object of my work was to get them to know what their bodies could do. I insisted that, in their rehearsals, they be conscious of what they were doing, and I felt this could be accomplished without touching their work. There was no need to tamper with their creative work; it was exquisite. I guess the clearest answer to the critics was the enthusiasm the dancers returned to me.

In addition to training their bodies technically, I set out to give them a professional attitude toward work. This involved teaching them how to use their time to best advantage, how not to over-extend themselves, how to approach rehearsals and performances. Briefly, this meant, in rehearsals, *sheket,* or "keep quiet." Regarding the performances, though I hated the task, I had to convince them that it was not professional to bring their families backstage during

a performance. This practice included tea and refreshments for everyone, at times making it difficult to get the dancers on stage at their
cues. On one occasion they were ready to go on strike if their
families were not allowed. "Factory workers work in the factory," I
told them. "You work in the theatre. It is the same thing." They
finally understood. I also worked with them on make-up and taught
them a respect for their costumes and the stage.

S. Hurok came in August to have a look at Inbal with a view to
arranging a tour for them under his management. It was very difficult to find a theatre for the performance (a common situation in
Israel). In the end a movie house was made ready, but I will never
forget the heat that night. The theatre was an oven. S. Hurok was
decidedly impressed, but thought that Inbal needed more polishing
before being seen abroad. For the next three years the work went
on, bitterly at times for Sara Levi-Tanai and the dancers who wondered if they would ever leave. But at last costume sketches were
solicited, costumes were made, sets were constructed, music was composed and scored, extra lighting was provided, as well as extra
technical personnel, and in August of 1957 Inbal sailed out of Haifa
for Marseilles. After touring Europe, they arrived in New York
at the Martin Beck Theatre under the auspices of the Foundation
and the management of S. Hurok. The critics sang their praises,
from Dublin to Toronto.

Inbal today is a going concern.* S. Hurok and the Foundation have
completed plans for another tour that will take Inbal to Japan and
back to the United States where the Western cities will have a chance
to see them. I was with them again in the summer of 1958, after
their first tour. They were still working hard for new dances, better
technique, better methods of touring. They are now installed in
their own studio in Tel Aviv, and they have a new, air conditioned
bus. It is delightful now to realize that all the effort, on the part of
so many, was worthwhile. The work of Inbal will continue to improve, particularly because the dancers love what they are doing and
because Sara Levi-Tanai shows no indication of running dry. Indeed, one of her new works, "The Desert," is exceptional theatre.

* As of Summer 1959.

As I have already stated, the bulk of my time was committed to Inbal, but from my first visit I had a strong interest in the other dancers. With them in mind, I have taught open classes in modern technique and choreography during most of my stays. Sara Levi-Tanai was, herself, quite eager that I do this, and gave me every assistance she could. I must say, too, that the teachers of Israel were genuinely helpful in seeing to the success of these classes, many of them joining the classes. All the classes were held in a high school gymnasium, it being the only place with a wooden floor, and were attended by dancers from all parts of the country, including some remote *kibbutzim*. Sometimes there were as many as one hundred in a class. They represented all the schools, modern as well as ballet, and included many folk and ethnic dancers.

With the launching of Inbal I was able, in the summer of 1958, to give much more time to these classes and, at the end of my visit, to present two evenings of my own works, "Session '58," to the music of the American jazz composer, Teo Macero, and "L'Histoire du Soldat," of Stravinsky. The Israel National Opera offered the works for which the new opera house was used. The dancers I used, from both ballet and modern schools, the actors, musicians, technicians, were all Israeli. Both performances were sold out and the press was enthusiastic. I think they point the way to further similar activity. Other outsiders should be encouraged to work with Israeli dancers.

This experience of mine is, I think, indicative of the progress the dance has made in Israel since Jerome Robbins reported back what he had found there. Among other things he had noted the need for outside companies to make appearances in Israel, as well as for Israeli teachers and dancers to go abroad for study. He had also proposed that some kind of institute of the dance be set up where the most talented students from all the fields of dance could go to further their studies and out of which a permanent company could be formed. Such an institute has not, as yet, been achieved. But there have been other signs of progress.

Several foreign companies have played in Israel. A number of American dancers have gone to live in Israel and are now teaching there. Quite a few Israeli teachers have gone abroad to Europe and America for courses. Many Israeli dancers have gone to study in Paris, London, and New York.

The Israel National Opera has a ballet company which gives evenings of dance twice a week in addition to its opera performances. Among the choreographers are most of the ballet masters of the country.

The Conservatory of Music in Jerusalem has a Dance Department which offers classes in modern dance. It opened in the Fall of 1958 with a two-week course given by Martha Graham. But it does not have a theatre.

In sum, much has been accomplished. All the dancers, like the Inbal dancers, are hard-working and full of energy. Like dancers the world over, their road is not easy. Aside from the activity I have mentioned, and the occasional musicals and plays-with-music in the theatres, there is not much they can do. They do need a theatre. Most of all, they need to perform, for progress can only come through performances before audiences. Without audiences, and I do not mean family-and-friend audiences, the dance becomes too much ivory-tower, too in-dwelling, with no healthy chance to expand. As I told the dancers last year, they must work, work, and work some more to better their techniques and their disciplines. They must not wait for theatres to be built for them. They must, by their own activity, create audiences, which in turn will demand theatres. This is the only way they will get a dance theatre. By activity I do not mean sporadic concerts. I mean steady performances all around the country, on *any* kind of stage they can find, and under *all* conditions. The people of Israel will support every kind of dance company, as they have supported my concerts, and as they support the opera, the theatres, and the orchestra. In the end, the kind of national institute Jerome Robbins envisioned will certainly come to be.

I intend to go back again. I intend to continue my work with Inbal. I intend to continue teaching the other dancers. I intend to do my own works, with Israeli talent. I trust other Americans will follow suit.

8

ON THE PLASTIC ARTS

MITCHELL FIELDS

It seems natural in beginning the account of my trip to Israel to wonder what made me want to go. For a sculptor who intends to practice there, the decision could not be an easy one. The trappings of the profession are complicated and unwieldy. The end product is huge and usually of prodigious weight. Altogether it is a time and energy consuming business, and fearfully expensive. It is not easy to answer the question I put to myself . . . why did I want to go? The roots go back too far, and too deep.

However, it is certain that I did not go to Israel with the thought in mind of promoting the culture of the country. No sculptor could afford that kind of altruistic luxury. As a matter of fact the "compelling necessity" would rather indicate that it was I who hoped to be the beneficiary, and I suppose it is an unwitting tribute to the Israelis that I sought artistic sustenance in the climate of the energy and vitality with which they are building their new life.

My good friend George L. Cassidy, the Executive Director of the America-Israel Society, gave me the idea of going to Israel. It never would have occurred to me. I never was a Zionist. As a sculptor it had been more natural for me to identify with those people to whom *sculpture* is or has been a language.

My meeting with Mr. Cassidy came about through the series of lectures on Israeli culture given by eminent speakers at Columbia University and sponsored by his organization. I am very glad I attended the art lectures, for through them and through meeting him my eyes were opened to a world I did not know existed. I had not been unconcerned about Israel, but until then I had been unaware of it as something close and personal.

The story of a new emerging art life in Israel fascinated me. I wondered if it could be the scene of the rendezvous that is every artist's dream—the place where art may be pursued because people care for it. So I took on the assignment in Israel very kindly proferred by George Cassidy. The long dreamed of "strategic withdrawal" became a mission of purpose.

Over the centuries, the Jewish people have always been culture-minded. They have been known as the people of the Book, to whom learning was synonymous with Godliness. They have made significant contributions to the cultures and civilizations wherever they were permitted to play a part. However there is one great and important field in which they played almost no part, until about the beginning of this century, and that is the field of the plastic arts. Short as this period was, it demonstrated a predilection for the plastic arts previously undreamed of. During this period, artists like Chagall, Soutine, Modigliani, Pascin (and "midwife", Gertrude Stein) rose to international fame.

This period, which saw the birth of an international style, actually dates back to about the close of the Victorian period. The world was still big then, though it was beginning to shrink. The spirit of the French Revolution and French humanist democracy were very important factors in attracting intellectuals in search of an atmosphere of freedom. They naturally gravitated to Paris from everywhere in Europe. Among them were many Jewish intellectuals who added their creative genius to form what came to be known as the École de Paris. It was therefore inevitable that the end product should have an international character. This very nature of their art removed them from concern with the art problems of their own people. The fact that the Jewish artists of Paris felt themselves to be without national roots made them able and willing through their contributions to belong to the whole world.

Although the art emanating from Paris involved intellectuals of France, Russia, Germany, Spain, Italy, and the low countries, it had little impact on the peoples of these various nations. Eventually, of course, some of their ideas filtered down (though not too deeply) to nourish the cultural life of some individual nations—those lands without rigid political barriers and those with a cultural climate sufficiently mature and to some degree wholesome.

At about the turn of the century, too, the settlement of Palestine began. The men involved were political and national idealists, the Zionists of Central and Eastern Europe. From the beginning, with the conscious striving towards nationhood, there was a deliberate effort to develop a national culture. The young artists of Palestine drew from the bubbling fountain of Paris too, but it was for the purpose of watering their own "seedlings." Their problem was new and different. It was as new and as different as their life was.

I wrote a short article on Israeli art that was recently published by the America-Israel Society Bulletin. I am including an excerpt to help round out the picture up to the time of my arrival: "According to Gamzu the noted Israeli critic, 'the pioneers of Israeli painting were Rubin, Paldi, Guttman, Shemi, Litvinovsky, Lubin, and Zaritsky. The members of this group wished to create in contact with each other, while stressing what was original in each of them. Their final objective was to give essential artistic expression to the old and new life of the country and to lay the foundation for an Israeli school of painting.' Subject matter was dominant then, and it had to be to fulfill their purpose. This, of course, was a serious point of departure from the direction of the then developing international style; for in Palestine content was crucial.

"From those beginnings the artists, each in his own way, developed with the tide of the times at home and abroad. The birth of the State, which brought with it a great influx of muscle and blood from all the corners of the world, recreated something of the spirit that had existed in the beginning. A new legitimacy, a new world acceptance imposed a new and greater responsibility uniting them as one people in one place and by the paths of their own choosing.

"Whatever the background of the newly arrived artist may have been, every artist felt himself in some way reborn when he touched foot on the ancient soil. There is in their lives a new concern with the contribution they make towards a new entity. The change may be in their style, on subject matter, or perhaps in the pervading spirit of their work. The sense of security in belonging, the sense of being wanted cannot help but have a powerful effect on their creative energies.

"Thus, at the ten year mark, the question is often put, 'Is there an Israeli art?' Of course there is . . . though the diversity of its roots and the breadth of its philosophic and aesthetic outlook precludes the possibility of its being an insular school of art. It is, nevertheless, the face of a people reborn in their ancient surroundings, rejoining their old stream of history in pursuit of a brave new goal as a national entity."

There can be no doubt that their greatest strength lies in the diversity of their art. Simultaneous with the founding of the State an *avant garde* group arose. Like a lusty, self-confident youngster beginning "to feel his oats," they determined to find their own paths. They are sometimes called "Young Turks" or "Secessionists," but their own name is more fitting: "The New Horizons Group." They sought to produce an Israeli art using the more advanced techniques. I have spoken with many former adherents who since then have developed to maturity. They explained their "defection" from the group with the statement: "The time had come to secede from the secessionists, for the whole body of artists had also grown and matured so that differences became indistinguishable. Thus, once again, the time has come when the artists should be 'expecting', and no one should be surprised by the howling of another new and healthy infant."

Hava Meketon is a young Israeli sculptor who very recently returned from a two and one half year study trip abroad. Her views, as she expressed them in a news item, reveal a critical and mature outlook. It reflects the thinking of a large body of the younger artists. To quote from the news item: "My own objective in travelling was to re-acquaint myself with original sculpture and to submit myself to any influences accruing from this observation. In addition to these positive influences, seeing a plethora of modern sculpture helped me clarify my own approach to the art. So many 'polished pebbles'—

sculptures by Arp, Brancusi, Moore, and others—and constructions of old pipes and waste metal make it clear that this form of sculpture is of historic importance only in an instructive elementary aspect . . . to clear the stage of the bric-a-brac of 18th and 19th century European sculpture. Today, I feel, we must go beyond these primary forms to a deeper and more significant expression." I only hope she has the gifts her profession requires in the same measure that she possesses the sensitivity to her responsibility as an artist. *Bon chance. Bon courage.* She needs them both.

I arrived in Israel in June, 1957. It had been a long journey and my first glimpse of Mt. Carmel overlooking Haifa was a thrilling and welcome sight. Going through the customs with my hand luggage was a simple and pleasant operation. Of course I had "hold baggage" too, about ten huge crates and seven smaller ones containing some equipment and my sculpture, a good part of my life's work. These pieces, about forty in number, were to be unloaded later and I was to return in a few days to have them cleared.

Bad news awaited me when I returned to Haifa to claim my baggage. Much of my sculpture, representing years of work and a considerable financial investment, was broken. This had come about as a result of improper storing of the crates when they were loaded on the boat. In my great disappointment and sadness, I seriously considered returning to the United States immediately, as one inspector indeed had suggested. Also disturbing was the fact that original sculptures (unlike paintings) are dutiable in Israel, and that the government takes a commission on whatever is brought into the country and is sold. The law requires the artist to deposit a sum equal to the amount of the expected commission. The legal difficulties involved in bringing sculptured works of art to Israel makes such an undertaking prohibitive. The only excuse offered is that this law has been inherited from the Turkish regime.

Among the first people I decided to see after my arrival in Israel was a sculptor, because I knew he would understand all the problems I would have to face. I knew the name of just one such person in Tel Aviv—Rappaport, a fine sculptor, the creator of the Warsaw monument erected in memory of the heroic ghetto fighters. Rappaport lives in Ramat Gan, a city in the outskirts of Tel Aviv, so I taxied out there in the hope that I would find him at home.

He was in when I arrived. It was siesta time, but he graciously forgave my intrusion. Rappaport, a man of medium height and stocky (like so many sculptors), is in his middle forties, energetic and bubbling with enthusiasm. We talked shop for a while. When I told him I had come to work in Israel, he was positively delighted. He welcomed me like a general in battle, who had just received an army of fresh reinforcements. "There is only one way for the people of Israel to learn to want good sculpture," he said. "They must be *shown* good sculpture, and they will want it." "And," he added, "it will help me too." Then he went on . . . "You won't make money here, but they'll love you." The President of Israel himself could not have made me feel better, had he said it.

On another occasion, I was introduced to a group of painters at the Milo Club. One of them remarked, "I'm so glad you came, we need you." Laughingly I asked, "Would you say that if I were a painter?" "Oh no," he said, "we don't need the competition. We have enough good painters." Of course I understood; the going is tough for artists there, though it is true that in Israel, sculpture has not attained the same high level that painting has.

The first few days in any new place are always the most thrilling. I cannot describe just what I expected. The Jewish people I had known in America somehow had become indistinguishable in the great variety of peoples there, but in Israel I saw them for the first time living together as one people. It was hard for me to reconcile myself to the fact that their national origins were more obvious than their oneness as a people. The Russian Jews looked Russian, the Austrian Jews looked Austrian, the Persian Jews looked Persian, and the Indian Jews looked Indian. The latter were some of the "dark Jews" I had never even seen before. Somehow I got a feeling of unworthiness, for there could be no doubt that I myself too must be very unlike the legendary people of the Bible.

During their dispersions, the Jews have had to learn to live together with other peoples. Therefore it is natural to assume they could live together with their fellow Jews, in spite of the differences which do exist among them. A genuine sentiment of good will arises from the simple statement, "He is my brother." It occurred to me that, in the near future, this population, a composite of national origins now gathered in one place, is destined to become the *altneue* soul of the people of the Bible.

I began the search for a studio in Haifa, I suppose, because it is such a beautiful city. There is something about its encircling hills which gives you the feeling of a magnificent creature opening her arms to embrace you. It is a fairyland terrain with the added vision of Abba Khoushy, Haifa's Mayor. I sought out the local artists' association in town for help and advice.

Chagall House is their headquarters. It is a new building built especially for them, with the city and its mayor taking an active part. The secretary, I found, happily was an American from California. I was cordially greeted, but most important, we could talk. He spoke with the quiet eloquence of a man who knows the drama of language in its application to life. Writing is his profession. America had become for him a place, far away, yet he wrote in the English language; for that is the language in which he kept up with international literature.

Soon after that meeting, I acquired a studio in Tel Aviv. About the same time I was able to have the huge deposit on my sculpture waived through the intervention of the Israel Foreign Office. Thus I was able to install myself in a picturesque alley in the older quarter of the city. My neighbors were mostly Eastern and North African Jews. Communication with them was not easy, but I managed with my native tongue and a limited knowledge of four other languages.

I had been offered the choice of several places in artists' colonies where I could have settled. I turned them down, because I had had enough of that kind of inbred existence at home. At any rate, I was fascinated and drawn to a kind of people I had never known except through my familiarity with the sculpture of the Middle East. I was fascinated by their children, too, and there were lots and lots of them in my quarter.

My sculpture arrived from Haifa late at night so that no one in my alley really knew what my "business" was. I believe I was rather glad about it, particularly since my skylight window to the rear faced the court of a synagogue. But this period of incognito existence did not last long. One fine afternoon three little boys climbed up on something under my skylight window and there I saw staring into my studio three wide-eyed little boys. I decided it would be best to let them have their fill of gaping. Finally two boys did go away but one decided to sit it out. I thought about it, and quickly decided upon a different strategy. I went to the rear and invited all three to visit me and to see my sculpture. Very happily they followed me in. Their spokesman and interpreter was a ten year old boy with the face of an angel, sparkling dark eyes and long curly *payot*.[1] After he had looked and looked . . . he exclaimed in Yiddish, "You can die, you can die, they're so beautiful!!" Before they left I explained that they were never to climb up to peep in my window, and that they would always be welcome when I was not too busy. I gave each of them some clay and off they went. In about three minutes there was a knocking at my door. Outside were five grinning faces—a little girl with her baby sister, a boy of about fourteen, and two twelve years olds. They marched in eagerly, giggling, and then the oldest boy took over. He acted like a seasoned museum guide—"Don't touch! . . . This is so and so . . . This is made of . . . Yes, with a hammer and a chisel." I gave each of them a large piece of clay, and explained that they were always welcome. Off they went. Five minutes later . . . well, this time I counted twelve. And so it went for the entire afternoon and on into the evening when the parents and grownups began to come. It continued until supper time. I have never had a happier and more rewarding "exhibition." I felt they were all quite proud to have me in their alley. In the days that followed I had visitors often. It is so nice to have people seek you out because they are interested in what you do.

Unfortunately, not all the inhabitants of our alley were glad to have me as a neighbor. I realized this one day when a group of men shattered a newly installed skylight and then proceeded to demolish the rear wall of my studio. My workmen ran to call the police and soon the attackers were taken away in a police wagon. Later I was

[1] Earlocks, which orthodox Jewish males never shave or cut.

given an explanation for their violent and unprovoked actions. My attackers held firmly to the biblical stricture against the making of graven images. Luckily, most of my neighbors did not take this position and, like most of Israel's citizens, took a positive interest in art even though many of them had no previous art experience.

The biblical stricture against making graven images is still prevalent among many people. I am aware that much of the sorrows of the Jewish people in historic times was due to the tampering of their host peoples with the Hebraic notion of God. I am aware that idol worship still exists in the world, but, I believe, there is no longer any danger of pious Jewish people succumbing to it. I suppose the fact that the stricture against sculpture has lasted for many centuries is a tribute to the grandeur of the Hebraic conception of the Almighty which is undefinable in concrete form. At the same time it is a tribute to the power of sculpture over the minds and hearts of men, and a tribute to the men who make it. It is time now that it be used for the pleasure that it can create in men's lives, and for the dimension it can add.

It is only fair to state that my reception by people varied. Shortly after I arrived, I was invited to show a piece of sculpture in Ramat Gan in a show sponsored by the city. When I came to the opening I was told that the mayor's representative in art matters wanted to see me. I was pleasantly surprised by the offer of a one man exhibition. "But," I said, "you haven't even seen a photo of any of my things. Can you judge by this one piece?" "It's enough for us," he said, "and we will be glad to pay all expenses." Ramat Gan, incidentally, has a fine, well-lit exhibition gallery.

Everyone everywhere loves flowers, and there are flowers everywhere in Israel. In Israel, however, it takes more than love and desire to have flowers: it takes water. Though water is so costly the people seem to pay the price gladly. So I wonder how much of a step it is from flowers to art. The bleak modern architecture and Spartan interiors cry for it. The large glaring walls exposed to the bright sun would soften with color and form. The ancient Persians and Assyrians understood it very well, for colored terra cotta was used extensively in their architecture. The glaring lack in Israeli parks and public squares is the warm human touch that art can give.

There are, however, some places in Israel where sculpture stands unmolested and where there is a thirst for more. These places are some of the *kibbutzim* and the city of Haifa.

I visited Kibbutz Ein Shemer when I first arrived at the invitation of Zvi Lurie, one of its founders. It is one of the older *kibbutzim* in Israel and is a veritable garden of Eden. As a matter of fact, a few years ago this *kibbutz* won the award for the best landscaping in Israel. The chief gardener told me that he was an artist who had given up painting pictures and used the entire terrain as a great canvas. Zvi, my guide, jokingly complained, "The paths he cuts are never straight from one place to the next . . . but the extra steps are exciting to take." As he conducted me about the place he pointed to two palm trees flanking the entrances and one other old tree. "When we first came, our *kibbutz* was an arid wasteland. Only those three trees were flourishing. For the first ten years we carted every drop of water from five kilometers away. Then we struck water and our crops and orchards bloomed, and that brought the bugs that brought the birds. We brought back the birds that nest in our trees and orchards." And I could understand how he felt when he said "Our gardens cry for sculpture."

There is a very interesting monument on this *kibbutz*. It is a huge bas-relief, which forms a sort of background for a stage. It is dedicated to the memory of one of their members who lost his life in the effort to land a shipload of new immigrants during the British occupation.

There are a few large monuments on some of the other *kibbutzim,* and several have erected museums. The Ein Harod Museum, the cooperative effort of three *kibbutzim,* is one of the largest. It is one of four important museums in Israel which constitute a circuit for traveling art exhibitions. Many American artists have contributed works to their permanent collection. I also visited Kibbutz Givat Brenner, where Louchansky lives. He is one of the great sculptors of this century who spent most of his life in France. I brought him greetings from his old friend Jacques Lipchitz. Givat Brenner has built him a lovely studio. Now in his eighties and still very active, he has been working there for quite a few years. One wing of the Ein Harod Museum has a large collection of his works on display. Kibbutz Hazorea is now completing a museum which will house a small but fine collection of Oriental and Near Eastern art. There are three painters living on this *kibbutz*. One of them, Rhoda Reilinger, I believe to be one of Israel's most talented painters. Hazorea is reputed to be the most culture-minded *kibbutz* in Israel. It was founded by a group of highly cultivated people who fled from Germany in the late twenties. The story is told that, if you were to call out to someone in a field where a large group of people were working, "Hey! Professor!", almost everyone would turn around.

Israel, in the beginning of its second decade, is not a ten year old infant as nations go. The people that compose it and their co-religionists outside its borders, who in some way contribute to its upbuilding, are largely a group whose experiences are associated with all the more advanced ideas of our times. The idea of nationhood, however, is young. That is to say, the application and adaptation of their experiences to the building of their own institutions and folkways are new for them.

Often "practical" people speak of doing "first things first," the inference being that art is not one of these. However, the truth is that art is a basic ingredient of the "first things." Art cannot be excluded from the shape and nature of all things. Art may be good or bad, but it is never absent. The plastic arts are of importance because for the first time in two thousand years the Jewish people have the freedom to create their own physical world in the image of their own desires. They are to art as water to the seed, for art is not heaven-sent; it is people-inspired. Their art will be the measure of their attainments as civilized people.

People everywhere somehow think of art as easel painting or free sculpture. It is true that these constitute a major part of art and that they concern themselves with aesthetic gratification in people's lives. But there are also endless useful applications of civilized life which take their form and color from the major arts. It can be taken as axiomatic too that the level of achievement in art is dependent on the participation of people and on the level of aesthetic develop-

ment. Michelangelo could very well have gone through life unaware of his genius if there was no need for him in his time. It is
undoubtedly true that quite a few people know his name today, but
few understand his achievement. It is certainly true that in our
country much too few people know the art of the artists of our
time. As a generalization, the same thing can be said about Israel,
though I was gratified to find that people in Israel are not apathetic
about this state of affairs.

The art of our time is characterized by a drive for personal expression. Architects too, feel much the same way. I think they are
inclined to look on sculptors, muralists, and creative craftsmen as
people who are trying to get into their act. All this, of course, is
childish nonsense since most artists know that they are obligated to
others for at least ninety per cent of what they themselves know and
do. The remaining individual contribution is sufficient to create a
masterpiece or a dud. Much of the austerity and coldness of contemporary architecture in Israel, as elsewhere, is due to this self-
imposed limitation. Israel has the added problem of limited resources
and materials. Employing the combined ingenuity of its craftsmen
and artists would therefore, seem desirable.

Beit Brodetsky, the Anglo-American hostel, was built by the Jewish Agency with funds raised by the British Zionist Organization.
It is, without doubt, the finest hostel in Israel, beautifully designed,
and surrounded by lovely gardens. Robert Bannet, the architect, does
what he can to bring art into the life of the guests of the hostel. He
has begun to buy paintings for the hostel, though it is not easy to
acquire money for this purpose. He plans eventually to assemble a
collection of paintings to hang in every room. It is his plan to let
each occupant choose the painting for the room. The guests may
stay at the hostel for as much as six months, so that it is a mark of
real consideration to defer to the tastes of the occupants.

Bannet is also the architect for the housing development in the
area of Beit Brodetsky. In the shopping center area he included a
small sculptured fountain. With this as a beginning, he hoped to be
able to convince the city administration to appropriate more funds

for decoration. He chose an abstract design because he wanted to avoid any religious controversy. However, from the viewpoint of creating a beautiful spot for the people of the neighborhood, I do not think it matters whether it is abstract in design or derives from nature. Either could be successful. What does matter is that one approach to design is taboo. Abstract art is not necessarily "safe" either. After all, we can't know what the fertile imagination of our precocious youth might dream up if they set their minds to it. It makes more sense, I think, to trust the common sense of people by discarding prejudice altogether.

There are only two or perhaps three legitimate art galleries in Tel Aviv, and a few dozen "art" shops that sell trashy pictures to the tourist trade and to the home trade, too. These pictures are called "buckeyes" in America, and they are done by specialists, but in Israel many good artists do them for reasons of survival. What is particularly evil about this situation is that many of those things get out of the country as examples of Israeli art.

This is just one of many things that Israeli artists do much like their American colleagues. They, too, are faced with the same battle for survival. It is safe to say that art in Israel would be dead if only those artists practiced it who are able to earn their way by their art alone. This refers only to city artists. The *kibbutz* group is in a different situation.

An artist friend of mine who did such paintings barely eked out a living doing it, so that he was quite responsive to a suggestion that was made to him to go into the school system to teach art. It meant taking many courses. After a few months when I met him again, I found a changed man, a happy, excited man. As he put it, "Even if I never teach I would not want to miss what I am learning." From his description, the preparatory courses in Israel for art teacher training are nothing less than brilliant.

By the end of the year, he already had been teaching as a part time substitute. His remuneration? The teachers' starting salary in Israel is about $100 a month. He didn't earn much but it does represent a gain in self-respect and even a small gain for the future. When his pupils grow up, they will have been educated to a better art under-standing. In the meantime, life is not easy for my friend as it is not easy now for Israel.

The *kibbutz* artists are in a much better position than any of the city artists. The basic problem of security and normal family living is solved for them through membership in a *kibbutz*. One of the most exciting exhibitions I saw last summer at the Tel Aviv Museum was an exhibition of *kibbutz* children's art. The high quality of the show was no accident. The results were a tribute to the ability and devotion of their teachers, the *kibbutz* artists. There can be no doubt that many of the future artists of Israel will come from this source.

The fine exhibition of Kibbutz Artzi [1] painters and sculptors shows a high level of creative ability. Indeed, among their number are a few of the best artists in Israel. Their "realism" exists in the thematic content of the material, though not strictly in their tech-niques which, for the most part, are free and experimental as one would expect in good contemporary art.

Israel is a tiny, dry, and stony land. Its hills and valleys, which its neighbors fiercely begrudge her, have been sacred in the thoughts of countless peoples over the centuries. The Jews are now returning to this land, bringing with them their hopes for a new life in dignity. The land, no doubt, will yield to their labors but, like all peoples, their greatest source of wealth is the creative mind of man pursuing his tasks in peace.

[1] A federation of those kibbutzim affiliated with the Hashomer Hatzair Movement.

9

PROBLEMS OF CULTURAL ACCOMMODATION

MARGARET MEAD

It was my good fortune to visit Israel as the guest of the Ministry of Health, through the courtesy of The Reubeni Foundation, for a period of three weeks—between the dates of July 1 and July 22, 1956. My itinerary was arranged by Mrs. Phyllis Palgi, in consultation with various other governmental agencies and voluntary bodies throughout the country.

The purpose of my visit was to consider the whole problem of the integration of immigrants of varying cultural backgrounds into contemporary Israel, looking at the question from the standpoint of cultural anthropology and as a specialist in interdisciplinary research and practice in the field of mental health. As the guest of the Ministry of Health, I was given a special vantage point from which to view this whole process.

Three weeks is, of course, only sufficient to place the general situation in Israel against a much more detailed knowledge of problems of immigration, assimilation, integration, and culture change in other societies. I was dependent at every step on the specific information which could only have been provided by anthropologists who had specialized in the study of particular ethnic groups and particular communities within Israel. Without such information, anything that a visiting consultant can say is too general to be useful in the actual policy making or practice such as that which daily confronts the Ministry of Health.

It appeared to me that the Ministry of Health was playing a pioneer role and assuming very major responsibilities in community development in Israel. Upon the success of the various health centers in relating their whole program to the local communities, and in introducing team work among the various disciplines and continuing utilization of the specialists in culture and community life, may well depend the future usefulness of the behavioral sciences in Israel. It would be, therefore, almost impossible to overestimate the importance of what the Ministry is doing.

I shall address myself first to some general comments on assimilation problems in Israel and conclude with some observations on technical problems of utilization of specialized personnel.

This first part [1] of my paper must be regarded essentially as diagnostic comment rather than the result of research in Israeli problems. Research and diagnostic experience in other areas of the world have been combined in an attempt to illuminate some of the cultural problems of Israel. My visit to Israel increased my capacity to interpret the work of Israelis who had been my students, and to use the existing written materials on Israel and also increased my understanding of the materials on Eastern European Jewish culture which had been developed in the Columbia University Research in Contemporary Cultures.[2]

The last few years have seen increasing attention by the human sciences to the problems of identity, especially to the self-image which a people have of themselves as members of a group and citizens of a nation. Israel presents an instance in which almost all of the crucial problems which have been classified under the heading of "Problems of Identity" are brought sharply into focus.

Group self-images are necessarily elaborated against some background or contrast group; isolated primitive people see themselves vis-a-vis the animals they hunt, or their ancestors who have died. In the modern intercommunicating world, the self-image of any

---

[1] Substance of a report presented at the Conference on Economic Planning and Social Policy in Israel, Harvard Center for Middle Eastern Studies, May 10–11, 1958.

[2] Zborowski, M. and Herzog, E., *Life is with People,* International Universities Press, New York 1952.

group is a compound of the positive evaluations of the members of the group, combined with the positive and negative evaluations placed upon this group by outsiders. During the 40's, in the studies of Jewish self-images, there was a preliminary emphasis upon "self hatred," as if this were a uniquely Jewish trait. However, subsequent consideration has shown clearly that members of any group, who are identified, commented upon and reacted to by members of other groups, necessarily incorporate and build up reactions to these judgments, and that one of these reactions will be a violent self criticism in the fields on which the judgment has been made. Americans, whose national state developed within some of the same conditions of critical praise and condemnation which accompanied the inauguration of Israel, have institutionalized self-criticism as the response of the educated and responsible, and have classified defensive overstatement of American virtues as the response to such criticism of the naive and ultra patriotic.

Many useful parallels can be made between the establishment of the national self-image of Israel and that of the United States, where also immigrants from other countries—within a partial framework of idealism that obscured the complexity of motives which brought individual immigrants to the country—developed a self-image under critical and often hostile appraisal from members of other countries, especially the countries from which the immigrants came. But it is important to temper these historical parallels not only by considerations of the special position of the Jews in history, but also by the special conditions of the mid-twentieth century with its glare of mass communication which means that each nation, and especially each new nation, must work out its cultural solutions, its political and economic difficulties, on a world stage. The participation of the world audience will, of course, increase as the success or failure of each effort of the new nation is seen in settings with meaning for the members of the audience: as the triumph of a member of the capitalistic, communistic or neutralist bloc, as a battle between East and West, as the victory or exploitation of the weak, in a context of religious rivalry. This glare of public appraisal, which bedevils the attempts at negotiation on the international scene, is intensified in the case of Israel at almost every level: the previous experience of Israelis as members of a special group historically singled out, subject to persecution, needing special measures to survive; the involvement of Europeans and subsequently of Middle Eastern Powers in Zionist ambitions, the fate of Palestine, and the formation of a Jewish State. Then there is Israel's special position between the extreme collectivist and totalitarian solutions of the Communist world and the anti-collectivism of the rest of the Free World. In Israel, socialist aspirations, which have gone down to defeat elsewhere, seem vivid and viable. Furthermore, the peculiar link between the settlers and their fellow Jews in other countries and the moral and economic problems of Israel's continuing dependence on the help of the diaspora mean that Israel, probably more than any other modern state, is intimately and continuously a part of the internal politics of other countries. All of these types of involvement intensify the problem. Additionally, Israelis, as Jews, have had a long experience of identification with the whole group, of recognition that what any Jew did, anywhere, would reflect to the credit or discredit of Jewry. (This is in strong contrast to conditions in Indonesia where before World War II group identity did not extend beyond the limits of one or a small cluster of Indonesia's 3,000 constituent islands. Even in old states, like Great Britain and France, in peacetime the strongest identifications of the stay-at-home parts of the population were with family and locality, possibly with religion, rather than with any larger group.) So it may be said that in addition to occupying the most exposed position on the world stage of any present-day nation, the Israelis, as Jews, have also the longest experience of occupying such a role, with all that this means in accepting the responsibility or repudiating the inevitability with which the individual had to suffer for the group, in excessive pride and self-conscious superiority, and in high attention to the valued attributes of the Gentile communities in the countries within which they had lived.

This problem of cultural identity, in addition to the twentieth century situation of action on a world stage, can be analyzed into a number of components. Nationhood, as elaborated in the western world, had always been associated with soil, with a deep attachment to a landscape, an attachment compounded of cultivation and ownership, battles fought in its defense, and the incorporation of natural features and names of places into art and poetry, mythology, and patriotic symbols. In the formation of new nations in new and unfamiliar physical settings—as was the case of United Kingdom settlements abroad in Australia and New Zealand, and for the settlements of Spain and Portugal in the New World, for the European settlements in Canada and the United States, and Dutch and English settlements in South Africa—the physical and spiritual tussle with the unfamiliar landscape has been an essential ingredient in the formation of a national culture, whether the emphasis has been on the conquest of nature, as in the United States, in a passionate and romantic devotion, as in New Zealand and South Africa, or in a dearly bought and grudging affection for an exceedingly inhospitable environment, as in Australia. For immigrants to Israel from outside the Middle East, the unfamiliarity of the physical environment, especially when combined with the unfamiliarity of agricultural labor, has been tempered by the historical knowledge of the country and the role it played in the early history of the Jews. Battles fought under desert conditions in the twentieth century became endurable when the route had been taken by earlier warriors. Each resistant, arid intractable condition was hallowed by its sacred past. Significantly, the centuries-old sense of alienness from Christianity, which had been nourished by persecution in Europe, yields—in Israel—to the inclusion of the events of early Christianity in the same physical landscape. The meeting place of Mary and Elizabeth is pointed out to the visitor—part of the new identity of Israel as a country.

The language of the newly settled country is usually a battlefield, though it be only the struggle against the "colonial accent" which develops in isolated new conditions, the struggle between languages—as in Canada—or the struggle to impose a dominant language on groups of immigrants speaking many languages—as in the United States or Australia today. The choice of Hebrew as the language of Israel, which originally partook of some of the disadvantages of the revival for every-day use of a language long restricted to special purposes, has provided indispensable background, like the history of the relationship to the land, for the reception of immigrants from Europe and from parts of the Orient. For all of these, the value position of Hebrew was such that learning was facilitated, although the lines of learning from European languages and from Arabic were so different. Israel has the opportunity to solve the question which has dominated the educational systems of small nations, like Holland or the Scandinavian countries, and which threatens to disrupt the newly acquired unity of India, by continuing habitual bi-lingualism for which each group of immigrants has been in some way prepared; all to honor Hebrew, all to expect to use one or more other languages. The work of mastering three of four languages—viewed as a necessary hardship in a country like Holland, and as quite impossible in the United States—has been established as a cultural expectation for Israelis, and is an enormous advantage in working out a cultural identity as Israelis and in maintaining a national position both in the West and in the Middle East. Israeli tri-lingualism would seem to be both necessary and possible.

We may next come to the question of physical stock, to the problems that beset a country whose immigrants come from many different racial or sub-racial groups and have to meet and adjust under conditions in which some groups think that their racial inheritance, real or fictitious, or the expressions of parts of that inheritance in skin color or hair form is a sign of superiority or inferiority. The inclusion of immigrant or aboriginal populations with widely differing physiques and resulting high visibility has proved a problem in every country in which such attempts have been made. Here again the Israelis are now in a favored cultural position. Due to its special nature, the Jewish religion emphasized biological inheritance, and so assumed the primacy of "Jewish blood" among a chosen people. This tended to replace active religious expansionism with defensive religious isolationism, and through the centuries has meant the continuing assumption of "racial" relationships among Jewish groups, who in actual physical type also resembled the inhabitants of the countries where they had lived for centuries. This was of course combined with an over-emphasis on whatever "Jewish" physical traits had been selected as differentiating both by Gentiles and by Jews, which tended to be overselected for, locally. Individuals who looked most like the local stereotype of a Jew were least likely to disappear into the wider community and marry Gentiles. The habit of assuming a racial tie with people who looked extraordinarily different and who conformed to the negative stereotypes—not of the locally defined differences between Jew and Gentile but to the local shared definitions of inferiority, e.g., dark skins as compared with light skins, or a difference in body build—has built up among European Jews a habit, often ambivalent, of seeing anyone who says he is a Jew, as a Jew, no matter what he looks like. However much this cultural expectation was strained and however much the dislike of the foreign and "inferior" physical traits were masked by intra-Jewish antagonisms to Jews of other nationalities, it remains as a deeply ingrained cultural commitment to the unity of the widely dispersed, physically differentiated Jewish "race," ready for use in the accommodation of immigrants to Israel, representative, in pigmentation and features, of all of the great races of mankind. The over-emphasis on the importance of race which was a negative contribution to any establishment of acceptance of man's common humanity in Europe has become a positive feature in Israel, counteracting, at least in some degree, the over-weaning sense of "white" or "European" superiority which the earlier immigrants brought with them. This acceptance of all Jews as Jews has not been complete enough to prevent negative self-identifications on the part of some of the newer immigrant groups nor attempts to follow the old masked pattern of physical discrimination under the disguise of different degrees of "civilization," as in the common dichotomy between Europeans and Asiatics or Orientals, or the new euphemism— particularly inappropriate when one considers the participation of the "Orientals" in the defense of Israel—of "veterans" and "new immigrants."

The traditional identification of "race" and religion, so much more characteristic of the Middle East than of Europe, yet sufficiently

developed in Germany and in parts of Eastern Europe to challenge
the attainment of cultural unity, has also made possible a new type
of cultural acceptance in Israel. "Race" could be and was accepted by
both Jew and Gentile in Euro-American culture in lieu of religious
belief and practice, and conversely conversion and circumcision made
it possible to join the Jewish race. Consequently, Israel can extend
absolute hospitality to all Jews and maintain an open door for immigrants who become Jews by conversion and also make a place
for non-Jews who wish to become Israelis. Although Israeli culture,
especially in some of its political expressions, has not entirely escaped
the problems solved by Pakistan in one way and Indonesia in another, which stem from historical treatment of religious affiliation
and real or aspirant nationhood as coinciding, the very ambiguity of
identification as a Jew in the past now provides a cultural climate
which makes possible appropriate 20th century solutions of the
acceptance of immigrants of many types, while an orderly place for
Arabs also to be Israelis can be found.

Perhaps the most serious barrier to assimilation and acculturation of the diverse immigrant and old resident groups in Israel is
the tendency of these ambiguous attitudes towards Jewish identification to mask themselves under notions about "civilization," "literacy,"
etc., in a situation where there actually *are* enormous differences in
type of "civilization" among the immigrant groups. The conflict
between the official idealistic ideology and actual attitudes, as expressed for example in the term "intermarriage," referring to unions
between individuals of different immigrations, results in a great
deal of confused thinking and refusal to face issues. This is generally the result of such a conflict of ideal and actual attitudes in any
situation of cultural and racial conflict, documented so fully by
Myrdal [3] for the United States in the treatment of Negro Americans,
but it becomes specially significant in a country where planning is as
important and as possible as it is in Israel. The treatment of the
older generation as people to be cared for but from whom nothing
can be expected, the over-emphasis upon youth and the extreme dependence upon the acculturative effects of weakening family ties

[3] Myrdal, G., *The American Dilemma.*

and of educational separation, and the failure to face the educational handicaps of immigrant children without a European cultural background are all examples of the obfuscating effects of an unadmitted set of "racial prejudices." There is a definite danger that such measures, which have much in common with measures adopted more implicitly and with less planning in the United States, which isolated the American-born generation from the cultural tradition of their forebears, and also with the methods of penalization and liquidation of historically doomed classes adopted in Communist countries, may counter-balance, in Israel, the very great advantages inherent in the long traditional continuity of Judaism. All three patterns of induced change—that of the United States, that of the Soviet Union, and that of Israel—have in common a distrust of the ability of adults whose learned cultural behavior differs from that of those in authority to learn the new patterns and to participate actively in them and to contribute to these patterns and change them, not from the cultural poverty of a limited and indoctrinated childhood, but from the richness of a mature past.

This final portion of my chapter contains the substance of my report to the Ministry of Health, my specific assignment in Israel.

It is clear that at every stage of the settlement program in Israel, there is need for an anthropologist who can deal with such questions as the way in which members of different cultures will meet urban or rural conditions, admixture of groups of different economic or educational status, and with the question of which groups can be placed in juxtaposition with other groups. A second set of problems arises in such matters as the ability to deal with long or short time expectancies; to tolerate greater closeness or greater dispersal of family members; attitudes toward money, status, help, community responsibility, the law; divisions between secular and religious life, traditional distribution of roles within the family; traditional methods of child rearing, food habits, theories of health, and practices of hygiene. Without a particular and detailed knowledge of each group of settlers, a health program of the depth and extensiveness of that of the Ministry would be deeply handicapped. Furthermore, an initial traditional study of the culture of any one of these groups, such as the Yemenites or the people of the Atlas Mountains, is only a first step in the process. Knowledge is needed also of the actual combinations of persons within any community, and of the characteristics of clusters of small settlements, the members of which interact in a larger administrative district. Furthermore, as each step of the program is introduced, and the members of each community learn to work together with the Health Team, and adopt new health practices which in turn will modify family relationships and patterns of living, the culture which they brought with them to Israel will be modified, in ways which can only be partially predicted, as they will be dependent upon the interaction between specified health department personnel and specific community personalities within the immigrant and Israeli cultural traditions.

The initial steps which the Ministry has taken are well designed to deal with these characteristics of the situation, including initial studies of a culture, the training of anthropologists in the actual everyday problems of the Ministry of Health, and the incorporation within the structure of the Ministry of the role of anthropologist, where basic cultural information and continuing information on change can be coordinated and imparted to the technical staff, in high-level conferences, and in teaching situations for young and new personnel. All of these functions of the anthropologist appear to have been conceived and set up in the development of Mrs. Palgi's role, for which I have great admiration. Under present circumstances, of course, the conception of what anthropologists can do within the program has been so imaginatively developed by Mrs. Palgi's energy that it makes extraordinary demands on the small number of people available. However, it may be hoped that the very striking usefulness of anthropology in the program will make it possible to expand the number of workers involved.

Specifically, I emphasized that, to be really useful, an anthropologist, unfamiliar with Israel and with the problems peculiar to the ambitious and inclusive health program of the Ministry, should have at least a year of working intensively with members of one immigrant culture, followed by comparative experience in other communities, combined with continual close inter-relationship with the team of health workers in his or her area. Younger anthropologists should be encouraged to interview, under supervision, older and experienced health workers, physicians, nurses and health educators who have been working with a particular culture or in a particular community. This will increase their understanding of the specific problems of health and community organization to which their research is to be addressed, and help members of the health team to clarify their own understanding of the habits of different ethnic groups, and of how they can use more cultural information.

This type of procedure should also have the advantage of dispelling the idea that an anthropologist or other social scientist can give useful advice without specific knowledge, and, on the other hand, of demonstrating the need for a disciplined and expert approach to the problem of cultural patterns which can come only from a basic training in anthropology, carefully applied to local situations.

It seems clear that the possibility of absorbing groups of such divergent cultural backgrounds and such different physical types is enormously facilitated by the self-definition of all of these groups as Jews, sharing a common religious historical tradition. The advantages of this common sense of identity can hardly be overestimated. Some of the advantages may well be lost, however, if the present tendency to speak of large sub-groups, such as "Oriental Jews," and "Anglo-Saxons," is perpetuated, either explicitly in vocabulary, or implicitly in practice. It would seem that everything is to be gained by the avoidance of any generalization of vocabulary or practice below the basic one of common Jewishness, and that even the distinction between "old" and "new" immigrant is undesirable. Such designations as "North African," or "Moroccan," which fail to make the necessary distinctions between—for example—people from the Atlas Mountains and the highly acculturated individuals from Casablanca, lead to the formation of prejudice, bitterness, and faulty community planning. The more specific and the more accurate the designation of each group, including sometimes such details as year of emigration and specific type of religious affiliation, the less danger there will be of inter-ethnic conflict arising. Thus, lumping all "Moroccan" boys together would fail to distinguish between early immigrants whose parents tended to send their problem children, youths who served in the army, and later immigrants, who, while showing cultural similarities, also present great differences owing to the period and conditions of immigration. There will undoubtedly be new distinctions introduced among immigrants in terms of their having shared or having failed to share each new peril.

The question of keeping families together, the desirability of resident youth groups compared with daytime youth groups, legislation affecting family responsibility, etc., all have to be looked at in terms of each specific cultural group. Some groups are ready for more responsibility to be taken by grown children for their parents, some groups should be helped to loosen family ties which are incompatible with life in present day Israel. Any policy which is followed across the board, without making distinctions of this sort, is likely to show enough failures to call it in question and bring a demand for a reversal. As the Ministry develops a clearer and ever more firmly based policy toward integration, it will be important not to apply any policy—such as single ethnic group villages, boarding schools for adolescents, separate housing for the aged—without specific attention to the ethnic group or groups involved and the date and detail of their immigration and settlement.

The application of such a policy of continuous adjustment of broad policy to specific groups means that field workers, with broad anthropological training and specific knowledge of cultural and social backgrounds in Israel, have to stay in touch with developments in the new settlements. In such new settlements, difficult situations often develop which have both local and national political implications. It is also most important that the role of the community specialist should be protected from any imputation of spying or informing, and yet kept specific enough so that local situations attributable to the interaction of identified local personalities can be studied, and, if necessary, measures can be taken to break deadlocks or to shift personnel. Experience has shown that such a protection of the anthropologist's role is best accomplished if the anthropologist reports findings to *all* the groups involved, that is, never reports only *about* a situation, but also to the people involved in the situation. Unless such precautions are taken, the community worker is torn between standards of professional integrity and an honest desire to have a given community or health program work well, and is likely either to abandon scientific work or to retire into the type of scientific detachment which has little relevance for an ongoing health program.

When present-day immigration conditions in Israel are placed against a historical background of immigration in other parts of the world, especially in the United States, it is possible to try to avoid in Israel some of the less fortunate aspects of immigration elsewhere. Israel, like the United States, is very successful at making the children of immigrants full members of Israeli culture, and there has been an understandable tendency to emphasize this successful integration of the young and to write off the old. Particularly because Israel has emphasized a protective system for the old, there has been less pressure to help the middle aged and old to learn to live in the new culture. Yet we know that the United States has paid a terrible price for this break between generations—in thinness and superficiality of contemporary American culture. When children are sung to sleep in one language and one idiom, and use another in school and at play, there is an inevitable dilution of the cultural stream. More emphasis upon the involvement of grandparents, on their ability to learn to speak Hebrew and to be carriers of modern Israeli culture before they die, would compensate for this. It is also important to distinguish between immigrant culture patterns which are so far removed from contemporary Israel that a total change is necessary, and those richer and more thoroughly literate traditions in which the adults are capable of adjusting without making a complete shift. The situation, in which a woman sits grinding on a cement floor and keeps half-cooked food in the shower, is one which is likely to perpetuate cultural distinctions which may lead to new rifts in the emerging culture of Israel.

It is also necessary to steer a middle course between recognition of some of the old values of the immigrant cultures and emphasis upon the new values of hygiene, exercise, dignity of manual labor, and service to the country instead of loyalty to one enclave. Both immigrant and health worker are likely to swing between these two extremes, so that European-trained doctors or nurses or social workers may start out with a dogmatic insistence upon European ways and a total repudiation of the old customs. Then, as they learn more about the problems facing the immigrant mother who must now care for ten living children instead of the four who survived out of ten, they may swing violently away from advocating cultural change, to a dogmatic and more irrational defense of the old. These responses within the community health services themselves may contribute to a pendulum effect in which nothing is gained, like the comparable swings in the United States, from scheduled infant feeding to unscheduled back to scheduled feeding, from open windows to closed windows in sleeping rooms. This pendulum effect can be overcome if there is a conscious attempt to make changes in style of this kind, in health practices, both specific as in infant feeding, and general as in types of staffing a health center, and so maintain a slow but continuous movement in a *direction of change,* so that temporary revulsions for or toward a particular practice never simply repeat a past level of achievement.

Closing the gap, in practice, between the newer and the old immigrant groups, presents a particular challenge to Israel because of the ideal of a single kind of treatment for all. Although this is most difficult, perhaps, in the field of formal education, where special classes for newcomers seem to be discriminating, while lack of special classes may place children at a permanent disadvantage and turn them into second-class citizens, this is also true when it comes to learning a new attitude toward health, child care, and community responsibility. Devices, such as the single ethnic group villages grouped around a school and health center, such as those developed in Lachish, are one way of avoiding this difficulty, although the single year in which little children go to school with their own language group seems insufficient. The type of town planning which is going on in new towns like Kiryat Gat, which may well result in segregating different ethnic groups, can be compensated for if

these local concentrations are then made the occasion for extra
efforts, which can be viewed as special privilege rather than discrimination, as they prepare the children and the adults of less ad-
vantaged groups to move out into the wider society.

The Arab population within Israel presents particular problems in
the way in which discrepant adjustment to the modern world is
being handled. The way in which trained Arab workers—physicians,
nurses, and social workers—were integrated into some of the discussion groups in which I participated was a model of inclusiveness and solicitude for any difficulties with language or concepts.
Yet there also seemed to be a tendency to demand for the Arab health
services far less local contribution than Jewish communities would
make and to treat some Arab nomadic groups with a considerable
amount of patronage. I fully recognize the extreme delicacy of the
problem and the possibilities of worldwide repercussion, but I think
the only safe course of action is to accord the Arab populations the
same type of expectation, privilege, and responsibility accorded other
Israeli citizens, for over-privilege can be as discriminatory and as
psychologically damaging as underprivilege, even though there are
fewer immediate ill effects.

In my visits to the various health centers, I was struck by the
inclusiveness of the task which had been assumed and by the possibility that difficulties might arise at high administrative levels because other agencies might feel that the health work had assumed a
global character, and at the community level where there might be
a tendency to leave all community responsibility to the Health Center
team. I found the local program at Kiryat Shmoneh, in which an
active regional committee had been involved in the planning, to be
one very valuable solution to the problem at the community level.
At the national level, cooperation in regard to any specialty between
agencies is, of course, partly dependent upon the presence of counterpart personnel in both agencies. As other national agencies make a
comparable use of permanent anthropological staffs, ease of cooperation should be increased.

It may also be useful to recognize that the idea of team work
is very modern, while the members of Health Center teams are of

different degrees of seniority, were trained at different periods of history in different universities and medical schools in various parts of the world, and so present contrasting styles of behavior. The introduction of team work—in the contemporary sense—into structures which have had a hierarchical pattern in the past (such as the relationship between physician and nurse, or between the medical and social services), presents a great many problems which cannot be solved by fiat or a declaration in favor of team work. Unless there is continuous and expert attention given to questions of team functioning, there is a danger that the whole new concept so essential to the Ministry's plan for the development of community health services may come into disrepute. I met some situations in which a group for whom a "free discussion" had been officially planned were briefed within an inch of their lives into inexpressive silence, and others in which the idea of how a "team" would relate themselves to an expert in discussion was muted by an expectation of listening to an authority.

In the emerging understanding of mental health in Israel, the present program of the Ministry of Health should make it possible to maintain a focus, which utilizes an initial concern for the mentally ill, as the motive power for the support of preventive services, stretching throughout community life, which prevent mental illness and are positively conducive to greater mental health.

In closing, may I emphasize how much I learned—in Israel—about the problem of applied anthropology. By seeing the anthropologist operating in a setting of such rapid purposive change, I was able to formulate more exactly than ever before the way in which the anthropologist cannot be simply an informant on the *status quo ante,* but must be part of any change that occurs. In evaluating the visits of experts to other countries, what the expert learns is at least as important as what he teaches—and this is especially so in Israel, where directed change is so consciously and responsibly pursued.

IO

SOME REFLECTIONS ON THE
ECONOMY OF ISRAEL

LEON H. KEYSERLING

In August 1959, I visited Israel for the third time within the past few years. The opportunity to be there is always an inspiration to anyone who believes in the infinite capacity of people to make progress under the institutions of freedom.

I have been asked to make a critical evaluation of my own participation in the great human adventure which Israel represents, from the perspective of the economist. It has been suggested that I deal fully with the successes and failures encountered in my work there, and also make some comments about the significance of the progress thus far achieved, the difficulties still to be overcome, and the potentials still to be realized.

It is not within the scope of my inclination to evaluate any small contribution which I may have made toward the treatment of Israel's problems. The people and leaders of Israel are better equipped than others to meet these problems as they arise. They have not read their history; they have lived it. They have worked hard and shed their blood. They seek in all things independence, not dependency, and they are moving rapidly along this road. It would, therefore, be an act of supererogation for me to pretend that I could hew close to the line of attempting to appraise my relationship to their tasks and their efforts, although my advice has been met in Israel with an engaging open-mindedness which is characteristic.

Instead, I shall use the method of setting down candidly my own reflections about the problems of Israel, especially the economic problems, and my own critical—though I hope sympathetic—appraisal of what the people there are doing. I feel that the discriminating reader will gather from my comments a fair appreciation of what I have said in Israel, and also of the extent to which my suggestions have fallen on receptive ears.

First of all, let us take a brief look at Israel's economic record to date.

The size of any economic accomplishment must be measured against the base from which it starts, and judged by the weight of the burden superimposed upon that foundation. Never within the history of economic development in any land has any people voluntarily assumed the task of more than doubling its population in little more than a decade, mainly through free immigration. The population of the State rose from 879,000 in 1948 to 2,054,000 by early 1959. This burden, assumed by the people of Israel, would have been difficult even if the State had long endured and long prospered before the commencement of the task. On the contrary, the State at that time was suffering from economic exhaustion caused by the struggle of its creation. In addition, it had been bleak and underdeveloped even before that struggle commenced.

Yet, during this slightly more than a decade, the increase in the output of industry and agriculture has far more than kept pace with the increase in population. Agricultural production has increased more than three and one half fold; industrial production has risen more than three fold. This would have been a phenomenal accomplishment even if the new population could immediately have been impressed into economic service, and even if the resources and tools had been available for their use. But the accomplishment has taken place with neither the resources nor the tools available at the outset, and with the new population constituting, initially, a manpower liability rather than a manpower asset, because it had to be housed and fed and to a degree equipped and trained before it could assume any economic responsibilities whatsoever.

The vast expansion of Israel's economic output during these years of strain is all the more remarkable because, even insofar as potentially productive tools and resources were available, they had to be diverted in an enormously large percentage of their total to the building of houses and roads and many public buildings as well, and thus could not be poured into the process of replenishing and revitalizing the economic assets of the country. In addition, although the War for Independence had been valiantly won, the burden of maintaining security against a ring of inimical and numerically superior powers, and fighting again in self-defense, has continued to exert a heavy tax upon the entire economic system.

But Israel during these years has faced not only the task of achieving economic growth; she has also faced the task of achieving economic stability. Serious shortages existed even in 1948, and magnified by the tremendous population increase, they would in themselves have created an inflationary strain. Moreover, the very effort to overcome these shortages by affirmative economic activity required the building of plants and machines, and this process of construction necessarily exerted additional inflationary pressures before the benefits flowing from their completion could be realized. On top of all of this, account must be taken of the effect upon Israel of the post-war inflation throughout the free world, including those strong nations from which Israel had to buy a large portion of her supplies for both consumption and investment.

Measured against these severely cumulative inflationary pressures, the unchecked expansion of which would ultimately have wrecked the young and fragile economy beyond repair, anti-inflationary measures have been drastic without being repressive, and far-reaching without being excessive. They have produced substantial results.

Mounting inflation, partly open and partly underground, has been replaced by a reasonable though not absolute degree of price stability. From 1956 to 1957, consumer prices rose 6.5 per cent; from 1957 to 1958, only 3.4 per cent; and during the first quarter of 1959, there was virtual price stability. Excesses in the money supply relative to the supply of goods have been substantially drained off. The Ordinary

Budget of the Government, which now includes most defense out-lays, has been brought into balance through improved revenue measures and attainable economies.

But the mere control of inflation is in itself only a neutral though important accomplishment, not only because stability without growth is insufficient, but also because stability in the long run cannot be maintained without growth. Consequently, growth programs are at the very core of all of Israel's economic efforts.

The manifest long-run purpose of all of these programs is to improve, on a sound and enduring basis, the standard of living of the people of Israel in the context of domestic freedom and international security. But this kind of sound and enduring advance in the stand-ard of living, if it is ultimately to be coupled with economic self-sufficiency, must be founded upon an increase not only in production to meet the needs of a growing population, but also in productivity, because advancing standards of living depend upon production in-creasing faster than population.

Thus, the shorter-run economic policy of the State of Israel, while preparing for and implementing the longer-run policy, may superficially seem inconsistent with it. For the accumulation of the plants and tools and equipment, both in the factory and on the farm, necessary to the expansion both of production and productivity, re-quires a larger relative level of investment and a smaller relative level of consumption than will be desirable when the under-develop-ment of the country has been appreciably relieved. It follows that, for now and some years ahead, the advance in the standard of living for which all free and progressive people legitimately yearn must temporarily be restrained though not abandoned.

In fact, Israel is a prime economic testing ground of whether a relatively underdeveloped free economy can under the methods of democracy make the hard choices which some other underdeveloped economies are making under the methods of dictatorship. We all know by now from observation that the totalitarian states have used brutal methods to repress consumption and living standards, in order to force enough internal savings to hasten industrial develop-ment through internal capital formation. It is much harder to do this in a free society (which values means no less than ends). Comparing 1958 with 1950, per capita private consumption has grown in real terms in Israel by approximately the same amount as per capita total national production. It might have been better if consumption had grown somewhat more slowly, thus leaving more room for internal capital formation. However, taking account of the human values and democratic procedures which animate the people and their Government, facile criticism on this score is unjustified. On the other hand, comparing 1958 with 1957 or 1956 rather than with 1955, it appears that per capita consumption has grown considerably more rapidly than per capita total national production. This seems to the writer to be an unfavorable trend which should be reversed. Yet outside economists do not need to point this out to those who are at the helm of the economic policies of Israel; those at the helm are fully aware of this problem, and are working vigorously to overcome it.

But since those at the helm in Israel cannot allocate resources in the brutal manner of the totalitarian states, and would not if they could, the amount of goods and services required to maintain a tolerable standard of living and to support the advance of production and productivity will require for some years ahead a very large amount of investments furnished from abroad, plus grants-in-aid and private giving—primarily from the United States.

The more adequately these varied forms of necessary assistance are forthcoming, the more quickly will Israel be able to attain relative economic self-sufficiency, to close or greatly narrow the gap in its balances of trade and payments, to provide for the common defense, to promote the general welfare, and thus to achieve those objectives of a free people which are explicit not only in the history of the new State but also explicit in the Constitution of the United States.

The short-sighted may mistakenly marvel at the ostensible ease with which totalitarian states can repress the standard of living of their peoples for the ignoble purpose of feeding their aggressive war machines. But those who are not short-sighted will be inspired instead by the capacity of a free people voluntarily to endure sacrifices and self-denial in order to build enduringly their economy and their state.

In economic affairs, both private and public, rectitude of intentions and courage and character in their execution are the most important requirements for eventual success. These qualities Israel is demonstrating. But in economic affairs, other qualities are also needed, and these reside in the ability to think clearly, to plan soundly, and to manage wisely. No nation, large or small, can claim perfection in these matters. But I do believe that the people and the leaders of the State of Israel—and I put the people first advisedly—are approaching their great tasks with clear intelligence, sound plans, and prudent management. Unless the general peace of the world is shattered by a third world war, nothing would seem to me more likely in the long run than that the economy and the people of Israel—if other free peoples who have joined in their effort through financial and moral participation do not shamefully withdraw—will endure and grow stronger and gradually achieve an ever-widening range of sound objectives.

The difficulties which Israel has already surmounted with slender resources relative to the task, and the remaining difficulties which Israel still faces in economic and political affairs—both domestic and international—should warn any person from another country that facile criticism could have no justification. But it may not be inappropriate for someone with the perspective which comes from distance—even if considerable ignorance is the price of that divorcement—to proffer some friendly analysis which should not be confused with aimless, reckless, or unsympathetic criticism.

The essential economic problem of the State of Israel in the future is to strike a balance between extremes. While this has been the objective of thoughtful people at least since the time of Aristotle, it is particularly relevant to the problems of a new economy which cannot afford the luxury of extremism because it cannot afford to make big mistakes. So I might most appropriately attempt to depict the salient problems still confronting Israel by defining the successive Scyllae and Charybdae between which the ship of State must steer, for while the wily Ulysses had to steer this course only once, the State of Israel will have to steer it continuously for many years.

The first middle course which Israel needs to steer is between a level of current enjoyment of consumer goods so high as to weaken the building of its productive strength for the future, and a level of current consumption so low as to impair morale or health or efficiency, thereby weakening the most vital factor in the whole productive process—the men and women who are doing the work.

A second and closely related middle course to be steered is between the objectives of the welfare state and the objectives of the efficient and productive state. This reconciliation may be described in other words as the proper blending of stability and growth, security and progress. Israel may find this problem of peculiar difficulty because, while most other nations developed the bases of their industrial structures before the concept of social justice was strong among them, Israel of necessity must deal with both of these aspects at the same time and cannot escape either. While this might seem to make the task more difficult, this very dualism is now, and will continue to be, a great source of Israel's strength, provided the proper reconciliation is made.

A more specific illustration may be found, in the economic sphere, of the need to reconcile stability with growth rather than to seek the extreme of one at the cost of excessive loss of the other. While greater price and monetary stability has been a signal accomplishment of the country thus far, it would nonetheless be a fatal error to derive smug satisfaction from this kind of economic stability, or to fail to place continuous and major stress upon dynamic economic growth. It is only through the well-balanced growth of production and its sensible distribution that any economy—whatever its form —can thrive and prosper in the long run. While maximum stability and maximum growth should both be sought, it is far better to have a little so-called inflation and a lot of growth than to have no inflation and no growth, if it should prove impossible to achieve growth in an absolutely stabilized (i.e. excessively controlled) economy. A stable or falling or rising price level, for instance, is not an economic *desideratum per se* under all circumstances. Other things being equal, an absolutely stable price level is most desirable; but other things are rarely equal in the real world as distinguished from the controlled exercises of the economic text books. And so, that price policy is most desirable which, in the long run, is most conducive to economic growth and social justice.

Still another middle course which Israel needs to follow requires considerable adherence to the grand and imaginative and yet practical plans being made for the further development of specific segments of the economy and specific projects. On the other hand, emphasis upon these segmental objectives should not blur the fact that, unless they are in total limited to the attainable, unless they are in total fitted together into a coordinated and consistent economic strategy which must include a firm sense of priorities, great words may be followed by small results, or by results in some fields accomplished at the cost of losses too great in other fields.

No one can fail to admire the daring and imagination which have led to the projection of these various segmental plans for economic development. But equal daring and imagination, and equal courage and practicality, are required for the task of planting a forest instead of a scattered bunch of trees. It is here that I find that the business of Israel, despite considerable progress, is indeed "unfinished business."

As a corollary to this, it needs to be realized that plans alone, or even plans plus money from whatever source, will not in themselves achieve satisfactory or even tolerable economic results. Plans and money provide the signal to go ahead, but they alone do not provide the labor skills and the managerial skills, or in one sense the engineering skills, required for execution. For some years to come the economy of Israel may import a great deal of financial economic assistance from friends in the United States, and this is proper and desirable under the circumstances. But Israel cannot in comparable measure import the skills and the know-how, the spirit of enterprise combined with the spirit of self-restraint, required to do the job. These must all be home brew.

In this particular process, Israel needs also to steer a middle course which distinguishes between the virtue of independence and the vice of provincialism. The justifiable pride which Israel takes in its own traditions and its superior knowledge of its own problems should not lead it to reject or fail to seek technological and managerial advice from its friends in America, particularly its business friends, just so long as the business friends want to offer advice and not to dictate terms.

But Israel should not listen too much to the council of those well-meaning friends in the United States who do not understand Israel because they do not fully understand their own country. There are those, even in the United States, who do not appreciate the role of planning, including government planning, in the successes of America.

I have no fear whatsoever that Israel will fail to continue to steer a middle course between the excesses of totalitarian planning and the excesses of the *laissez faire* philosophy masquerading under the guise of responsible freedom. Israel should constantly bear in mind that some few people in the United States who call Israel "socialistic" when it pursues this middle course have been applying the same epithet to the same course of action in the United States—under Republican and Democratic administrations alike.

Of course, these suggestions that Israel must move along the middle way may be complicated by the fact that different people have different definitions of the middle way. The conservative who says that he is the only "true liberal" finds the middle way a little to the right of his own path; and the liberal who says that he is the only "true conservative" finds the middle way a little to the left of his own course. But most of those exercising responsibility in Israel, according to my observation, will be neither bothered nor frustrated by these ideological difficulties, because they are pursuing ideals rather than adhering to ideologies, and because their pragmatic preoccupation with hard problems day by day and year by year permits them neither to indulge in theoretical speculations nor to become frozen into any doctrinaire positions.

And for this very reason, those Americans who are considering the placement of their investment funds in Israel (one of my major interests in connection with Israel), either through private channels or through the purchase of Bonds of the Israel Government, should never fear that the State of Israel will gradually evolve policies inimical to their investment interests through the gradual emergence of doctrinaire positions either economic, social, or political. On the contrary, the current trend in Israel is accelerating in the opposite direction—toward recognition that a mixed economy, with ample room both for responsible enterprise and responsible government, is absolutely essential to the reasonably swift progress of an under-developed but highly civilized area toward economic self-sufficiency, a rising standard of living, and its fair share in trade among nations on a truly competitive basis.

In 1955, 57 per cent of all gross domestic investment was public, and only 43 per cent was private. This was not an unusual admixture, considering how large a part of investment in a very young and so rapidly growing country had to be devoted to purposes which are not "profitable" in a private sense. But by 1958, the public and private portions of gross domestic investment were about equally balanced. In the future, the planned evolution of the economy, in-fused with a variety of policies and programs designed to encourage private investment, is likely to result in an admixture more similar to that found in more highly developed economies organized on the Western model.

The foregoing identification of some of the major problems for which Israel must find ever-improving solution was not conceived by the writer primarily in the United States. Instead, these ideas became crystallized during time spent in Israel. While naturally the ideas herein expressed are my own, and while I cannot insinuate that others bear any responsibility for them, nonetheless it is my personal feeling that a majority of these ideas—as well as the prob-lems and possible solutions to which these ideas relate—occupy an important status in the thinking of some of the leaders of the State of Israel as they grapple with their hard tasks.

In short, my observations within the State of Israel have con-vinced me that here are an economy and a nation which, both in their definition of the problems lying ahead and in their efforts to meet these problems, are exhibiting a blend of vision and practicality. The people of Israel are dealing with the tasks of today while pre-paring for those of the future, using the lessons of the past to retain what has been proved good and to shed what has been proved faulty, and combining responsible free enterprise with responsible free government. These efforts, in happy combination, offer fair promise in this troubled world of achieving those results in material well-being and in the perpetuation of the great basic liberties toward which aspire all those who love freedom and value the worth of the individual.

I I

DESIGN FOR ISRAEL

JAMES S. PLAUT

I have yet to encounter the man who, once invited to Israel as a "foreign expert," does not attain a sense of close personal identification with the destiny of the young State. First of all, this kind of assignment can hardly fail to inflate the ego (a human condition that induces fulfillment of certain base satisfactions). Going a bit deeper, one tends to date the *true* growth of the State from the earliest moment of one's *own* involvement in its progress, and this too, I suspect, is an inescapable human failing. A common bond that unites the many disparate types who have seized the tail of this bright comet—some holding on longer than others—is the exhilaration of a fabulous flight. All of us, I imagine, also share the illusion that by leaving our own mark on the development of some facet of life in Israel, through some contribution of skill, wisdom, or experience—no matter how flimsy or marginal it may be—we have somehow rubbed shoulders with history. In our time, this constitutes an especially precious and appealing privilege.

My own adventure, which began in 1951—during the first cycle of Israel's statehood—was wholly unpremeditated. In 1948, the Institute of Contemporary Art in Boston, whose affairs I then directed, had formed a new industrial design unit—the "Department of Design in Industry"—in order to give disinterested advice to American manufacturers with respect to the education of designers and the conditions under which a productive climate for

126

design might evolve within a company. The concept upon which
the Institute's program was based was new to American education
and industry. It led quickly to the establishment of constructive
alliances of the Institute with American manufacturers, and the
experiment was followed with interest in professional circles here
and abroad.

However, a phone call from Washington in the late autumn of
1950 took me by surprise. The speaker was Theodore Kollek, then
the Israeli Minister to the United States. It seemed that Mr.
Kollek had heard of the Institute's program and wanted to talk about it.
Could we not lunch together in New York?

I saw "Teddy" Kollek for the first time a few days later. He was
the first Israeli I had met, and I was unprepared for his bland and
youthful appearance, masking the weighty compound of past experiences and present responsibilities that is the hallmark of the
youthful leaders of Israel and sets them apart from their contemporaries in every other society. As Teddy talked, it was hard
to associate this relaxed, smiling, boyish person with the Zionist
youth leader and underground fighter that he had been, and the
mature negotiator and responsible political and economic representative that he had now become. Had I known then as much as I
do now of the resourcefulness of Israel's younger leaders—especially their uncanny ability to ferret out and enlist vital sources
of assistance in every domain and from almost every corner of
the world—I might have been less astonished by the breadth of
Teddy's skills and enterprise.

I dwell on this first contact because of its strong emotional
impact and because in the most important sense it set the stage—
psychologically and substantively—for my entire subsequent involvement. In the course of a single lunch hour at a New York hotel,
Teddy Kollek asked me if I would go to Israel to inspect its
infant industries and determine the feasibility of a national effort
in industrial design. This might serve to ameliorate an unfavorable
balance of trade by making Israel-produced items more attractive
and thus more saleable in foreign markets. He suggested an initial,
exploratory trip, and I accepted his invitation without even think-

ing—to say nothing of letting him know—of my abysmal ignorance of the two essential ingredients: Israel and foreign trade. In any case, I flew to Israel for the first time in February, 1951. I had never before been in the Middle East, apart from a four day, war-time conference at Cairo in 1943. I remained for two weeks, conferring with government leaders and educators, and visiting factories and workshops. Returning to Washington, I gave Minister Kollek an optimistic reading on the potential for an industrial design program in Israel.

Several months later, in April, 1951, I secured a half year's leave-of-absence from the Institute in Boston. Taking our two children out of school a bit early in the spring, we embarked *en famille* for a longer sojourn in Israel. We decided to live in Jerusalem in order to be near the government, which was then moving its principal departments from Tel Aviv in order to give substance to its desire to establish the Israel-held sector of Jerusalem as the new capital. A charming apartment in an old Arab house—whose thick walls provided superb insulation from the blistering summer heat—became our home for six months.

Israel, in 1951, had not yet overcome the ravages of her War of Independence, but it is impossible to imagine a more dynamic moment in the growth of a new nation. The heady excitement of hard-won statehood was still in the air. Immigrants were pouring in daily, new villages were springing up overnight, the cities were mushrooming. Swamps were being drained in the North, the desert reclaimed in the South, and forests planted on the rocky mountainsides in between. The emissaries of the new State were going forth to take up important political responsibilities in the world's capitals, and the government was attempting to carry out the myriad tasks which confront the responsible leadership of a new republic. Foreign experts of every hue were coming to Israel to assist in the solution of an endless chain of national problems, ranging all the way from sewage disposal to taxation.

Reason could not hope to yield a mature, full-blown nation over-night, so the Israelis resorted to faith. Since the coming to statehood was everywhere regarded as a miracle, there was widespread confidence that a series of lesser miracles would take care of the infinite number of lesser problems which now beset its people. This was also a moment of great austerity in the national life. Successive waves of immigrants had placed upon their new homeland a heavy burden, which had to be shared by every Israeli. The nation lacked foreign exchange and credits, her currency was soft and volatile. The bare requisites of life itself—minimum shelter, clothing, and provisions for the swollen population—could not be found within the country and had to be secured abroad. Foreign trade was virtually a one-way street, so dependent was the nation on the importation of such essentials as machinery, building materials, and foodstuffs.

In consequence of shortages in all commodities, a drastic system of rationing became essential. The rationing laws were applied with great severity and accepted by the populace philosophically, if not cheerfully. The Israelis demonstrated exemplary self-discipline; there was remarkably little grumbling and only limited recourse to the black market—over a period of several years, when only a few grams of poor meat and two or three eggs a month, or a single pair of shoes, constituted the normal adult allowance.

In this atmosphere of tension and deprivation, first things had to come first. The State, first of all, had to survive—politically, militarily, and economically. The immigrants had to be absorbed, settled, and given a productive role in the nation's social evolution. And, as Israeli produce could not sustain the population, industry had to be developed as the handmaiden of agriculture if the national economy were ever to become viable.

I have long since become convinced that 1951 was not a propitious time for the introduction of industrial design as an additional national problem to be dealt with. The moment was indisputably premature, for a leadership so deeply and properly concerned with the very survival of the nation could hardly be expected to worry over the color of a toothpaste tube or the size of printing on an olive oil tin. Yet such seeming trivia were to become increasingly significant if even a modest volume of exportable products was to be achieved, and it was felt that Israel, in order to gain any measure of *economic* independence, must soon "export or die."

In the early stages of my activity in Israel, I worked closely with the staff of the Ministry of Trade and Industry, notably with Yehuda Eylath, a dedicated man who had been a department store executive in Germany prior to his arrival in Israel in the 1930's, and who, before the formation of the State, had occupied a position with the Jewish Agency comparable to that which he now held in the government. Eylath headed a small unit in the Ministry of Trade which was expected to carry out liaison with Israeli manufacturers with a view toward the maintenance of reasonable standards of material and workmanship in the production of export items. But Eylath believed that he had a more fundamental mission —to use all his strength and influence to elevate the taste of the nation and thereby create a natural, popular demand for higher quality in the articles of everyday life.

Eylath was a stubborn, single-minded idealist, who confronted his enemies—those who deprecated or ignored the urgency of his mission—with the same wholesome, pioneering spirit that was the very soul of Israel's progress in many other, less abstract, enterprises. Admiring Eylath's rectitude and zeal, I did everything I could to advance his cause. I believed in the man and his philosophy, and felt that Israel was fortunate to have in its midst a qualified professional who, if properly supported, could give momentum to a vital program.

But progress was painfully slow, by the American yardstick. In 1951, good design could not logically occupy a high place on the priority list of national objectives. Israel's industrial leaders were preoccupied with the financing and procurement of raw materials and basic machinery, and with the training of inexperienced workers. The management group itself was new to industry, having come largely from commerce and the professions. And the government, although it was anxious to stimulate industrial expansion and recognized the need to divert the national effort from an unrealistic over-dependence on agriculture, lacked both the means and the

experience to render adequate assistance. Another disquieting factor
was the lack of continuity in personnel and policy. So frugal was
the economy that a series of ministers sought to alleviate the
country's pitiful material shortages by successively contradictory
programs—control followed by de-control, belt-tightening and then
relaxation, artificial respiration giving way to "self-levelling." No
arbitrary legislation or economic theory, of course, could overcome
the shortages, a rising population curve, and an undeveloped industrial potential. The "miracle" eventually came in the form of
German reparations, which furnished Israel with the machines and
materials to prime the pumps of national development, released the
country from desperate privation, and supplied a breathing spell for
the economy. Simultaneously, a slow-down in immigration brought
the first opportunity to make adequate provisions for the new
settlers.

My work with Eylath and his associates was handicapped by the
continual and rapid turnover of responsible officials in his Ministry.
Ours was a new and difficult concept, and the objectives of our
program had to be explained in considerable detail whenever we
wished to enlist the support of any individual or organization.
From 1951 to 1955, if memory serves correctly, the portfolio of
Minister of Trade and Industry changed hands four times. Each
Minister, in turn, brought in his principal associates, so that in four
years, let us say, there were four different Ministers, four Directors-
General, four heads of the industrial and export divisions, and so
on down the line. Each time the team changed, we were obliged
almost to start over again, for any development program must
depend, in the end, upon the enthusiasm and dedication of its
leaders.

It is probably fair to say that during my initial stay of six
months, in 1951, we were able to stimulate a national consciousness
of the *desirability,* at least, of good design as an aid to the economy
and a prerequisite of a rising culture. Seminars were used as a
device to bring producers and designers together for free discussion;
lectures were offered to the public, articles were prepared for publication in trade journals, interviews were given on the radio and

in the press. Education had to precede action, and instruction as to method and opportunity had to be widespread.

In a memorandum of June, 1951, to Yaacov Geri, then Minister of Trade and Industry, summarizing my activities to date, I said, in part:

"I do not think that it will serve any useful purpose to give you herein an analysis of the level of design in Israel's industrial products today which is based on personal standards of taste or on esthetic consideration alone. I wish to emphasize, however, that the standard of design in Israel products manufactured today for export purposes leaves a great deal to be desired from many points of view. Since your Ministry is concerned primarily with the economic rather than the esthetic implications of design, I shall dwell for a moment on what I consider to be the fundamental failing in the design of articles for export. Virtually every manufacturer with whom I talked interrogated me on the condition of the American market as related to his products. No single manufacturer appeared to have any conception whatever of American consumer attitude, taste, purchasing power, or general response to, and need for, his product. Israeli goods, in other words, are being produced today in a kind of vacuum, on a hit-or-miss basis. Your manufacturers are conducting no market research abroad and have no opportunity to do so. In the fabrication of tourist and gift articles—ceramics, metal ware, etc.—the only measuring-stick is that of the sentimental market for Jewish religious and ceremonial objects. In this area, your manufacturers and designers consider themselves on sure ground, since Israel must be regarded as the source or fountainhead for all such material.

"But even here, very little practical thinking has taken place, in my opinion. In the first place, if Israel plans to confine its exports of decorative and luxury goods to the area of ceremonial objects, it would seem that *not more than five per cent, at the outside, of the potential foreign market will be reached.* It is undeniable that Jews all over the world will buy Israeli products, to a certain extent, on sentimental grounds alone, but the tendency to think of this market as an important and exclusive outlet for your products is dangerously limiting, and does not begin to take into account the actual export potential of the country.

"When I say that your manufacturers are working in a vacuum I mean also that, for the most part, they seem to have no idea of the level of quality, price, and other competitive factors which they must consider.

There seems to be a widespread conception among your manufacturers that they can compete successfully in foreign markets on a mass production, or at least a quantitative, basis. Manufacturers of lighting fixtures, ceramics, metal ware, and other products, in discussing the American market, for instance, all talked of competition in the *low-or-middle-price brackets.*

"This tendency seems to me to be the second fundamental fallacy in the design aspect of your export program. I am not a trained economist, but I am nevertheless thoroughly convinced that Israel's products for export must have a special appeal; that they cannot be competitive on a price basis; that they must have a character which will identify them as of Israel origin; and that they will be purchased on the basis of *quality and individuality alone,* without consideration of price. In a recent letter to the "Jerusalem Post," written by one of your manufacturers returning from abroad, it was said that Israel must export on the "Rolls Royce" level. I am certain that this is sound doctrine, and that an emphasis on luxury products for special and discerning consumer groups will in no way limit the 'dollar volume' of your return.

"There is one further consideration in this connection. You will doubtless wonder how Israel can compete with European and American producers of luxury goods. What special qualities or characteristics can be imparted to your products to set them apart and make them desirable purchases in competition with the refined and coveted products of other countries, possessing a longer experience in this area? I consider that there is a vast potential here. At present writing, I would suppose there are at least a dozen highly gifted, well-trained designers available to you. There is also a rich and positive Palestinian design tradition which—while not strictly Jewish—goes back thousands of years, unmarred and uninhibited by superficial European influence. There are museum specialists, historians, archeologists, and students of applied art in Israel today who can be exploited for their professional knowledge of source material for design and its proper application. No other country possesses this potential; but unfortunately, the few individuals who recognize its value have had no opportunity to make use of it and the general tendency on the part of designers of commercial products has been either to ignore or to misunderstand it. What I am attempting to convey is that, with proper direction and integration of your native traditions, your artistic potential, and your productive capacity—as all of these factors exist today —*products for export can be evolved which, by their special quality and*

appeal, will compete successfully with the luxury goods of other countries.
"I have stressed from the outset that a successful long-range program
for industrial design cannot be expected to evolve overnight. Before
recommending certain measures which may well be taken on short notice,
and which may be expected to produce early results, I believe it is appropriate to warn against the illusion that a program of permanent value
is a simple matter. It is possible to utilize existing talents and facilities and
to start something significant on a modest basis. But a long-range program
is one of education at three levels—education of the industrial management group, education and training of designers for industry, and general
enlightenment of the public."

I left Israel in the autumn of 1951 to resume my duties in Boston,
but returned at regular intervals in the years following to do what
I could as a part-time advisor. I recall the return visit to Israel in
February of 1952, when Dov Joseph, who had succeeded Geri as
Minister of Trade in the interim, presided at the initial meeting of
the National Council for Design Development. Eylath and I had
worked hard to bring this Council into being and to establish its
sphere of operations, because we felt that a representative national
body would give weight to our efforts and focus public attention on
the problem. The Council has functioned more or less continuously
since its inception. Operating without adequate staff or funds, it
has managed, nevertheless, to enhance the general awareness and to
carry on useful propaganda in behalf of the national design program.
After suffering many vicissitudes, it has recently been subjected to
renewed scrutiny by the country's leaders, who look to its revitali-
zation as an active force.

I was back in Israel for a brief stay again in the autumn of 1952,
and in February and September, 1953. By then, a pattern of semi-
annual visits had become more or less regular.

At the very beginning of the year 1954, Yehuda Eylath died, with
terrible suddenness. His death came as a great shock. He was in his
late 40's and left a young wife and teen-age daughter. I have always
felt that he literally gave his life to the cause of beauty. He had
devoted all his energies for almost twenty years to the thanklessly

slow, often exasperating, task of improving the living standard of his countrymen. In the end, a heart so full of desire to help others could not sustain him.

I returned to Israel late in February 1954, very shortly after Eylath's death. It seemed to me that his untiring efforts tragically had failed to secure a permanent place for design in the minds of the leaders, although his associates were carrying on his work and the Ministry assured me that his Department would continue to operate. I called on Eylath's widow and told her that his life-long devotion had already borne fruit, but that the true measure of his achievement would not be felt until Israel was further along the road to economic and cultural maturity. Although I felt obliged to assure her of my own continuing interest, I had to admit to myself that we had probably reached the end of the road. In three years, I had encountered no one who had anything even approaching Eylath's skill and sense of dedication to this work. Without his leadership, I felt sure that the design program would vanish into thin air, and it seemed to me most unlikely that I would have further reason to prolong my own association with Israel.

However, I had come this time to explore ways and means for the continuation of the design effort with the knowledge that Eylath would no longer be there to guide it. This realization made the obligation to carry on all the more compulsive. Also, after three years of abortive progress and indifferent success, it seemed to me that a sharp change in direction had become mandatory. I had felt for some time that government was a less than ideal vehicle for the prosecution of this experiment, and that private enterprise had been insufficiently aroused. I had also come to admire the dynamism of the Technion, Israel's growing technical university at Haifa. Before leaving the country, I believed that I should try to enlist their interest. The Technion had already established itself as a central force in the nation's growth. It was creating a new cadre of scientists, engineers, and architects and, like its older sister institutions in the United States, it had proved itself capable of conducting research applicable to many requirements of the nation's economy. Moreover, the disciplines of the engineering and architectural curricula were fertile ground for the training of industrial designers.

Early in March 1954, I conferred with General Dori, President of the Technion, and Dr. M. Levy, its Secretary, and won their agreement in principle to have the Technion develop a program for the training of designers, "in partnership" with the government, assuming long-range educational responsibilities in the field, and to have the government continue its efforts to establish a suitable climate for the application of better design in the nation's industrial output. Two days after the meeting at the Technion, I was obliged once again to leave Israel for Boston.

The second and present phase of my involvement in Israel's design movement began unexpectedly at a party outside of Tel-Aviv the following September. I had just returned for a brief visit and had been invited to dinner by Temple Wanamaker, then the Economic Attaché at the American Embassy. The newly arrived administrator of the United States Government's foreign aid program in Israel, Lincoln Hale, was among the Wanamakers' guests that evening. Dr. Hale had heard that an industrial design program was "under way" in Israel and wanted to know more about it. We agreed to meet again the next evening so that I might acquaint him with the history of the project. Dr. Hale, after many hours of discussion in the ensuing days, concluded that it would be desirable to utilize American public funds available for the furtherance of technical assistance in Israel (under the "point four" program) so as to give real substance, for the first time, to our efforts. He felt also that it was consonant with American policy to encourage the development of active long-range relationships between private institutions in the United States and the "host country" (Israel). Dr. Hale, a retired college president, was intrigued with the Technion, and fell in readily with the idea that an intensified industrial design education program should be based on the Haifa campus. The guiding American institution would be the Institute of Contemporary Art in Boston, which had already become the spiritual parent of this activity in Israel and had "lent" me to the cause.

A full year transpired before a contract materialized with the International Cooperation Administration, the Washington headquarters of the U.S. foreign aid program. In essence, this contract —signed on September 1, 1955—envisaged the establishment of an "Israel Institute of Industrial Design" at the Technion. The new Institute would have two principal functions: to carry out professional instruction in design within the general framework of the Technion's School of Architecture, and to operate a design information and exhibit center for the public. The Boston Institute would provide a qualified American as Director of the Haifa Institute, and an Israeli Co-Director would be named at such time as a suitable candidate could be found. The Boston Institute would also make its cumulative experience in the field of industrial design available to its "younger sister" in Haifa and would furnish the basic materials for the new undertaking. To round out the picture, an American industrial design firm would establish an office in Israel.

In December 1955, John Cheney of New Hampshire and Massachusetts arrived in Haifa with his family to take up residence and direct the affairs of the new Institute. Cheney is a sculptor, craftsman, and chemical engineer with a wide-ranging mind. A dedicated teacher and inventor, he seemed the ideal choice for this exciting assignment. As I write, John Cheney has rounded out three productive years at Haifa, interrupted only by the Sinai Campaign, which brought on his evacuation from Israel with all but a handful of the American officials and technicians then in residence. Sinai temporarily halted the activities of the Haifa Institute, although they were resumed before it was possible to persuade the United States Government, after a hiatus of six months, to permit Cheney to return. The first Israeli Co-Director was Nathan Shapira, a brilliant young architect, trained in Rumania, Italy, and the United States. I had first met Shapira in 1954. He had recently received his doctorate in architecture from the University of Milan and was in Israel to organize the Israeli Section of the 1954 "Triennale," the great international exhibition of design and applied arts held every third year at Milan. Shapira came to the United States the next year on a Commonwealth Fellowship. When Lincoln Hale returned to Washington for consultation, I was able to bring them together for a meeting. Hale and I decided that Shapira looked promising as Cheney's counterpart, and we encouraged him to return to Israel upon completion of his studies in the States. When Shapira was ready to go, Sinai had already erupted. En route, he conferred with Cheney, "exiled" in Italy, and arrived in Israel early in 1957 to take up his duties without benefit of Cheney's presence.

Coincident with Cheney's arrival in Haifa to head up the new Institute, the Pittsburgh industrial design firm, Peter Müller-Munk Associates, under separate contract with the American Government, established a "branch office" in Haifa, under the direction of Paul Karlen, a Müller-Munk partner. The Israel Product Design Office, as this firm is called, is an operating industrial design organization whose staff is preponderantly Israeli. I.P.D.O. has moved its offices from Haifa to Tel-Aviv, but maintains salutary and complementary relations with the Haifa Institute.

An integral element of the design development plan in its "point four" phase has been a study of the opportunities for Israeli producers to enter the American market. A "standards evaluation program" was formulated under the direction of Dr. Kenneth L. Heaton of Philadelphia. Dr. Heaton and his associates have conducted surveys in the United States and published reports (which were subsequently translated into Hebrew and given wide distribution in Israel) on such promising categories of potential Israeli export as ceramics, packaging (of soap, chocolate, and olive oil), metal giftware, leather goods, textiles, and apparel.

A recent report on the activities of the Institute at Haifa is a far cry from my 1951 memorandum to the Minister of Trade, from which I quoted earlier in this chapter. Here are some excerpts:

January 1959

"TO: International Cooperation Administration, Washington, D.C.

FROM: The Institute of Contemporary Art, Boston
SUBJECT: INSTITUTE TECHNION INDUSTRIAL DESIGN
PROJECT Quarterly Progress Report for Fourth Year,
First Quarter (September 1–November 30, 1958)

I. *Field Design Expert's Activities*

  A. Exhibition Center

    The Packaging Exhibition, which opened on August 27, continued through September and October, with a total attendance of 2570 visitors during these two months. Since only a limited amount of publicity was directed to the general public, the majority of these visitors were graphic artists, designers, and manufacturers. A large number of manufacturers from all sections of the country came to the Exhibition Center daily, seeking new ideas about package engineering, graphics, and development of new packages for contemplated products.

    During the period of October 23–November 1, final preparations were made for the exposition of Durable Consumer Goods which opened on November 2. The attendance of 4560 at this exhibit during the month of November almost doubled the Center's September–October record. This show included fabrics from the United States and Europe, and locally manufactured tableware and furniture. The seven leading Israeli manufacturers of furniture were visited in preparation for the exhibit, and approximately 25 pieces of furniture were displayed, as well as a selected group of ceramics, tableware, and metal giftware. All of the exhibited products were photographed and entered in the new Design Index.

  B. Israel Institute of Industrial Design (at Technion)

    The *Forms from Israel* Exhibition, sponsored by the Government of Israel in cooperation with the American Cultural Foundation and the Crafts from Israel Committee, was shipped to the United States on September 19 to begin its nation-wide tour. Dr. Nathan Shapira left for the U.S. at the end of September to make final preparations for the December opening in Baltimore, Maryland. The Exhibition is comprised of approximately 175 examples of Israeli craft and design produced since 1948, such as: ceramics, metal work, weaving, mosaics, and designs in plastic, calligraphy, and typography. Photographs from Israel and of the individual craftsmen at work are included in the exhibit.

    The special display unit for the Traveling Package Exhibition was completed in October by Mr. Alexander Pollack, design trainee. The exhibition was on display at the Z.O.A. (Zionist Organization of America) House in Tel Aviv during November. Catalogues were prepared which accompanied the display.

The fabrics for the State of Israel Bond Drive were completed during November, and the finished models were sent to the United States to be entered in the Bond Drive Fashion Show. Six Paris couturiers were selected by Mrs. Miriam Finemann, National Director of the Bond Drive, to fashion models from Israeli-produced fabrics. Ten Israeli designers submitted fabric designs to the I.I.I.D., and from these the works of three designers were chosen. Mr. Cheney supervised the preparation, dyeing, printing, and finishing of the fabrics.

II. *Activities Planned for Fourth Year, Second Quarter* (December 1, 1958, February 28, 1959).

The second exposition of durable consumer goods will open at the Exhibition Center in December. This exhibit will feature locally produced textiles, lighting fixtures, and toys. The consumer goods will change every four or five weeks.

The Traveling Package Exhibition will be shown in the Ministry of Commerce and Industry in Jerusalem during December.

The model of the folded corrugated carton building will be placed outdoors for weather testing during the winter. Further research into methods of converting this project into a commercially feasible item will be continued, perhaps in conjunction with the Technion Research and Development Office.

Preparations for the furniture design contest, sponsored by the I.I.I.D. and the Interior Architects' Association, will continue. Agreements will be made with local furniture manufacturers to purchase for production the designs which are submitted.

On June 30, 1959,[1] upon completion of the Technion's academic year, official American support of the Haifa Institute came to an end. John Cheney will remain in Israel for some months as advisor to the Government, and a competent group of Israelis will take over the reins. The Technion and the government will finance and operate the Israel Institute of Industrial Design as a permanent national resource. Nathan Shapira, who has recently brought to the

[1] This chapter was written in the summer of 1959.

United States the exceptional exhibition *Forms from Israel,* will enter private practice as an architect and designer. The Cheney-Shapira team will be succeeded by Daniel Havkin, an able, young Israeli architect, Technion-trained. Havkin will become Director of the Institute and continue as a member of the Technion's Faculty of Architecture.

In 1957, Lincoln Hale retired from the directorship of the U.S. Operations Mission in Israel, a post he had held for three years. For him, as for so many others, Israel had become a personal crusade, a way of life. He came home to Connecticut and died a few months later, almost as if, separated from the country to which he had given so much of his life in such a short span of years, there was nothing left to live for.

And so, by strange coincidence, and without ever knowing each other—for Lincoln Hale did not even arrive in Israel during Yehuda Eylath's lifetime—two men no longer with us gave full expression to a pioneering venture in the great human tradition that has seemed always to light Israel's path.

When John Cheney and Paul Karlen leave Israel, the design counselors of the "first generation" will have completed their tasks. They will leave a going concern in the hands of capable leaders. Daniel Havkin will be aided by experienced, senior members of the Technion Faculty, such as Dr. M. Levy and Professors Neumann and Mansfeld. Paul Karlen will turn over his design office to an Israeli staff. And there are admirable allied institutions whose history parallels these, such as Maskit, the growing home industries enterprise headed by Ruth Dayan, the wife of the intrepid General. Maskit becomes increasingly important in the life of the nation by stimulating the creative effort of Israel's craftsmen and providing a substantial market for their production.

The Boston Institute looks forward to a long and productive association with Haifa. As for myself, Israel is in my blood and under my skin. I hope I shall never have to cast about too hard for an excuse to return to Haifa to see how things are going.

12

THE VISION OF A CITY

PHILIP KLUTZNICK

In July 1957, I entered the office of Prime Minister David Ben Gurion for an appointment which we had made to discuss a development program in Israel. I now believe it to be the largest of its kind undertaken in any country in the postwar era. As I remember, soon after I had entered the office, Mr. Ben Gurion said to me, "I thought you were interested in culture, in B'nai B'rith. I thought you were interested in young people, and now I find that you are interested in making money."

I was somewhat taken aback. I said, "I'll give you a blank check now, and later you can fill in whatever sum I make from my interests in Israel." At this point, Mr. Ben Gurion became very serious. "This must not be," he answered. "It is important to Israel that American businessmen profit from their activities here."

I agreed with him, of course, but I was overwhelmed by the Prime Minister's directness. We changed the subject and began discussing various other topics. About ten minutes later, in the middle of another subject, his whole background got the better of him and he said, "Of course, you must not profit too much."

As far as I am concerned, the "Vision of a City," the program for the development of the community of Ashdod, is not motivated by the capitalistic instinct. Without in any way reflecting upon the economy of Israel or in any way suggesting that it is unsafe to invest there, I would submit that there are in the United States more inviting opportunities from purely a profit point of view. One does not travel 7000 miles from home base to seek the privilege of building a town or a city or a concept of this character for money alone.

On the other hand, I think it would be most unfortunate if, in the years ahead, a closer relationship is not developed between men of business affairs in this country and those in Israel. We must develop an interaction out of common interest and utilize each other's talents. Israel will benefit from sound business transactions—transactions on which it must come to rely—rather than on the essential gift dollars on which it has had to depend to such an extent until now. Deep in my consciousness is the feeling that this program can develop meaningful human relationships around a business enterprise with social and economic objectives, and it may also serve to unite segments of the business community of Israel. And out of it I hope there may develop the conviction that Israel should rely on economic fortifications created for economic reasons, rather than out of sentiment or an abundance of historical and traditional love and affection.

The site of Ashdod was not my choice. In Israel, as elsewhere, you sometimes have limited areas of decision when you come as a stranger. For two or three years, I had been talking with my friend, Oved Ben Ami, the former mayor of Natanya, who has become my business associate, about the idea of undertaking a slow-paced project to build a town between Natanya and Haifa. For a year and a half, we were in negotiation with the owners of the concessions, the Rothschild interests. In the midst of it, certain officials of the Israel government quite persuasively called Ben Ami's attention to the desirability of shifting his sights geographically—to the South. The reasons should be clear to anyone who knows Israel. The Negev means everything to the future of the country. Whether or not Israel can become economically sufficient—and I think it can—depends upon the application of genius, industry, and money to the Negev. Whether or not Israel can absorb its future population depends, in large measure, on what can be done with the Negev. I must agree, therefore, with both the social and economic vision which diverted attention to the south.

There was a second consideration—Israel has a long, exposed

coastline. Actually, the miles and miles of Mediterranean coastline constitute one of its greatest assets. However, today, Israel has but one real port on the Mediterranean—the port of Haifa. If the Negev is to be settled, if it is to expand, if it is to produce, it must have a ready outlet to the Mediterranean. The government itself chose this southern location of Ashdod. Once, in ancient times, it was a buzzing, teeming port of commerce.

In Israel, much is done as a result of what is read in the Bible. Thus, this selection was made with but limited engineering background. Frankly, I accepted this edict because it seems that so many of the Israelis' conclusions are supported by subsequent events. When American and French engineers were retained to study the area, we hoped for the best. I can tell you now that their preliminary analysis confirms the facts of history. It is a good site for a port.

There was a third consideration that guided the selection of the site. During the time that the discussions were taking place, the possibilities of a port using the Gulf of Aqaba were in everybody's mind. However, I believe that even Mr. Ben Gurion in his most optimistic moments did not think there would be a usable outlet to the East so soon. As events transpired, there is now a port at Elat that faces to the East. This suggests the need for an economic outlet to the West. The distance between the two must be kept as short as possible to make the whole route available as a competitive route for trade between the Orient and the West. The events that took place in 1956 and early 1957 thus make Ashdod that much more important. When I was at this site in August 1957, I put my foot on the last section of the eight-inch pipe line that connected the East with the West as far as oil is concerned.

All of these considerations guided the selection of this site. However, there was still this fundamental question. How does one go about planning the building of a city that will ultimately accommodate 150,000 to 200,000 people? This sounds very challenging. When some of my friends say with awe, "But look, it's a two million dollar program," my answer is, "It's only two plus naughts. The principles are the same." Whether it is 150,000 people or 200,000 people, the principles fundamentally are the same as though you were building for 5000 or 10,000. In some ways, the principles are almost the same as though you were building for yourself. We must not be frightened by astronomical figures. What is needed is an idea, people, money, and material. The idea existed. The most important second requirement was people. Who was going to do the planning? What sort of creativity had to be encouraged? We found the people. Out of this came a lesson that I believe is significant.

If you come from out of town, you are usually considered an expert. Some of my Israeli friends and associates suggested that we get the greatest experts in the world to plan this community. I have had the experience of observing planning across the United States. During a rather critical period in the life of our country, I was responsible for some 2500–2600 community developments. I learned then that, even within the indigenous area that we call the United States, a planner from Cleveland is not so valuable in San Diego as an able native. You must have the feel of the aspirations and the hopes of the people for whom you plan. You can get it best by being a part of them. If any one decision was made in Israel of which I am proud, it was my insistence upon using Israelis for this job.

In 1950, when I was involved in a housing survey, I came to the conclusion that Israel did not need us nearly as much as was commonly supposed. They needed money and assets, but they had the experts. They had the people with the talents. If they were not good enough, they would become good enough. Growing *their* way would be better than growing *our* way, because they were going to live in their land, not in ours.

So we selected local talent. Except for the compromise of having the staff of my own shop check their work and Albert Meyer, a New York expert, review it, the planning of Ashdod was and is the responsibility of architects, engineers, traffic experts, economists, water experts, sanitation and sewer experts, and landscape experts, who live in and are part of Israel.

Let it be said to their everlasting credit that they came up with a plan which, in my experience at least, is as solid and sound as anything I have seen in recent community planning. Certainly, it will require adjustment in construction. But essentially, the lesson to be learned is that, if you do not walk into Israel with the idea that all of the knowledge is elsewhere, you can find what you need substantially in the way of talents right there.

Having found the people, the next question was: for what are we using their talents? Remember that we are talking in terms of the creation of something that will serve, to a limited degree, this generation and, to its greatest degree, the generation to come. What does this mean in a stabilized country with clear trends in specific directions, with a long and settled history, and with a stable population? Even in such a situation, it requires considerable ingenuity. But when you take a country that is in flux, beset by tremendous political problems, with economic problems that have not leveled off, with trends that begin to show themselves but cannot be considered permanent—how do you imagine and what do you assume you are building for? This was the big question.

Somebody has to be fool enough or smart enough to say, "These are the assumptions on which we proceed to plan." You never plan for yesterday or today. You plan for tomorrow. You plan 10,000 acres of sandy beach, scrubland and wasteland. You must conceive of it as being one of the great urban centers of this little country in fifteen, twenty, or twenty-five years. You plan against a shore line where you must imagine teeming commerce, and what that means to this area. You plan against a hinterland that has its own problems, and you must conceive of what its relationship will be to Ashdod.

People say, "This must be exciting and challenging." Perhaps. You simply must decide that you have enough courage to make whatever mistakes you are going to make. You must have enough faith in what you are engaged in to assume not minimal goals, but goals that reach for the top.

There are several assumptions on which Ashdod has been planned and on which the plan itself will proceed to execution: We assumed that within the generation, instead of an uneasy *truce,* there would be at least an uneasy *peace.* The first premise, then, on which we proceeded, was that there would be peace in the Middle East within a generation. If not, the plan would be partially invalidated—but only partially.

The second premise was that the population of Israel, within its present boundaries, would at least double within twenty to twenty-five years. Israel would then be a nation of at least four million, instead of today's approximately two million. This premise is perfectly sound and conservative. It has nothing to do with upheavals or revolutions in Eastern Europe. It was predicated upon health standards being maintained and the resultant increase, and natural immigration during a period of peace.

This brings us to the third premise—that the economic level will increase and the standard of living in the next generation will improve. With higher economic and living standards, there would be a natural tendency for population growth to accelerate.

Another premise was that there would be more automobiles in Israel. This may sound unimportant, but it is very important. Projection as to how much travel there will be by foot, how much by public transportation, how much by personally owned or shared vehicles is basic to the planning of roads, parking areas, sidewalks, cycle lanes, and related space allocations. While we do not believe that in twenty to twenty-five years Israel will have the traffic problem of midtown New York City, we do believe that the relative ratio of automobiles to population may well approximate that which prevailed in some of our metropolitan communities in the United States immediately before World War II.

There were certain other assumptions. Let me put them all in a nutshell. We concluded that the transition, which took place in the United States from the period immediately following World War II until today, represented a norm that could be applied in terms of increments in the next generation to a place like Israel. Under conditions of peace and natural growth, the next generation will telescope into twenty-five years an evolution and progress that have taken as many as four generations in prior periods of human history. Science, thought, techniques and medicines have developed to a point that leads at least a conservative planner to assume that their impact on civilization, ways of life, habits and society within one generation will be as great as that over any previous hundred-year period.

Armed with these assumptions, the planners went to work and produced on these 10,000 acres a concept of a flourishing community as it should be twenty to twenty-five years hence. We hope it will be sooner. And it will—if peace comes a little earlier, the economy grows a little faster, the birth rate is a little higher, and if people can pay their bills a little better. All of these factors can combine to accelerate or to decelerate the program.

In this future period, we envision a thriving port city with a large industrial area. We envision a city with roughly sixteen distinctive residential neighborhoods, served by a north-south railroad, with the existing railroad station incorporated into the plan. A power plant that is already there will be one of the cores of the industrial developments. Light industry will be concentrated to the south of the city to avoid the burden of all traffic going one way. Every one of the neighborhoods will grow its own green belt. In addition, every neighborhood will have its grade schools, synagogue and *mikvah* (ritualarium).

We are not prepared to gamble money on the proposition that the future civilization of Israel will not have prevailing Western characteristics. Our planning was based on what we considered to be the reality—that many aspects of the civilization of Israel, as it will develop from the seeds that have been sown, will have more in common with the West than with some of the archaic Middle Eastern habits. This is not to foreclose the hope that other countries in the Middle East may also move in that direction in the next generation.

The master plan is now complete. It is being dissected bit by bit by all of the government bureaus. This is as it should be, and I am not complaining. It is done in the United States, and I do not know why Americans complain when the same thing happens to them in Israel. We ask for no special privileges in government review. Some of the review is intelligent and some of it is not. In this respect too, it is not different from the United States.

The initial construction has begun. What are its characteristics? In Israel, there can be a lot of water for a minute and no water at all for a long while. The water always runs where you want to build.

So the first thing that had to be built was a bridge to cross what was no water last August, and what is a flowing stream every winter. To enable us to build in the winter, we had to have a bridge.

The second thing that we had to build, and which should be completed soon,[1] was the access road across the bridge into the first residential neighborhood.

Third are the houses which are necessary but which are uneconomic from a private builder's point of view. These are the houses for the new immigrants. A certain portion of the first houses will be for new immigrants. 1000 of those are in construction now, and in various stages of completion. The first 600 units to be made available for those who can afford to be owners of homes are about to be constructed. The plans are nearly completed.

The first shopping center is in the process of final design. The first school, the first synagogue, and the first *mikvah* are in a similar stage of development. The port itself should be in the process of initial construction before the end of 1959. The completion of the port is a four or five-year endeavor and will involve substantial commitments, both public and private. These commitments, I hope, will be made before the end of 1959.

Thus far, I have made no reference to resort facilities. When there are miles of beautiful beach comparable to the Riviera, it would be unrealistic not to recognize that the hinterland, Rehovot, Jerusalem, Beersheba will need access to the sea. For what? To relax. The day will come, if it is not here now, when an increasing percentage of Israelis will quit working twenty hours a day and rest a little bit. They, too, are not superhuman. The recreational area, to the south of the port, is planned for development four or five years hence. However, the demand for bathing and resort facilities is so pressing, that we have negotiated a contract with a French group who will build a 120-room motel. We hope it will be finished, at least in part, before the end of 1959. This will be incorporated into our plans for the northern section of Ashdod.

If we are not frowned upon too much by external events, this town should achieve the status of a community of 12,000 to 15,000 within

[1] This report was written in June, 1959 and covers developments to that date.

two years. From there, it must go as goes the economy. The subsequent growth rate is dependent upon a complexity of events, involving the rate of stabilization and growth and the prosperity of the State of Israel. The vision is there to keep pace with anything that anyone is imagining, but the pace itself must be related to the reality.

The vision of a city is not really the vision alone. I hope that this reaches the skies, but that it keeps its feet on the ground. Anything else would destroy rather than build.

I conclude with a true story. The negotiations with the Israelis took place over a period of a year, preceding the events of Sinai. In the spring of 1956, I agreed in principle—on behalf of my company —with Ben Ami and his associates and with the Israel government on the broad basic outline that would enable progress to be made.

But these are very complex matters. The contracts were being drafted and re-drafted. Studies were also being made. Then along came the events of October of that year. I forgot about Ashdod; I thought everybody else forgot about it.

In December, when nothing had been definitely settled, as far as I could see, with respect to the Suez and Aqaba, and with Israel on the firing line at the U.N., I received a cable from Israel that the government had signed the contract. At this point, I asked myself, "What kind of people am I dealing with? They don't know what the world is going to do to them tomorrow or the next day, and yet they take time out to put their signature on a contract to build a city for the next twenty-five years."

I wrote a letter to my partner, Ben Ami, and said, "Look here, what's going on? How come I received this cable from Eshkol?" He answered in typical fashion, "In these difficult days, the morale of the people is very important. I think the government was wise in pointing out that, when it was in greatest difficulty from a military and a diplomatic point of view, it was still concerned with the future of the people." When I read his letter, I was ashamed of myself.

With this spirit, I do not believe it possible for our vision to remain a vision. It will have its failings, it will fall short of some of its objectives, as it will exceed some of them; but with the kind of spirit demonstrated by the people of Israel and their leaders, the vision will be translated into reality.

13

THE ARMY *

S. L. A. MARSHALL

I have recently returned from an examination of the Israeli Army in the field and I have been studying it and the whole military balance in the Middle East at first hand for the last three years. My best estimate is that the Israelis are strong enough to discourage Arab nationalist military adventures near their borders for about five years—if the Army's fighting power can be kept up to its present level. Within that time it might be possible to work out a settlement reasonably satisfactory to all the nations concerned.

But if Israel's deterrent force is allowed to dwindle, then a war —with unpredictable but terrifying consequences—seems to me much more likely. During the August (1958) crisis, I saw for myself that the weight of the Israeli Army was one of the main supports for stability in Jordan. Any conspirators plotting to overthrow King Hussein must have realized that they might well be denied all the prizes of revolution by a military reaction from Israel.

This does not mean that Israel was eager to leap at the established Jordanian government, as some of the news dispatches from Jordan suggested at the time. On the contrary, I can testify that both the Israeli Army and government were normally tranquil. Senior staff members took their vacations on schedule, and maneuvers were held to a reduced program decided a year earlier because of a tight budget. In sum, Israel reacted like a neighbor desiring to keep Jordan at peace.

* This chapter appeared in Harper's Magazine, October 1958.

Moreover, Israel's request for the right to buy arms and equipment from the West does not indicate any plan to build up its fighting power. Its main purpose is simply to replace machinery now wearing out, and to fill its dire need for trucks, half-tracks, and medium tractors. If this equipment is obtained, the Army will be ready to give as splendid an account for itself as it did in the one-hundred-day war it fought against the Egyptian Army on the Sinai Peninsula in 1956.

Ever since I first went to Israel to make a study of the Sinai War, I have been asked by American military experts: How did the Israeli Army do it? And now that American troops have actually touched on Middle Eastern soil, the question seems more pertinent for Americans to ask than ever. Whatever virtues our own forces may have, one thing seems certain: our training and our tactics—the demands we have made and the performance we expect from our soldiers—are radically different from those the Israelis have employed with remarkable success.

My conclusion while in Sinai—and it stays unchanged—is that Israel's Army did it by extending the limits of military daring. Hitting forces traveled farther over more formidable country in less time than any other combat body in history. Decision was won in three days. By the fourth day some of the brigades (the Israeli term for regiment) were mopping up two hundred miles beyond their assembly points.

This alone is a feat at which to marvel. A fortified area about half the size of Nevada and far more repellent than the harshest wastes in that state was conquered by a small field army fighting as it drove forward almost at the rate of an unopposed motor caravan. Even the few paved roads in Sinai lack level gradients and follow a tortuous course according to the rise and fall of the terrain. Of this land little comes to man but trouble.

The mediocrity of the opposition had something to do with the phenomenal pace of the invading army. But it is only through the close range view that the opposite and more significant truth stands clear: The soldiers of Israel invariably looked their best in those hours when they were beset by the greatest combat difficulty and the enemy pressure became such that total disorganization should have ensued.

Motorization and tracks made possible the record marks in mobility. Without tanks, without half-tracks, Israel's Army could not have started. But there is no bright new magic in that. The United States Army, which has had such vehicles for a generation, has not assured itself the same sustained mobility.

What made the difference? Certainly not professional zeal and efficiency, for Israel's Army is not professional in the way Western nations use that term. The campaign was not aided by any new secret making possible a more adequate supply in the fighting zone. Israel's ranks are not particular wizards at motor maintenance and battlefield repair.

To the contrary, Israel's Staff professes an ignorance of logistics, which in more sophisticated circles has become a kimono-like word, covering everything and touching nothing. Staff members claim—so earnestly as to invite skepticism—that the governing principle is to "send the combat force against the decisive object and then order the supply people to keep up."

Within their training system there is relatively little schooling in the problems of field maintenance, and in the field no such elaborate echeloning of technical skills and parts-stores as we know. During fighting operations the fighters do most of the repair. They explain, "Many of us are farmers. We learn the knack on trucks and tractors."

Briefly then, Israel's Army is a fighting body in spirit and not a balanced aggregation of highly trained specialists. In a frontiers sort of way, it looks the part. Its men are clean but not neat. From top to bottom, the establishment has no frills of any kind. The office of the Chief of Staff is a bare-walled cubicle. No elevator operates in its many-storied headquarters building. All ranks wear only the austere, rough woolen field uniform.

Smartness in dress is impossible. Smartness in bearing is given only lip service. By Western standards, this Army, while radiating human warmth and the high courtesy native to the country, is wholly lacking in the outward forms of discipline. An enlisted man may appear unshaven, with his hair looking as if he is on strike against the barber. The man on sentry guard may be seen munching an orange as he walks his post. An officer may wear striped civilian socks with his uniform.

All that counts is the end object which discipline elsewhere is supposed to serve—undeviating performance of the task. Israel gets that from its soldiers without polish or spit, except as the latter is applied to the hands. During the Sinai campaign troops had a saying: "Fear of the higher command is worse than fear of the enemy."

The Army's deviations from traditional military practice seem perfectly suited to the temper of a force which is more civilian than soldier. Israel's so-called "Regular Army" is scarcely more than a cadre of higher NCO's, warrant officers, and those relatively few commissioned people who love the military life, have demonstrated superior skills, and are therefore asked to renew their contracts periodically. There is no enlisted volunteering. The body of the "Regular Army" is that draft of inductees which happens to be getting its two and one-half years' steady training in the going period.

Recruit training is threefold tougher than in the United States Army. But the only stiffness is in the soldier's aching back after a full day. Men salute—occasionally. Orders and directions are stated in the simplest words possible, with a minimum use of technical phrases. The recruit hardly puts on his soldier suit before he learns to refer to his highest commanders by their first names. Within the officer corps the habit of using nicknames is so in-grained that proper names are too often forgotten. One assistant Chief of Staff explained the high degree of co-ordination in Israel's battle forces in these words, mystifying in their simplicity: "We give and take more easily because we're all friends."

This Army, composed for the great part of men who had to spring from the plow or rush from the office, was given only three days to form and move on Sinai. In that time, its reservists had to assemble, equip, deploy, and get such limbering-up training en route as the hours permitted. Brigade and battalion commanders were read into the plan only after mobilization and movement were well under way. With rare exceptions, their own parts—including sectors and in some cases main objectives—were not pre-assigned. They still had to shape their attack plans, contrive such basic reconnoitering as was possible, and issue their orders.

On still another count, as to infantry-armor action, the campaign was unique. Commanders were told to keep battle losses minimal and not encumber their columns with prisoners if it was more opportune to let them get away. All efforts were to be directed toward squeezing out and destroying opposing fortifications. This stricture, imposed because it suited both the political nature of the fighting problem and the moral standard of Israel's troops, made an utmost requirement of movement, while lessening the normal accent on fire.

It would work if communications held up most of the time and if Egyptians, with their advantages of owning the high ground, where they were relatively safe under deep earth cover, fronting flat fields of fire, were not overly resolute. Both calculations proved accurate. Communications broke down a few times, and usually, as is to be expected, at the highest pitch of the local fire fight. The Egyptians broke down more frequently, giving way time and again in the same minutes of heaviest pressure.

Strength overcame disorganization because Israel's Army fights that way. When the attack becomes disjointed, when radios are muted by fire and lower commands are out of touch with the steadying hand higher up, Israel's soldiers nearest the enemy invariably follow their standard procedure. They close upon the defender's works.

That is the main lesson from the battle story. The phenomenal mobility of Israel's Army isn't generated out of machine power but out of the unanimous acceptance and application of a fighting doctrine which of its essence becomes unifying in the hour of greatest danger. Gidon's band may have held to the same simple rules. There is not one new idea in the doctrine. The startling tactical pace of the Army comes of applying sedulously those methods and precepts which all armies tell their infantry and armor will best maintain unity in battle. The difference is that Israel's soldiers hear and believe.

It's a short list:

. . . Leading means moving to the point of main danger if decisive pressure is to be maintained. There is no excuse for holding back.

. . . When orders can't get through, assume what the orders would be.

. . . When in doubt, hit out. The short route to safety is the road to the enemy hill.

. . . Don't attack head-on; there is usually a better way.

. . . If you must go in head-on, don't present a broad target.

. . . When troops are truly exhausted, hold back and rest them.

. . . Waste no energy in useless movement. Maintain the pace of the attack so long as physical resources seem sufficient.

. . . If the force designated to attack is not suitably armed to overrun the position, pull off and call for what is needed. Avoid useless wastage.

. . . Don't delay the battle because of supply shortages which lie beyond its probable crisis.

. . . Keep your sense of humor if you would save your wits.

. . . When trapped by sudden fire, movement means salvation more surely than a foxhole.

. . . Always try for surprise in one form or another.

. . . When local surprise is possible, don't expose movement with premature fires.

. . . In the attack, risk, risk, risk.

Israel put nine brigades into Sinai. All but one were used in combat; the extra brigade arrived too late. There were two main battles, one of which decided the campaign as a whole. Eight brigades engaged in sharp and casualty-laden actions and wore through approximately a score of moderate-to-heavy skirmishes, without violating any of these combat commandments. Of the eight brigades, only three were "Regular Army."

The broad design for the campaign as drawn by the High Command was all-inclusive. That is to say that by its end, within less than one week after the first shot was fired, the nine brigades were to stand unchallenged over the whole of Sinai, with every enemy position taken and all resistance ended. All of this was "according to plan." The remnants of Egypt's Army withdrew to the Canal only after its brigades had been broken in trying to hold their defenses. The battlefield story is the final refutation to President Nasser's claim that Israel's swift advance was a hollow victory because he had ordered his Army out of Sinai. Thereby he discredits his troops, most of whom tried to hold their ground, and some of whom fought bravely, although their commanders showed no initiative whatever.

Egyptian conscripts are drawn mainly from the fellaheen or farm laborers. The fellah is illiterate, not interested in fighting, lacking any real bond with his officers, and so undernourished that he is not really combat material. But at least these forces had numbers, solid earth-and-concrete protection, favorable defensive ground invariably fronting on flat fields of fire, and sufficient modern arms to annihilate infantry and perforate medium armor. At all main positions—as post-battle inspection revealed—the Egyptians were over-gunned and over-munitioned.

The campaign was won in a whirl by such slender forces that it is almost a miracle they were not beaten by space alone. They did it on nerve more than with fire and deception. It does not cheapen their performance that the resistance was spotty: full courage is not a relative thing. But the record is not without blemish. Here and there a leader hesitated, trying to command from too far back or bending his ear more to the beat of danger than to the call of tactical opportunity. When detected, he was relieved. No excuses tolerated. No explanations asked.

Israel's High Command says: "Success comes when leaders lead instead of push." The Army guides by that rule on the battlefield. Squad, platoon, and company commanders go first into the fire. Should the attack temporarily stall because of strong resistance, or become unhinged from severed communications, battalion and brigade commanders go posthaste to the center of action and restore movement. If there are two points of disarrangement, the second in command also goes forward.

Measured in bodies only, the cost of this code comes high. Of Israel's soldiers killed in the Sinai war (less than two hundred) half were leaders. Yet the Army believes that this ratio of expendability among its best-qualified fighters is more to be honored than deplored. The Staff says: "That kind of leading, exemplified at all levels, inspires more men to become leaders."

How does the Israeli Army go about teaching its leaders to lead—and its soldiers to follow—so successfully? Here are brief summary notes on some of the more significant training practices I saw being employed in Israel. They will, I suspect, hold some surprises for those who have passed through American military barracks.

Standards for Induction: Israel's Army believes that it takes a minimum of thirty months' hard training to make a fit combat soldier. Every reservist has that much steady service behind him before qualifying for stand-by duty in a home-town unit.

There is no minimum educational requirement for induction. There is none for promotion or for elevation to, and within, the officer corps. All officers are made from the ranks. The average field-grade officer has less than a twelfth-grade education.

There is a minimum intelligence requirement for retention in the Army once the man is inducted. Every recruit must pass a basic examination designed to test his common sense, reasoning power, and reaction time.

During training, the soldier is thrown more on his own than under the United States system. All instruction is pointed toward sharpening the power of decision in the average individual. Physical exercise and lecture courses are aimed to test and increase personal initiative. Israel's trainers believe that teaching the man to think clearly, observe keenly, and report accurately is the main object in the school of the soldier. Accordingly, relatively little importance is attached to perfection in the manual of arms, parade-ground drill, and other routines familiar in Western armies.

Troops are kept moving about in open country as much as possible. The average recruit is strong in the legs, having hiked around since childhood. From the hour of his entry into service, he needs that muscle power, for it is pushed hard.

The Army wastes no time in road marching, believing that a thirty-mile movement across ridges does more to condition troops than seventy miles on the flat. Most marches are an approach to a combat exercise. Even when the reserves take their periodic training, they are kept in the open and are put over rough ground, traveling by night. Every camp is an armed bivouac on a position suitable for defense; no time is spent at a training base. Say the trainers: "That would be a waste. The men would be put on police tasks; we don't call that training." While in uniform, the reservists live away from their families, as would soldiers fighting a campaign, and they seem to like it better that way.

During training, the reservist subsists on hard field rations. No blankets or overcoats are issued for the bivouacs. The Staff feels that the toughening process is furthered by letting the men sleep cold on the ground.

What the Army requires physically of its troops is illustrated in the testing course given the recruit, after it is decided that he is potential NCO material. Such aspirants are divided into packets of three; then each member of the team is put under a twenty-pound load, including his rifle and ammunition. Next, the team is given a march schedule which keeps it moving forty miles per day for three days running, through sharp ridges, such as are found in the Galilee country.

Two-thirds of the route is covered by day, the other by night, the whole taking approximately thirty hours of the three days.

In another test, the body of NCO candidates must march forty miles and finish in eight and one-half hours. No starter is permitted to fall out. If he shows signs of faltering, his comrades must help him along. If he fails, they must carry him.

Though a night-fighting body, Israel's Army follows the principle that programs of night and day training should be balanced realistically. As things work out, about one-third of all training is done at night. But if, for example, it were estimated that 95 per cent of all combat mine-laying would be done during the daylight, mine-laying would get little attention in night training schedules.

Upon entering the Army, the inductee must serve at least six months as a private. But he may be tabbed for leadership immediately because of his personal qualities and a high IQ showing.

In that event, he is sent quickly to section-leaders school, where he spends five months learning to handle what Americans call a squad. Every week he works fifty-two hours or more.

As a basic soldier, he is paid ten dollars per month, with no allowance to his family. The reservist is paid the same, but gets compensation for his family from both government and his employer, which brings his total income to 80 per cent of civilian pay.

After being made an NCO, the soldier must work at non-comship for at least six months even if he is unmistakably officer material. If he has the quality, he can go before the officer selection board, provided he first signs a contract to serve as an officer for at least one year.

Israel commissions about eight hundred men annually, of whom approximately three hundred enter infantry service. The same school trains officers for the combat arms and the technical services; the tech officers are given an extra polishing later. The age for conscription is eighteen. The average age of the newly commissioned second lieutenant in the standing army of Israel is nineteen; in the reserve, twenty-three. A company commander's average age is twenty-three; battalion commander, thirty-two.

The basic course for officership lasts six months. The classes are sent for a week at a time into mountain country, where they practice patrol leading, approach marching, and leadership of the platoon in the attack. They march twenty-five to thirty miles each night and get their rest (except for debriefing practice) during the day.

All training programs, including the first instruction given the recruit, stress the conservation of human energy during combat and the danger of overextending operations by assigning tasks which are not within the physical limits of men.

"Never overload the soldier; rest him whenever possible." Reiterated at all stages of training, the two rules become ingrained in the junior leader. Says the Staff: "We learned the hard way that this is the road to salvation."

During training, one-third of body weight is the maximum load permitted the soldier. That includes uniform, pack, and all else.

During combat, the load is lightened, according to the theory that his energy will be less under fire, rather than more.

"Don't be too eager; don't pile on the pressure," has an odd sound, coming from a General Staff. It's said in Israel to junior leaders by way of emphasizing that men should be rested at every opportunity instead of settling on them that extra fatigue during the mounting-up process which comes from needless anxiety in the command chain.

Elsewhere it's a too familiar story. The colonel says "Be ready at 0900." So the captain tells his platoon leaders, "Be ready at 0800," and they tell the section leaders, "Be ready at 0700."

Israel's Army shuns this practice like a plague. The recruit, on his way to become an NCO, is told that if he checks his men, and they look relatively ready, even though they are still sleeping, it's a sign of weakness in him if he routs them out ten minutes too early merely to further his own peace of mind.

There are eight snipers in each infantry battalion and the Army values them as "worth their weight in gold." They are trained to take up ground individually, working well ahead or to the flank of the company in the attack. They become expert in scouting, map reading, the interpretation of frontline intelligence and use of the rifle. The sniper-scope is carried in the pocket and slips onto the weapon in one click.

Recently the General Staff has looked at a new problem: "How do we get aimed fire at night?" It is seeking the answer in an original system of muscle and eye co-ordination and is confident that the results are justifying the experiment. Under training conditions, according to the Staff, with this new method the average Israeli rifleman can be fairly sure of hitting a kneeling man at night three times out of four at seventy-five yards range. The theory and method have not been proved in combat. But the Staff believes that the solution lies in sharpening the senses of the rifleman rather than in the use of infra-red scopes or other special equipment.

In Israel's Army there is a higher proportion of women in service than in the United States Army. Eligible, physically able young women are drafted, though there are exemptions because of religious scruples, married status, etc. After entering upon training, they are employed according to their talents. In contrast to what is done in the United States services, they are fitted into the lower combat echelons, as signalers, clerks, etc., when they are emotionally disposed toward this kind of work even though it is attended by danger. Their presence in the zone of fire is believed to have an uplifting influence on the morale of the fighting force. Even the male fighters say so.

The literature, radio, and other conditioning influences in Israel put less accent on glamor and sex than is the case in the United States. The Army's problem is eased proportionately. Soldiers say, "We get along better because there are more women around than in other armies." But that doesn't half explain it. The association between men and women in service is marked by a mutually supporting comradeship, high respect for the dignity of every other person, and a common decency. The males act neither protectively nor superciliously toward the females. In the field, the attitude is as natural and relaxed as if they were together in a college classroom.

Women soldiers assigned to combat units are trained in the use of weapons. That is a safeguard rather than a key to their employment during fighting operations; they are used in the field on support tasks such as radio operator, supply clerk, or cryptographer. A few women soldiers have qualified as paratroopers mainly because the General Staff couldn't resist the pressure to grant them this measure of equality. However, no woman soldier was parachuted into Sinai. During the Sinai occupation the women were used in all kinds of security missions interchangeably with the male soldier.

Once a month, the Education Department of the Army's GHQ publishes a pamphlet about the land, its social problems, political goals, etc., for the benefit of troops.

The information is the precis for an orientation lecture. Each unit commander is supposed to give such a talk to his troops at monthly intervals. Like the average American officer, he dislikes the chore, tries to brush it off and sometimes succeeds.

Though Israel is a new nation and a melting of peoples with many tongues coming from everywhere, the Army attaches relatively little importance to the proposition that training for better citizenship—and clearer understanding by the soldier of his cause—is the one best way to build military unity and stimulate the fighting spirit.

The General Staff regards indoctrination as one more means of habituating officers to stand before their own people and talk—the chief value deriving from the program.

Toward heightening the power of decision in all ranks, the Army's doctrine as published by High Command, or expressed by a section leader, emphasizes task, mission, objective above everything else.

"The battle will never go as you planned it; but you still have your task," epitomizes the main idea. When given a mission, the leader is told that he will exercise his own judgment about how to perform the task if his instructions prove unsuitable. But he cannot withdraw without permission.

Such phrases as "at all costs" are avoided in Army orders because of their ambiguity. The patrol sent to reconnoiter with instructions to avoid detection may return at will if sighted by the enemy. On the other hand, a patrol of the same size, if sent to destroy a roadblock, must stay with the task as long as any chance remains that it can be accomplished.

The patrol can't quit simply because it has been badly shot up. But if in the judgment of the leader, it has taken so many casualties that the able-bodied have been immobilized by the weight of the wounded, he may withdraw without permission, and his decision will be accepted if the facts prove consistent with the Army's rigorous standard.

The radical disregard of supply sufficiency which marked Army operations in the Sinai campaign directly reflects teaching by the Army trainers. Leaders are told: "Logistical means are of secondary importance. Things are never perfect. It's more risky to wait. So go on and hit. Don't drag your feet because supply is short. The means will come to you. You've got to take a chance."

During the Sinai fighting, the General Staff concluded that reserve officers have less capacity than "regulars" for a quick shift of direction amid battle and the making of a bold decision.

The civilian leader undeviatingly responded to orders. He was less apt to see the opening clearly and change his line abruptly when the battle became fluid. That was understandable; thirty days' training per year provides too little exercise in "adaptability."

So something new was tried to test and make more acute the decision-making command-post exercise which starts at a slow trot and finishes like a cavalry charge.

The battalion commander is taken into the field with his staff, communications people, his company commanders, and their operations network. Then he is given a tactical exercise-capture of a tank-defended town, attack on a fortified ridge, breakthrough of a fortified pass, destruction of a major roadblock, etc.

On the first day, all of his means for careful calculation of decision are present. He is given twenty-two hours to form a plan. Air photos and maps are available. Any amount of reconnaissance is permitted, as is unlimited consultation with his staff, though all hands must act as if they are in the presence of the enemy. He commands through written orders. Control officers are down with his company commanders and they feed back information about how the situation is developing. In the end, he delivers his plan, and movement order, to the brigade.

At that moment, he's told, "Everything's changed. Your H-hour remains the same. But the brigade is making a ninety-degree change in direction. It's been stopped on the right. So that's your target— that hill over there. There's no time for reconnaissance. Here are the maps and air photos. You'll have to move in thirty minutes. We want your decision before then."

In the interval, the control officers are shoving information to the companies and it comes back to battalion in full flow while the chief and his staff are weighing what to do. The pressure builds up, up, toward the climax.

The worst bump comes as the battalion commander presents his second plan. He is told, "Again, everything's changed. The enemy is cracking on the right. You've lost half your force. You attack straight ahead against Hill 300. There's no time for map checking or staff talk. We want your decision right now."

In the final phase, the statement of enemy strength and the distance to be traveled makes sound solution of the problem barely within his limits of time and men. It remains just possible to take the objective. The commander's decision therefore initiates a workable plan only if, in his mind, speed of thought presages rapidity of movement and daring improvisation. The primary idea is to sharpen faculties; the secondary idea is to test their sufficiency under emergency conditions.

Some battalion commanders, given this processing, become completely shocked. Others meet its challenge without turning a hair. Along the road, higher command learns which officers excel at planning, which at on-the-spot improvisation and which at control. As personal weaknesses become revealed, further training is directed toward producing balanced "adaptability."

In Israel, force levels are not set by law. There is no such problem as the Army having to fight for its existence; very few members of the Knesset are actively anti-military. The armed establishment is given a lump sum appropriation according to the availability of money. It is then up to the General Staff to write the equation—how much can be spent on reserve training, what size standing force can be supported, what must be apportioned to procurement, etc. The Army figures that it costs five times as much to maintain a professional soldier as to train a conscript. Hence the continuing tendency is to narrow the standing force while broadening and strengthening the reserve manpower base.

Due to the high cost of the Sinai campaign, however, and the need for structural reforms indicated by the mobilization, that aim is being temporarily diverted. The funds won't stretch far enough to pay for conversion and still maintain old standards. Israel's Army has about decided that the most practical economy is to slash reserve training.

Here is another risk-filled decision. Readiness in its civilian soldiery has been the rock of Israel's security since the reserve was first formed and given its character in the design drawn by the inspired soldier-scientist, General Yigael Yadin.

Israel's law prescribes that a reservist shall not be given more than thirty days' continuous training per year and one day refresher training per month. That legal limit doubles the training stint of the average U. S. National Guardsman. But it's merely the statement of an ideal standard.

Prior to Sinai, the average civilian soldier in Israel got not more than two weeks' training annually. The look of greater combat readiness in its reserve is hence not to be found in length of training time but in the stern use made of it.

Under the new economy, the Army proposes to limit reserve training to officers and NCOs, down to section leader. It reasons, perhaps from necessity, that training money spent on part-time private soldiers is largely wasted because they forget too easily.

Reserve battalions will be called up separately twice yearly for three-day training intervals. Men and officers will get one day's schooling in weapons handling to quicken their technical knowledge. After that, the formation will go into a tactical exercise, such as the attack on a fortified position. Though only one battalion will be present for maneuver, the brigade exercise will otherwise be conducted full-dress—with pyrotechnics, bangalores, and live ammunition in the supporting weapons. In a first attempt, several of the participants were wounded. Staff observers marked the experiment "successful."

No matter how rugged, realistic, and ingenious a training program may seem, it is never proven until soldiers who have been through it must move forward and take ground in the face of the enemy. All over the world the operation which swept Sinai clean has been praised as a "masterpiece of mobility." But statistics never win a battle. The proof of whether a masterpiece was made by the mobile mind and the willing heart, rather than by machines, is to be found only in the small picture of the fighting under fire.

The picture that has emerged out of the Sinai war is one that deserves close attention from the soldiers and statesmen of other nations. It demonstrated how enormous group power can be generated by consummate daring in command. To the limit possible, leaders looked to their own forces, kept check on the sufficiency of supply, sought all information which might be helpful. But when forces seemed too few, supply drained low, and intelligence of the enemy was lacking, they still marched forward.

The men of this small Army did the best possible with what they had. They responded as if what is all-important is to live fully while one may. To regard their effort in any other light is to miss what counted most in the Sinai adventure—and in the Israel Army today.

14

THE LAND

WALTER C. LOWDERMILK

During recent years, "The imagination of the world has been caught by the concept of interchange of skill across frontiers and oceans, the miraculous ingredient of international cooperation whereby nations, by pooling together a portion of their resources and their know-how, are able to help each other without hope of reward or profit or gain." (Report of U.N. on Technical Assistance)

It is misleading to say that *some* nations are under-developed, and in need of technical assistance, for this sets up a complex barrier of inferiority and superiority that is difficult to surmount in international relationships. In a larger sense, *all* nations are under-developed in terms of the full use of their lands, water, and minerals. All countries have much to learn and to share in development and use of resources for advancing the common welfare of mankind.

Israel, one of the newest and smallest in the family of nations, is demonstrating this higher principle of collaboration within the United Nations and its Expanded Program of Technical Assistance. Israel has requested and received technical assistance in those fields for which she lacks trained personnel or man-power, while she supplies available experts to the United Nations in those fields for which she has professional and recognized specialists, who render technical assistance to less developed countries.

My assignment to Israel by the Food and Agricultural Organization of the United Nations covered five years work in two separate periods of two-and-one-half years each—1951–53 and 1955–57. For me, these assignments were the fulfillment of a dream of many years. I had visited Israel in 1939, while making a survey of land-use in the old world for the United States Department of Agriculture, in the interest of our Soil and Water Conservation Program. I had seen the usual winter rains wash soil from slopes, scour gullies through farm fields, and flood streams which dumped their silt-laden waters into the Mediterranean, discoloring its blue waters to a chocolate brown as far as the horizon. Precious soils were being lost forever in this process of land destruction that had gone on for centuries. No adequate measures were then being taken to retain the heavenly blessing of rain or to save the soil of these Bible lands, to keep them in place on the fields for crops. The dream of doing something about this stayed with me as the project I wanted to do after my retirement from the United States Department of Agriculture Soil Conservation Service.

An assignment to Israel is stimulating. After two thousand years, its people are free citizens in their own country, small though it be, and can work their own land, free from the injustices that have been heaped upon them by Christendom since the Crusades and by Moslem countries for over a thousand years, and free from the late horrors of Hitler's gas chambers. To see first hand the reaction of a people gathered in from the ghettos and mansions of some seventy countries is a profound and inspiring experience. There is a spirit of devotion to redemption of the wasted land and an appreciation of freedom and liberty which people in many countries either have lost or take for granted.

Specialists assigned to Israel in technical assistance find their work made easier because three important factors come together at the same time and at the same place. First, the Israelis are faced with the necessity of making full use of all resources to satisfy the enlarging demands of their increasing population. Second, they have the intelligence to recognize this necessity, and third, they are willing to work.

In the past, common opinion has held that Jews are not good farmers, because they have followed business and professional occupations. (It must be remembered that, in the Middle Ages, ownership of land was denied to them.) But in Israel, in their own country, they have proved to be excellent farmers and are working hard to improve.

The recent movement of Jews of many lands to return to the land of their patriarchs, has brought in more than a million people during this century. Their traditional love for this rocky, badly damaged and misused land which requires great sacrificial labors and high costs to reclaim it for production, has motivated an amazing migration of modern times. The dedicated, pioneering spirit of Israel redeems rocky slopes, malarial swamps, and drifting sand dunes, and irrigates dry lands to meet the needs of people that have come and are continuing to come.

The continued rate of immigration in Israel has increased its population two-and-one-half fold in ten years. It also imposes a critical and impelling urgency to make full use, with conservation, of the country's land, water and mineral resources to supply food, clothing, shelter, water supplies, sanitation, transportation and all kinds of services and jobs to earn these good and useful things. Rapid resettlement and rehabilitation of immigrants, especially on the land to supply these basic needs, has been and is a major task for the young state. It is a challenge to all agencies of government and the enterprise of its citizens. To meet this challenge, Israel has requested help from the United Nations and its specialized agencies in Technical Assistance, and from the United States Point Four or I.C.A. Program, and has made good use of all such assistance supplied.

My first assignment for F.A.O. (Food and Agriculture Organization of the U.N.) to Israel was in response to this request in 1951, and it continued for two and one half years. Upon my arrival in 1951, there was no means for transporting men engaged in field work, and no budget for purchase of the necessary equipment. By special requests to Jewish and Christian friends, we were able to get gifts of nine jeeps and pick-up trucks and one car, giving great impetus to field work. The young Soil Conservation Service was allotted more and more equipment, tractors, terracing graders, bulldozers and surveying and mapping instruments. The service under leadership of Nathan Gil gathered to itself a fine group of personnel.

They were enthusiastic in their devotion to the new science and technology of soil and water conservation that is basic to increased and continuing production of abundant crops for the needs of the rapidly growing economy of Israel.

Technical assistance of this sort to a "less-developed" country at its request called for a variety of undertakings. When a soil conservationist undertakes to design and plan for the installation of a program of soil and water conservation in an old and damaged land as was Israel, he sets out to evaluate existing conditions of its land and its waters. He seeks to reconstruct as far as possible from evidences and from records, the original condition of the landscape as to its forests, its grass and other plant cover, its soils, its climate and rains, its streams and their regimen of flow, and its geology. From such a survey, it is possible to judge the damage that has been done by man and his herds and other agencies, what processes are active, and to estimate what reclamation works are practical and promising.

In making this evaluation in Israel, I drew from many sources of information and from close inspection of actual conditions of lands and streams in the field. I found much valuable information in the Bible, in published reports of former students and archaeologists, and in personal examination of archaeological diggings or "excavations" with the late Colonel P. L. O. Guy, Dr. Nelson Glueck, and the late Sir Flinders Petrie.

After studying what the pioneer settlements, established during the British Mandate, had accomplished, we needed an inventory and classification of all kinds of land of the new state. Such a classification is necessary in formulating a program of land development for cultivated crops, for orchards and plantations, for pastures and forests, together with necessary precautions and measures and works of soil and water conservation.

This inventory of lands was begun in 1951 and completed in 1954. Today, no country has a better inventory of its lands than has Israel. The country is now able to locate quite accurately those areas most suitable for irrigation, for dry farming with supplemental irrigation, for dry farming entirely dependent on rains, for grazing, and for re-seeding to indigenous and introduced grasses for better pasturage.

This inventory also established possibilities and areas of hill and mountain lands for settlement of people, where ancient terraces may be repaired or new ones built which would permit planting of vines and orchards. Lands unsuitable for agricultural uses because of severe erosion or steep rocky slopes are designated for forest plantations, where rainfall is sufficient.

This inventory pointed up Israel's shortage of good farm lands and the need to put a stop to further extension of cities, towns, industrial sites, and sub-divisions on the best farm lands. Such growth is now being directed to areas of low productivity and especially to make use of the extensive sand dunes along the coast of the Mediterranean.

Reclamation of over-grazed lands is a task that applies to the largest area of the country. The biblical description of the land as "flowing with milk and honey" was realistic. However, after centuries of over-grazing, native nutritional grasses and shrubs were almost completely grazed out of the ranges, for what sheep do not eat, goats will, and what goats do not graze, camels eat. Thus, after long dry summers, vegetation was eaten into the ground year after year.

One of the first works started by the new Soil Conservation Service was the establishment of a large grass nursery. Others were established later. At first, scattered seeds of forage grasses were gathered for reseeding. Now Israel grows these seeds by ton lots for re-seeding of wild grass lands to increase the carrying capacity for herds. Seeds of special grasses and forage plants are also introduced from America and South Africa. Israel has made a detailed survey of about 875,000 acres of natural grazing lands of less than 14 inches of rainfall per year, as a basis for a national range management program.

Reclamation of eroding lands called for special works. The Government of Israel is now committed to a Soil Conservation Program, including contour farming, and will not grant development loans for new plantings of vineyards and orchards unless these are laid out and planted on the contour. Also, in areas designated as critical, the Soil Conservation Service is required to prescribe and lay out measures of contour farming and storm water disposal. Already the demands for such services far exceed available trained field men.

Reclamation of lands of deep soils, encumbered with stones that hinder cultivation, has been a challenging undertaking. Erosion of soil over large areas has left stones at the surface and makes such areas unsuited for cultivation without reclamation works. Israel's manpower and machines have performed Herculean tasks in removing stones and piling them in heaped ridges laid out on the contour or near contour, with a slight gradient to keep down the velocity of storm waters as is done in broad base terracing. This costly reclamation is justified in Israel by high returns from fruits in the hills and for support of strategic settlements.

Reclamation of deforested lands has been the most popular work. One of the most striking damages to the original condition of this region was the general destruction of forests and trees during past centuries. Tree planting is a useful type of project in Israel, carried out locally to give unskilled newcomers jobs and a love of the good earth. Some 35 million trees have already been planted on formerly naked hills which now are emerald green among rocky slopes. Solution pockets in the limestone hills retain the fertile soils which tree roots seek out, and trees still grow today, much as in ancient times.

Reclamation of coastal sand dunes is a big challenge to the country. Some 75,000 acres of active sand dunes are moving inland from the Mediterranean coast, while an area much larger lies inland in the southern Negev. Coastal dunes offer good building and industrial sites as at Tel-Aviv, Holon, Natania, and the Haifa industrial area, among others. Carob trees grow well on sand dunes in some localities, but only a beginning has been made to grow this tree with its useful products, and in reclamation of the dunes.

Restoration and modification of ancient rock-walled terracing on hills and mountains is an undertaking without precedents. It is my opinion that the Phoenicians were the first to encounter soil erosion in clearing and farming slopes, and at the same time they were the first to control soil erosion by applying the principle of the contour to rock wall terracing of cultivated slopes.

Most of these ancient measures of terraces in Lebanon and in Israel are now in ruins, but where maintained to the present time, they are still being cultivated to crops as in Ein Karem near Jerusalem. But they are suited only to hand labor. Accordingly, some modification was needed in Israel to permit the use of powered farm machinery, for Israel is pioneering on high wages. The practice now is to knock down the ancient Phoenician narrow terraces and, in their stead, to pile stone from old terraces and from stone-clearing into ridges laid out on the contour or near contour and 60 to 120 feet apart. The interspaces between these new Jewish National Fund terraces are presenting some problems of soil erosion, but studies are underway to work out suitable measures to bring this type of erosion under control.

Drainage of marshes and swamps was one of the first major undertakings in reclamation by early settlements. Newcomers to Palestine found lowlands depopulated by malaria. Arab farmers were cultivating uplands and were quite ready to sell pestilential swamps and marshes. Though malaria often killed off the first wave of Jewish settlers, volunteers persisted until all such marshes were drained. These marshes are now healthy and productive farm lands, surrounding populous centers—such as Petah Tikva, Givat Brenner, Hadera, and Nahalal, among others.

Drainage of the Huleh swamps in northern Israel is the crowning achievement of all such works. This major work, begun in 1952, has been completed in its major features. The Jordan River channel, as it leaves the southern end of Lake Huleh, was widened and lowered so as to drain the lake and the marshes. Miles of main and subsidiary canals were dug to lead waters of the three tributary streams directly through the swamps and out into the new Jordan River channel. In addition to some 16,000 acres of agricultural land reclaimed for intensive cultivation by drainage, the reduction in surface area of the free water of marshes and Lake Huleh will also reduce the high evaporation losses of these Jordan waters. This saving of about 50,000 acre feet [1] annually will be enough to irrigate 17,000 to 25,000 acres of land, depending on the rainfall of the district to which these waters are delivered.

---

[1] "Acre foot" is an irrigation term meaning the amount of water that will cover one acre to a depth of one foot, or 43,560 cubic feet.

We attended the celebration of the "first plowing" of these newly drained, fertile peat soils in 1955. The first crops were grown and harvested in 1956 with yields three times the average for sorghum grain and peanuts. Here it is possible to grow two and three crops yearly. When fully developed, the Huleh will become a veritable Garden of Eden.

Irrigation of dry lands, especially those with scanty rainfall, is one of the most remarkable developments since the Independence of Israel. The area of irrigated crops has increased from 74.250 acres in 1948–49 to 250,500 in 1957 and is planned to reach more than 411,000 acres by 1960. Water is the life blood of Israel, and, like Southern California, Israel has more good land than there is water to irrigate it. Rain falls in the winter and the summer is long and dry. Storage of waters for irrigation in summer is necessary. The fertile loessal lands of the South, with scanty rainfall but with a long growing season, justify extensive works to divert waters from the north to these lands where settlement is rapidly taking place. Waters are brought from the Yarkon River through 66 inch and 70 inch concrete pipe-lines. Most irrigation is by sprinkling systems under pressure, which does not require levelling of the land. Flat lands make it cheaper to use border irrigation. Irrigation is being extended as rapidly as possible on dry lands that were never before irrigated.

Control and reclamation of flood waters is provided for under the Master Water Plan. Flood waters are surpluses to conserve, to store in surface reservoirs or in under-ground aquifers to supplement natural recharge of ground waters. There they are made available for pumping in the dry season. Floods cause damage to life and property, erode quantities of fine top soils from fields into the sea and cause serious losses to the country. Control and conservation of flood waters in Israel is being founded on measures and works of watershed management and upstream control of "little waters" [2] integrated into a land-use and soil conservation program.

With the establishment of the State of Israel, an intensive study

[2] A term in watershed management meaning water courses in their beginnings, creeks, brooks, and intermittent stream channels, as distinguished from "big waters" —main stream channels, and rivers.

was undertaken to develop a Master Water Plan for the country. Tahal, the Government Water Planning Agency, was entrusted with the task of drawing up a final scheme for over-all irrigation development. All earlier schemes were studied, including my plan for a "Jordan Valley Authority" Power and Irrigation Project, which included the entire drainage of the Jordan for the benefit of Trans-Jordan, as well as Israel. Tahal combined the most satisfactory features of all schemes that could be put into effect within the border of Israel without the collaboration of neighboring countries, which refused to take part in a comprehensive scheme. After seven years work, this over-all Water Plan was approved in February 1956. It envisages more than doubling the present water supply for irrigation, industrial, and domestic uses. This plan will utilize the waters of all springs, streams, and rivers; store flood waters in reservoirs behind dams; pump from deep and shallow wells and will recharge underground aquifers during winter months of rain. Also works have begun for rectification and re-use of sewage waters.

Israel uses her own manufactured cement to build the 108 inch, 70 inch and 66 inch pipelines from northern Israel to dry but fertile areas in the south, where many settlements are being established on newly irrigated lands. The Jordan 108 inch pipeline is the primary feature to which all five satellite projects will be joined.

The newest type of agricultural settlements are Regional Development areas. This requires large blocks of land with sufficient water for irrigation. An over-all plan links one settlement to another organically. They form a net work of inter-dependent settlements with a town as a service center. The Lachish development in the region of ancient Ashkelon in the south, the Ta'anach project of the Valley of Jezreel, and the Adullam area of the hills south of Jerusalem, are proving the success of this method of settlement. By 1960, Regional Development should embrace a considerable proportion of Israel's farming.

Agriculture is a way of life and a necessity for Israel, as for other countries. Today there are more than 750 agricultural settlements, and their number increases monthly. Lands that are a wilderness one month may be dotted with scores of white farm houses the next month, and shortly thereafter become a green irrigated oasis. As the prophet Isaiah proclaimed, "The wilderness and the parched land shall be glad; and the desert shall rejoice, and blossom as the rose." (Isaiah 35:1)

While population has increased more than two and one half times during the first ten years of the State, the number of agricultural settlements has increased in number many fold. These farming activities have added to Israel's food crops, and will increase faster than the population. In 1951, Israel imported most of her food at high costs, but in 1957, the country grew 75 per cent of her requirements and exported the equivalent of millions of dollars worth of oranges, eggs, peanuts, "cut flowers" and the like. Israel is becoming more and more self-sufficient in agricultural products, but will not be able to grow all the grains and meats required. These imports will be offset with agricultural exports of high values. To sustain such expanding production, however, the program of soil and water conservation must likewise be carried on with greater refinements and wider application.

At the end of the first half of my assignment under F.A.O., as consultant to the government of Israel in Soil and Water Conservation and Land Development, Israel had made excellent progress. In 1951, the newly organized Soil Conservation Service of the Israel Department of Agriculture was the smallest in size with the lowest budget of any department in government. Two and a half years later, it was the largest with the highest budget. By that time, an efficient Soil Conservation Service was in action with a fine group of dedicated young men. The Grass Nursery was a success, tons of seed of nutritious grasses were harvested yearly for re-seeding of wild range lands, and contour farming was spreading over the countryside.

At the Agricultural School at Midrasha, short courses were given to train technical foremen to direct a labor force of unskilled newcomers, similar to our CCC Camps, to do various kinds of work on the land. These short courses attracted the attention of the Government of Cyprus, which requested that ten of its technical men be permitted to receive this special training. The F.A.O., upon the request of the Israel Government, sent Mr. William H. Bender to Israel to train these leaders and settlement representatives.

The inventory of land-use capabilities of all lands of Israel north of the true desert of the southern Negev was completed and had become the basis for settlement planning of land. Demonstration areas in soil and water conservation in various parts of Israel were installed, using modern techniques of contour farming, broad base terraces, storm disposal ditches, check dams, and all required measures to save the rains and soils for the maintenance of a permanent agriculture. Also, various methods were devised to educate city folk as well as farmers and school children in the problems of erosion and need for conservation, by radio, lectures, articles in the papers, and special studies in schools.

With deep satisfaction, I watched the progress of various features of the "Jordan Valley Authority" Power and Irrigation Project which I had outlined in 1944 in my book, *Palestine, Land of Promise*.[3] Part One envisaged full development and use of all available waters, as has been described in the above Master Water Plan. This is being carried out in a splendid way within Israel. Part Two, which called for diversion of the Mediterranean Sea waters through lined canals and tunnels for 26 miles, to be dropped into the Dead Sea through hydro-electric power stations with a fall of 1296 feet to generate about 600 million kilowatt hours of electrical power per year, must await the cooperation of Jordan, or it may be omitted for a time if atomic power is economical. Part Three of this JVA, which called for a program of full development and conservation of land resources to make the most of the soils and rains that fall on them, is advancing as rapidly as technicians can be trained to do the work. The major part of this Part Three is being carried out by agencies of the government and the Soil Conservation Service as previously described.

My second assignment was a natural sequence to the first two-and-one-half years as consultant in planning and organizing soil and water conservation work throughout Israel. The bottleneck in this urgently needed work was lack of trained agricultural engineers to carry out the various measures in the fields and to work up basic data

[3] Harper and Bros., N.Y., 1944.

for conditions in Israel. This required technical training, accuracy, and thoroughness of work; for running water never forgives a mistake or an over-sight in lay-out or in maintenance of water control and conservation measures. Ten times more work could be done if sufficient trained personnel were available. There also was a need for trained professional agricultural engineers in mechanized farming and in farm structures and buildings in agricultural settlement planning. Israel could not afford to hire foreign trained men, nor would it be good policy. It was necessary to train her own eager youth to do this work.

The Government of Israel asked the F.A.O. for assistance. Professor Philip Manson was then sent to review the situation, and he recommended the collaboration of the Hebrew University Faculty of Agriculture at Rehovot and the Israel Institute of Technology at Haifa (Technion) in training men for the relatively new profession of agricultural engineering. Professor Manson's recommendations were followed.

Plans for developing this new Department of Agricultural Engineering included an assignment for me by F.A.O. as visiting Professor to serve as head of this department—to organize and to develop a school of college level, and to work out a curriculum that would integrate agriculture, hydraulics, mechanics, technology, and works. Such works include adequate mechanization of farm operations for maximum production per farmer and per unit area; appropriate and efficient farm buildings and structures, and agricultural settlement lay-outs; irrigation and drainage; erosion and flood control, and soil and water conservation. So complex is the subject and so great its diversity that agricultural engineering was broken down into three occupational divisions—1) Mechanized Farming or Farm Machinery, 2) Farm Buildings and Settlement Lay-outs and 3) Soil and Water Conservation Works. These works and services all call for well-trained engineers with a good understanding of agricultural crops, measures and practices that should be integrated into programs of land-use and agricultural production.

The world will look more and more to this new profession to make the most of land, climate, and water resources for production of foods, fats, and industrial crops, to meet the enlarging demands of rapidly increasing populations. Israel has become a Pilot Area, for she is forced to solve problems that other countries sooner or later will meet as the requirements of their populations make more demands on natural resources. What is being done in Israel has significance for the entire Middle East and for over half of the earth's inhabitants who are on the verge of stepping out of subsistence agrarian to industrial economies.

To meet these requirements for Israel, the Technion, through its newly formed Department of Agricultural Engineering is responsible for basic training in general science and engineering techniques, while the University's Faculty of Agriculture at Rehovot teaches agricultural sciences and practices. This is an excellent example of cooperation in Israel which gives this exacting training at a cost much lower than that of a combined program in either institution.

Training is built up at three levels. The first level deals with the major activity of the department: training professional agricultural engineers. A four-year course was planned, but this will soon be extended to five years. During the first two years, the basic sciences of mathematics, chemistry, physics, geology, and biology as a prerequisite to agricultural subjects are taught at the Technion. In the third year, engineering students are transferred to Rehovot, where the Faculty of Agriculture instructs them in agricultural subjects of Soil Science, Agronomy, Horticulture, Plant Protection, Soil and Farm Management, and the like. For the fourth year, the students return to the Technion campus to take specialized subjects in the Division which they have selected.

To qualify for a diploma as a professional agricultural engineer, the graduate must carry out, in addition, a Diploma Project during his first year of employment, to the satisfaction of his employer and to that of a Diploma Committee. Upon satisfactory completion of this Diploma Project, this professional agricultural engineer is qualified to carry on exacting work in his speciality. Such graduates are in great demand—for employment by farm machinery companies, by farm implement repair shops, by agricultural institutes, and by the Soil Conservation Service. These trained men are also employed by drainage authorities, by cooperative settlements, by cooperative farms, by research institutes and by the Colonization Agency.

The second level is concerned with post-graduate degrees of Master of Science and Doctor of Engineering Science, under supervision of the Graduate School at the Technion. This will fill a twofold need in Israel; first, the building up of a body of adequate basic data, together with scientific information, and second, the training of competent scientists to conduct research and to train others in research in engineering. This combined department of Agricultural Engineering is strong and growing, with some 120 under-graduate students and 8 graduate students engaged in significant research, as of 1957. This department collaborates with government services and settlements in improving mechanized farming, and in experimentation and instruction in advanced land-use with conservation of soil and water.

The third level of instruction is in short courses, for special students, farmers, farm managers and field technicians of colonization agencies who wish to take a three to six months course of intensive practical training in specific occupations. When these trainees have completed their courses, they return to their jobs better equipped to carry on their work.

The Division of Soil and Water Conservation includes the subject of Watershed Management, as it integrates the measures and works for several purposes within a watershed, drainage basin, or other physiographic unit of land development and management.

The lack of adequate buildings for instruction and research has been a handicap. Money has now been designated, and plans for an Agricultural Engineering Building on the new Technion campus at Haifa were completed before I left Israel. The building is planned for efficiency, to serve adequately the growing activities of this new and exacting profession.

The new Agricultural Building will have three wings: one for class rooms and laboratories, one for offices and library, and the third for farm machinery, with display and research laboratories. Special mention should be made of the 60 foot tower for research in studies of rain drops and their velocities and energies as they strike the ground on various soil surfaces. There will be a fan to create down-drafts and up-drafts of different velocities to control effective velocities of rain drops. These studies of the dynamics of rain drops open up an approach to phenomena of infiltration of rain and of sprinkler irrigation, of rain splash and soil erosion in its first stages, that will lead to a far better understanding of these phenomena where most can be done about them.

Down a slope from the paved court, two lysimeters, with miniature watersheds with maximum gradient of 20 percent, will be set up. These lysimeters will be filled with soil to a depth of three feet. Provision will be made to collect and measure surface run-off with eroded soil and bed-load, and percolation through the soil, collected as ground water discharge. This set-up of a pair of lysimeters, with provision for artificial rain of different intensities and duration, on soils treated with contour furrowing, and the other without such treatment, will serve to illustrate to students, visitors of Israel and foreign countries, some of the problems involved in watershed management.

An effort was made to give all students who enrolled in this new Department of Agricultural Engineering a feeling of solidarity and common interests. This was done through regular parties for students, wives, and sweethearts, together with the faculty at a campus recreation hall. These regular festivities became very popular. All faculty members, and wives, as well as each senior class, were invited to dinner at our home each semester. A splendid spirit developed among students of the Department and in their relations with the faculty.

My two F.A.O. assignments to Israel, so stimulating and satisfying, came to an end in 1957. It was gratifying to know that the soil and water conservation work, begun in 1951, was being continued at increased tempo by an efficient Soil Conservation Service, and that the young Service could carry on satisfactorily and prepare for the future.

As I looked over these Bible lands, now increasingly farmed on the contour, with rows of vineyards, orchards, stone walls and broad bench terraces on the level around slopes, I felt my dream of 1939 was coming true. I had written my biography, not with words, but with land and water conservation on the slopes and fields of this sacred land.

The Department of Agricultural Engineering, now well established to train the eager young men who would continue these works on the land, could carry on and advance without my further councils. With great satisfaction, I could turn this new Department over to my well-trained, able, and efficient successor, Professor A. De Leeuw. May the adage come true—the greatest success lies with the successor.

15

THE AMERICA-ISRAEL SOCIETY

THEODORE R. McKELDIN

Every man can look back on moments of more than usual significance in his life. One of these moments came to me in the early summer of 1952, when my secretary laid on my desk an invitation from the Government of Israel to visit that State which had won its independence barely four years earlier.

I had long been familiar with the events that led to the rebirth of Israel as a modern nation. My own city of Baltimore, of which I had been Mayor, was the birthplace of an American lady who had contributed as much as any man or woman to the return of Jews to the Holy Land. She was Henrietta Szold. The flame of her conviction enabled her to bring into being the great work of Hadassah in the encouragement and preparation of youthful Jewish pioneers.

Years later, Baltimore was the port from which more than one ship set out for the Mediterranean to engage in the rescue of refugees from the Hitler-made horror in Europe. One of those ships, the President Warfield, was rechristened the Exodus. The story of her voyage and her attempt to run the British blockade will always live in the memory of those who are moved by courage and sacrifice.

Later, when the British gave up their mandate over Palestine, I, like many other Americans of Christan faith, read accounts of the conflict between the Arabs and Jews with anxiety. I was thrilled to hear of the heroic resistance of the Jews against the attacking armies of the Arab World. Many of those who were fighting with hardly more than their bare hands had relatives in Maryland, some of whom were friends of mine. They shared with me the letters that they received from the Front. I could rejoice with them over the announcement of the establishment of the State of Israel by the United Nations, and could appreciate their relief at the end of the fighting.

The Israel Government's invitation stirred me at the prospect of seeing at first hand the result of so many years of trial and effort. The thought of observing with my own eyes the use the Israelis had made of their first few years of freedom was indeed tempting. I hesitated only because of the weight of my duties as Governor of Maryland.

With the aid of my staff, however, and with the ready cooperation of the heads of various State departments, the affairs of my office were so arranged that the trip became possible without serious inconvenience to public business.

I felt, too, that my usefulness as a servant of the people of Maryland would be enhanced by on-the-spot observation of the character and sinew strengthening of developing democracy in Israel. On our trip to the Middle East, Mrs. McKeldin and I were accompanied by our long-time friends, the Honorable Simon E. Soboloff and Mrs. Soboloff.

In many subsequent speeches, I have sought to translate into words my experiences during that visit to Israel. I fear I never have quite succeeded in describing the exaltation that was mine as I set foot on the ancient soil at the aiport of Lod. It was a sensation that grew, rather than diminished, as we traveled from place to place, for each name had become familiar to me in the long-ago and through the years from my reading of the Bible.

I found that what I felt was shared by almost every Jew whom I met in Israel. I was not surprised, of course, but I was moved when I found so many references in ordinary conversation to the holy traditions of the places that surrounded us on all sides.

One of the most striking things about Israelis is their sense of history. Whether religious in a formal way or not, a surprising number of them live with the Bible as a constant influence in everything that they do. The officers and men of Israel's army actually have used their Biblical knowledge in the conduct of their campaigns. General Yigael Yadin, the soldier-archeologist who was Chief of Staff during 1958, credits many of the successes in that desperate struggle to the precedents of Biblical history. Many an erudite churchman could learn from the leader of a remote *kibbutz,* as a collective settlement is called, or from a vendor in the streets of Jerusalem.

Equally impressive was the Israelis' sense of the future. Awareness of the meaning of the past, that saturates every inch of ground in their homeland, does not conflict with their equal determination to build just as meaningful a future. Wherever we went, we encountered inspired men and women who proudly showed us what had been accomplished since the establishment of the State, but who described even more proudly to us the plans they were making for next week, next month, next year, ten years hence. It was almost as though the present were unimportant—there was so much to do! Nor was this passion for the future confined to leaders. Israel is the only country I know where nearly every individual man, woman and child consciously feels that he is taking part as a person in the construction of a great edifice. When a taxi driver in Tel Aviv refused a tip, he explained that he felt it was his duty, his part in helping to make the stranger feel respect for his country. A brick-layer, spreading mortar at the side of a new hotel on the Mediterranean shore, said he felt that every brick he put in place gave him a part in building not merely a house or a hotel but in rebuilding the Temple!

As I have been concerned with government for so many years, I looked for certain practices that seem to me to be vital in any system. To me, no government is good if it shackles the people. Here I found guarantees of religious freedom, of equal participation of all adults in the election of representatives, of equality of the sexes, of protection of the rights of minorities, of scrupulous fairness in the administration of Justice. As Herman Wouk has written, nowhere in the world is there a deeper appreciation of the worth of the individual as a person, nor a greater respect for the value of human life. This is the reason why Israel does not inflict the death penalty—not even for treason.

Those were some of the impressions of my first visit. Since then, good fortune has brought me back to Israel many times. Now I know, from my own observations and constant study of the news, that these basic guarantees are not only embodied in the law but are effective in practice.

What I learned on my first visit was enough to make me feel that I should help to bring Americans of every faith to recognition of what was being created in Israel. It seemed to me the accomplishments there, from the point of view of citizens of our own country, was a good in itself, a contribution in vision and in advancement of civilization itself. The achievements in Israel were being made by Jews, stimulated by utter necessity and the recent memories of horrors. Yet the position of the Jews, who had come to Israel from the far corners of the earth to build a home in the mountains and valleys, swamps and deserts of a long neglected land, was much like that of the pioneers of our own country scarcely two centuries ago. They, too, needed aid and encouragement from across the seas.

So it was that I consulted a number of friends as to the best method of putting my wish into action. It was obvious that I could do something by taking a stand as an individual, speaking and writing wherever there was an opportunity, and giving my support to the organizations that were helping the people of Israel in their struggle, as it was then, for survival. I wondered whether I could not make some special contribution, something of new and lasting value. At first it seemed that existent groups were concerned with almost every aspect of Israel. Then it became apparent that there was one lack.

There was no organization in existence that was composed of both Christians and Jews, dedicated to interpreting the culture of Israel to Americans and the culture of the United States to Israelis. Friends, both Israelis and Americans, suggested that such an organization could prove of real value to the advancement of mutual understanding. They pointed out that the English Speaking Union has made a major contribution over the years toward clarifying the similarities and differences between the culture of the United States and that of the British Commonwealth. Why should there not be an organization to do similar service for our country and Israel? After considerable further consultation, I decided to see whether it would be possible to form such an organization.

From the very beginning, it was clear that such an organization should be independent; that it should avoid lobbying and controversy; that it should concentrate on education in the broadest sense; and that it should gain the interest and support of leaders in government, the arts and sciences, industry and labor. One of the first to seize upon this idea and to work unselfishly with me during the formative period was F. Joseph Donohue, a former chairman of the Board of Commissioners of the District of Columbia. He has continued his interest and has given time and wise advice ever since.

We were lucky to obtain the services of the Reverend Howard M. LeSourd, who took a few weeks leave of absence from Boston University to conduct the extensive correspondence that was necessary to enlist the interest of a group of Founders, and of Charles Van Devander of New York to handle our relations with the press. We decided to suggest that the new organization be called "The America-Israel Society." We thought that this name would immediately communicate our conception of our new organization's function—to interpret, with equal concern, our country to Israel and Israel to our country.

Response to our first communications was good. Within a very short time we had the enthusiastic concurrence of forty outstanding persons, leaders in their fields in many parts of the United States. I then sent out invitations for a dinner meeting in Government House, Annapolis, official residence of the Governor of Maryland. Nearly every person invited expressed the intention of being present. However, they reckoned without the weather. January 21, 1954 brought one of the worst snow-storms in years. Only those whose travel arrangements were the least affected by the atmospheric inclemency were able to get through: Governor Christian A. Herter of Massachusetts; Governor Robert B. Meyner of New Jersey; Mr. Donohue; George T. Newell, Vice-President of the Manufacturers Trust Company of New York; Rabbi Abba Hillel Silver of the Temple, Cleveland; Dr. LeSourd; Professor Howard Mumford Jones of Harvard; and Judge Soboloff. The remainder, finding themselves grounded, sent telegrams bearing reassurances of continued interest.

Although the storm howled outside, lashing the waters of the Chesapeake Bay into white-capped waves and piling the snow high, we had a very pleasant meeting. Professor Jones made a statement of aims which he later expanded and which became a beacon for the future. We decided to incorporate our Society under the laws of the State of Delaware. I was chosen President and Mr. Donohue was designated Chairman of the Board of Governors (Directors) to be elected later. It was all very informal but hopeful. Thus Mr. Van Devander was able to send out the news that The America-Israel Society had been born.

Most of those present accepted my invitation to remain through the night in Government House. Rabbi Silver was assigned a room and bed in which, I informed him, the late Cardinal Gibbons once had slept. When the Rabbi came down to breakfast the next morning, I inquired whether he had spent a comfortable night. "I had no theological difficulties whatsoever," he replied with a smile. Another good omen!

Soon thereafter, we enlisted George L. Cassidy as Executive Director of the Society. Mr. Cassidy, formerly chief roving correspondent of the New York Post, had spent an entire year in the Middle East, with his headquarters in Jerusalem. We decided to launch our activities by having a large public dinner as a way of introducing the Society—a kind of "coming-out party"—in the Nation's Capital, where we intended to have our headquarters. The late Maxwell Abbell generously gave us a room in the Willard Hotel for our office. The Willard is still our home.

Our first national dinner was a success. Its theme was one of tribute to the pioneer spirit of the Israelis, and it was held in the

Washington Statler on the eve of the Fifth Anniversary of Israel's independence.

But a debut, no matter how brilliant, does not guarantee a lifetime success. After the first national dinner, the America-Israel Society consisted of the original forty-one members. Very little was left of the small sum that we had raised to cover the initial expenses of preliminary organization. We still were operating as a trusteeship, and we had no assurance of tax-exemption.

There were only two sources from which we could hope to derive an income that would meet the basic operational expenses of a national organization: donations and membership dues. Furthermore, unless we were able to begin the program of activities that our goals demanded, the America-Israel Society would die at birth. Thus the remainder of the first year of our Society's existence was devoted largely to securing a membership and sufficient donations to stay alive. It was a battle against time. A.I.S. would not have survived this first twelve month period, if it had not been for the sympathetic help of the late Louis M. Rabinowitz of New York, Dewey D. Stone of Boston and several others who made substantial contributions, as well as for the support of those perceptive persons (both Jews and Christians) who became sponsors and members. Our reluctance to make promiscuous appeals for aid made solution of our financial problems even more difficult. These problems are still with us, but are not quite so acute as in that period.

Since then, our Society has been able to do more to carry out its objectives. Our membership has spread to such an extent that the Society is truly national in character, with business firms, associations, labor unions, as well as individuals, participating in thirty-nine states and the District of Columbia. Recently, our Board of Governors authorized the formation of regional chapters. Four have been organized: Maryland, New Jersey, New York and Pennsylvania. They have a liberal degree of autonomy, within the requirements of our national constitution and by-laws, and have been conducting good programs of their own.

Despite limited funds, the America-Israel Society has been able to do a good deal to advance mutual understanding between Americans and Israelis through the interchange of cultural information. We would like to do more. Some of the things we have done necessarily have been experimental in nature, and, I believe, we have learned some valuable lessons. Our achievements cannot readily be measured arithmetically. It is not easy, as the psychologists have discovered, to apply yardsticks to minds and emotions.

One of the Society's most important accomplishments has been to bring persons, whose interest in these matters heretofore was very slight, into close association with various aspects of the cultural relationships between Israel and the United States. This includes non-members as well as members. Among the activities that have served this end, I would note:

Providing services to other organizations interested in some aspect of our own objectives;

Encouraging or actually sending American leaders in various fields of culture (broadly interpreted) to visit Israel. They have contributed to a better understanding of the United States there, and, upon their return, have brought enlightenment in their lectures, writings, and appearances on radio and TV;

Making available appropriate platforms and hospitality for distinguished visitors from Israel;

Cooperating with our Department of State in its exchange of persons program;

Participating in the national conference on this subject conducted by the Institute of International Education;

Conducting symposia on Israel culture in institutions of higher learning;

Sponsoring concerts by Israeli musicians;

Distributing, on occasion, books and articles on aspects of America-Israel cultural relations to carefully chosen persons and institutions;

Publishing a monthly bulletin for A.I.S. members and others;

Showing educational films at Chapter meetings and before other groups;

Acting as a center of information insofar as the Society's limited staff permits.

Opportunities for the expansion of our Society's program and activities would be without limit, if finances were available. My experience to date convinces me that it would be highly desirable to increase ten-fold the number of carefully selected persons who go to Israel under the auspices of the America-Israel Society. We have found that those who visit Israel with a specific subject for investigation do much to correct misunderstanding. Then, too, there is a great need for the establishment of Visiting Lectureships at the graduate school level in our institutions of higher learning for Israelis of professional standing. It is not only that governmental aid is wholly insufficient, but that private enterprise in this area is highly desirable. The Society's distribution of its own publications also could be increased with benefit both here and in Israel. It is hardly needful for me to labor the point that A.I.S. could do more.

The accomplishments of the America-Israel Society have been made possible only through the expenditure of a great deal of time, energy and resources by those who have dedicated themselves to its objectives. Every founder, sponsor, officer and member has made his unique contribution. I have enjoyed every minute of my association with these splendid men and women. Looking back over the brief history of the Society, I am certain that our investment has been worthwhile. It is my conviction that the advancement of mutual understanding is a factor in making peace possible in the world, and that there is a special value in preserving and deepening understanding between Americans and Israelis, two peoples who have so much in common through ancient heritage and shared aspirations.

16

"SENTIMENTAL JOURNEY"
(A Dramatic Reading)

DORE SCHARY

CAST OF CHARACTERS

NARRATOR
FIRST MALE VOICE ⎫
FIRST FEMALE VOICE ⎬ (NOT SEEN)
SECOND MALE VOICE ⎭
ISRAELI POLICEMAN
NEWSPAPERMAN
SOUTH AFRICAN LADY
OLD MAN
  (Yiddish Accent)
YOUNG SABRA
SOLDIER
MAN WITH *SHTRAYMEL*
CULTURED MAN
BUTCHER (KATZ)
EGYPTIAN MAN
  (Druggist)
EGYPTIAN LADY
  (Dressmaker)
YOUNG MAN FROM KIBBUTZ

ANATA (Girl)
ARTIST FROM SAFED
(Goatee)
CHRISTIAN MAN
HEBREW TEACHER
THIRD MALE VOICE   (NOT SEEN)
(Angry)
NARRATOR'S WIFE
BENNY BUDENSKY
MR. MAYOL
(British)
MISS KALLARAH
(Painter)
JACK BERLIN
SCHLOMO ROSEN
(Hotel Man)
YEMENITE SCHOOL TEACHER
(Woman)
MEYER WEISGAL'S VOICE (NOT SEEN)
PROFESSOR #1 AT
WEIZMANN INSTITUTE
PROFESSOR #2 AT
WEIZMANN INSTITUTE

FOREWORD

In the spring of 1957, my wife, our son Jeb and our younger daughter Joy, traveled with me on our first trip to Israel. The journey to and through Israel was the most exciting and stimulating event in my life. During the visit we kept notes and I wrote letters to our older daughter Jill and her husband Jon and to some of our friends.

In the fall of that year I was asked to speak to the friends of the Weizmann Institute in America about my experiences in Israel. As

I reflected on what I wanted to say, my thoughts fell into the form of a dramatic reading. What follows herewith contains most of my impressions and introduces you to new friends whom I met.

This sketch, therefore, is hardly a definitive analysis or thorough commentary—it pretends to be neither. It is merely a happy visitor's look at a new and busy nation, written by one who came with an open mind and an open heart.

(An orchestra softly plays "Sentimental Journey.")

NARRATOR: It is a languid song the orchestra is playing—an American popular tune—out of reach, out of sound, out of tempo with Israel. But last spring as we boarded a ship at Venice to go to Haifa, a three-piece Italian band played that song—and all of us, the Americans, English, French, Brazilians, Spaniards, Italians and Israelis, listened to it—and to each it meant something else—and yet to all of us it meant the same. We were all on a journey—the lady from London going to a cemetery near Safed to look, as she has looked each year since 1948, at the grave of her son, killed fighting for freedom in Israel; the Spanish Catholics bound for a tour of the Holy Land, the Brazilian going to Tel Aviv to see his cousin whom he wanted to take to Brazil so they could prosper together:

(THE MUSIC FADES OUT)

"Three times," he said, "I have gone—three times the answer has been, 'no.'"
"Then why do you go?", I asked. "Because," he answered, "It is pleasant in

Israel. Each time I go, I understand my
cousin's 'no' better." And the English
telephone expert was going to Cyprus to
put in new wires and a new system. He
had been in Cyprus many times. He was
quite sentimental. And then there were
the two of us, my wife and I. We had
listened to the music, too, as they played
"Sentimental Journey." Sentimental—this
trip to Israel? My wife hardly thought so.
"Why Israel?", she had asked. "Palm
Springs with less air conditioning!" And
what about me? I knew Israel. Of course
I knew it. I had listened to many speakers at U.J.A. dinners and at Bonds for
Israel. I knew Israel because I had listened—listened well—

A VOICE: (Quite ponderous)
In Israel at the present time there are two
million arable acres converted to use by
modern irrigation and planting methods
in order to provide food for—
(It fades away)

ANOTHER VOICE: —There are in Israel today one million
(A Woman's)   eight hundred thousand inhabitants. Of
this number, one hundred and eighty
thousand are Arabs. Some thirty percent
of the remainder are native-born—*sabras*
—and the rest are immigrants who came
to Israel as long as forty-five years ago
and as recently as yesterday. These people represent a diversified citizenry that—
(The voice fades)

STILL ANOTHER   (Very precise)
VOICE: —And each month some eight to ten

	thousand new refugees flood into Israel. This is their only door—their only passage—
NARRATOR:	Of course I knew Israel—all about it—and—*nothing!* Nothing at all.
A POLICEMAN: (In Israeli uniform)	I saw him when he landed at Haifa. He was dressed too warm for April—so was his wife. I think I know what he felt. Here was Haifa—and everywhere he looked he saw sailors—stevedores—taxi drivers — policemen — merchants — soldiers—truck drivers—newsboys—and they were all Jewish. I think that's what he felt—because that's what I felt when I came from Italy to Israel in 1950—and if I felt it—he did—because—we're both Jewish.
NARRATOR:	The Officer is right. He has reached the thirty-two thousand dollar plateau. Suddenly, as I walked onto the dock, the endless discussions (academic, philosophical and theological) were at an end. I was in Israel. Who could discuss why it was? —should it be? It was here—a pulsing, vibrant nation—and the air swept around us like a *tallis* [1] and we breathed deep.
NEWSPAPERMAN:	(English-Israeli accent) How do you do. My editor asked me to get answers to some questions. Is this your first trip?
NARRATOR:	Yes!
NEWSPAPERMAN:	How long do you plan to stay?
NARRATOR:	Two weeks.
NEWSPAPERMAN:	Not long enough—but better than a week.
NARRATOR:	I want to see as much as possible.

[1] Prayer shawl.

NEWSPAPERMAN:	You'll see more than is possible. Once you start moving—you'll never stop. They won't let you.
NARRATOR:	Who won't?
NEWSPAPERMAN:	Everybody. The U.J.A. people, the government officials, the Bond people, the Israelis—everybody.
NARRATOR:	Well—
NEWSPAPERMAN:	Have a good time. *Shalom, shalom.*
NARRATOR:	Like the policeman, the newspaperman was right. I never stopped—I saw it all—I went by car, by foot, by plane—to cities—*kibbutzim—moshavim—ulpanim,* deserts and ports—villages and resorts—plains and hills and valleys. I saw it all—and it was suddenly and deeply a sentimental journey. In each place I asked and was asked questions.
A LADY:	(South African style) If you were asked to describe Israel in one word, which word would you use?
NARRATOR:	One word?
LADY:	Yes.
NARRATOR:	That's hard.
LADY:	Very.
NARRATOR:	One word?
LADY:	Nu?
NARRATOR:	Vitality.
LADY:	Good. That's a good word.
NARRATOR:	Vitality. Israel fizzes with it. It's like living in a glass of Alka-Seltzer.
LADY:	*Bome-bah!*
NARRATOR:	My Hebrew is not that eloquent. *Mah zeh Bomebah?*
LADY:	*Bomebah* is our word for swell—great—

	sensational—cool. All of those things and more—*Bomebah!*
NARRATOR:	Thank you. Now I'd like to ask you a question. Who is Israel? Not what, but who?
LADY:	That, too, is a hard question.
NARRATOR:	I give you more than one word to answer.
LADY:	Well—
NARRATOR:	Nu?
LADY:	(Slowly at first)
	We are Israel. We who have come here, not because we ran away from anything —but because Israel was here to be lived in. We've brought some talents—some skills—some culture—some money. We're giving Israel a new look.
A MAN:	(With a broad Yiddish accent)
	Excuse me, Lady. We can do without the new look. The old one is good enough for us.
NARRATOR:	And who are you, sir?
MAN:	I am the *chalutz* who came here a long time ago, when that charming South African lady wasn't even born. We came here and plowed the fields of *Ha-Emek*—the plain. We planted the first groves, dreamed the first dreams. Without us, there would be no Palestine—no Israel. That's who I am.
A YOUNG SABRA:	Let the old man talk. The old like to live in the past. But I'll tell you, my old neighbor—*"Al teh-kash-kesh bah—koom —koom."*
NARRATOR:	I beg your pardon?
YOUNG SABRA:	I was addressing him—not you. I said—

"*Al teh-kash-kesh bah—koom—koom.*"
A Hebrew phrase.

NARRATOR: Meaning?

THE MAN: (With the Yiddish accent)
It means, "*Hock mir nisht cane chine-nik.*" [2] That's a Yiddish phrase.

SABRA: And Yiddish is the language of our grandfathers. Don't speak Yiddish— "*Daber Ivrit.*" Speak Hebrew.

THE MAN: Oh, the young are so very snobbish. They wear their Hebrew like a new sports coat. Listen, my young friend, I know Hebrew better than you. After all, I've spoken it for thirty-four years. If you are eighteen you've probably spoken it for sixteen years.

SABRA: I've spoken it for seventeen. I'm bright.

THE MAN: *Chochem!* [3] Listen to me. You are here because of what we put into the earth— into the air—into the ears of men. You breathe because we gave you breath. The Israel you love—we gave you to love.

SABRA: And it is true. What you say is true. But finish the truth. Don't leave the truth unsaid.

MAN: What is unsaid?

A SOLDIER: You know what is unsaid. What of us—
(with red beret)   we young ones who fought in 1948 and in Sinai? Look at the quiet beds of stone in the military cemetery at Mount Herzl. Read the ages on the granite pillows: 13–19–15–18–21–14–17—boys and girls who died fighting for freedom. Take away their guns and their bayonets and they

[2] Literally, "don't bang the kettle," meaning, stop making noise with your prattle.
[3] Smart fellow (wise guy!).

would have continued fighting with hands and teeth. They died to keep your Emek. The Israeli flag is washed pure (blue and white) with their blood. Go to the borders and see their images standing firm. Go into the *kibbutzim* and hear their voices. In the quiet of the Negev night, hear the crack of their rifles and the cries of their voices as they resist the invader. Yes—we, the young who guard the borders and drive the tanks and fly the planes and plow the seas with our warships—we are Israel—because without us there would be no Israel—there would be only the wind blowing over the ruined cities and uprooted earth—there would come only the *chamseen* [4] and the sigh of the shifting sands.

(A PAUSE)

Does that answer the question?

THE MAN WITH THE *SHTRAYMEL*: [5] (He speaks rapidly—with a broad accent) Pouiee!! That's how it answers the question. Pouiee!! *Soldaten!* Soldiers—farmers —Israelis—Pouiee!! They defile the holy tongue, speaking it on street corners, in bars, brothels and banks. *Goyim!* [6] They ride the streets on *Shabbos* [7]—they eat *Trefe* [8]—they go to the *movies,* not to the synagogue. They don't know the difference between *Kiddush* [9] and *Kaddish!!* [10]

[4] Hot east wind.

[5] A fur-rimmed hat.

[6] Hebrew for nations; in yiddish, as used here, has come to mean one who does not observe the religious law.

[7] The Sabbath.

[8] Un-kosher.

[9] Prayer over wine.

[10] Prayer receited by mourner.

A MAN:

(Cultured voice and reasonable)
Hold a moment. Don't laugh. I, too, am an Israeli and I say to you, don't laugh at the man with the *shtraymel*. Sometimes to me, he is irritating and wearisome. As I walk into his synagogues and listen to him pray and sing, I feel as remote as a New Yorker must feel in Tibet. But this man is part of the spine in the body of Israel. He has nurtured "The Book" and "The Word." He has guarded it in ravaged cities and in concentration camps. He is stubborn, but take away his devotion to the faith and will faith remain? Who in Israel will carry his knapsack of religion? Who will live the law and pass it on? Don't laugh, my friends. There is, of course, a nation called Israel, but there is also a faith called Judaism. Can Israel live without Judaism? If it can, will it be the Israel that is in the minds and bones of Jews outside of Israel? Judaism has been a pipeline that has brought a precious ore of truth and ethics into Israel. More, it has brought funds and muscle to Israel. If Judaism diminishes in the Heartland of Israel, will interest in Israel become spavined or varicosed? So hold your smiles at the man with the *shtraymel*. His strong, orthodox hand may be supporting a necessary wall.

SABRA:

We have all listened to these kind of arguments. But we are Israelis and we will create a new kind of Judaism—a Judaism that works for us. We have strong roots in the faith of our fathers, but so much of this faith was written at a time when we were scattered and dispersed. Now we are again a nation and perhaps our religion must be refashioned to these new times. We speak of *changing* dogma—our faith is as hardy as the cactus for which we are named—*sabra*.

NARRATOR: Those were some of the answers, to only one of the questions. Answers came quickly and as you have heard—different answers—moving and stimulating. As they say on television: "The views expressed on this program do not necessarily represent the opinion of the sponsor." I traveled and I listened and heard so many things. There were, for instance, my journeys into the transit camps—*Ma'abarot*. I asked a man—what brought you to Israel?

THE BUTCHER: (Accented speech)

I'll tell you. Some of it makes me ashamed—but I'll tell you. I am a Pole, I ran away from Warsaw before the big trouble. See my face. It is not what is called a Jewish face. I worked in farms and in other cities. I worked for the Russians, and after the war I was free to settle in Poland again. I was married. My name was now Zubriskie, a good Polish name, and my wife—well, she too was Jewish but had kept it a secret. And in 1947 we had a baby—a daughter. She grew up with our name, Zubriskie, and her friends were hand-picked—she didn't have many. Last year when she was nine years old she came home from school crying and her face was scratched. Some children had slapped her and pushed her and called her "Jew"—"dirty Jew." Then I knew that the running and the hiding was of no use. The changing of my name had fooled no one but me. So we came to Israel, with some suitcases, a little money and only a thimbleful of pride. All my life, it seems, I've run—but here in Israel I will run no longer. I will never run again. My name is Katz—not Zubriskie. I am through running. I may die, but I will not run.

NARRATOR: Mr. Katz is a butcher—and now he has also been taught to operate a machine gun. He has strong hands. Now meet one of the new Egyptian refugees whom I met in Bat Yam.

A MAN: (With a soft voice—timid and shocked) Only some months ago I owned two drug stores in Cairo. Two stores. I was doing very well. I am an Egyptian. What am I doing here? Everything I own is in Cairo. What has happened to my two stores? What has happened to me?

NARRATOR: What has happened to you, my friend? The same sad thing that happened to Jews in many lands in many times. I am sorry—but Israel will heal your hurt, restore your senses and fire your courage. Once in a while it takes less time, like with the lady from Alexandria.

EGYPTIAN LADY: How do you do?
(Very smart &
well groomed)

NARRATOR: How do you do? How long have you been here?

EGYPTIAN LADY:	Three weeks. A long time in this bare house.
NARRATOR:	I see you have a sewing machine.
EGYPTIAN LADY:	Yes. I'm a dressmaker. I had a shop in Alexandria.
NARRATOR:	Do you intend to do dressmaking in Israel?
EGYPTIAN LADY:	Of course. I hope one day to have a shop in Tel Aviv. Israeli women lack style in their clothing. When I leave this transit camp I hope to settle in Tel Aviv, take my three children and open a fashionable shop.
NARRATOR:	Where are your children?
EGYPTIAN LADY:	Presently they are in an Ulpan.[11] I miss them very much.
NARRATOR:	I can understand. Where is your husband?
EGYPTIAN LADY:	My husband was killed.
NARRATOR:	When next I visit Israel I'm certain this lady will have a shop—and I'm equally certain it will be a fashionable and popular one. She not only has good taste, but she is indomitable.
	(A MUSIC CHORD IS HEARD)
	Chaim Weizmann said: "A state cannot be created by decree, but by the forces of a people and in the course of generations. Even if all the governments of the world gave us a country, it would only be a gift of words. But if the Jewish people will go and build Palestine, the Jewish state will become a reality—a fact." Well, the Jewish state is a reality—it is a fact—and a

[11] School in Israel giving intensive course in Hebrew language.

YOUNG MAN:

young man in the *kibbutz* said something to me that must be included in this report. I do not know what you mean when you ask if I am a Zionist. I am an Israeli. Tell me, sir, in America do you have an organization pledged to support an American revolution?

NARRATOR: No.

YOUNG MAN: Of course not. Because America won its revolution a long time ago. We do not care if it was a religious or a political mandate that gave us birth. All we know is that we are here—Israel is a fact—it is a nation—it is a reality.

NARRATOR: This is what the young man said to me and then others repeated the same thought. I do not dare interpret this for you. I only report. If you are to know Israel you must hear all that is said. You must listen to all the attitudes, because knowing Israel is knowing more than how many arable acres and how many people fill the land.

(THE ORCHESTRA PLAYS
A SAD POLISH SONG)

One day we visited Yad Mordecai—a *kibbutz* near the Gaza Strip. In 1948 this thriving *kibbutz* was overrun by the invaders, who blew up a concrete water tower on the brow of the hill. The Israelis recaptured the *kibbutz*, rebuilt it, replowed it, replanted it. It is today a place of verdant beauty. On the hill they have left the wreckage of the destroyed water tower, but next to it they have erected a figure of Mordecai—of the Warsaw Ghetto. He stands there—a proud figure in bronze—his garments are rent, his right fist is clenched and in his left hand he holds a grenade. He is a symbol of defiance and of strength. Yad Mordecai is more than a memorial to Mordecai; it is a memorial to the unquenchable spirit of Jewish people everywhere, who have either endured or fought against the plague of bigotry.

(THE MUSIC IS OUT)

Near this place is another *kibbutz* called Eretz. On the way to Eretz we met a young girl. Her name was Anata. She was seventeen.

ANATA: Are you new to Israel?

NARRATOR: Yes, we are visiting from America.

ANATA: How long are you staying?

NARRATOR: About two or three weeks.

ANATA: What can you see or learn in two or three weeks? You should stay a year.

NARRATOR: We don't have the time.

ANATA: You must make time. How often have you been here?

NARRATOR: This is our first trip to Israel.

ANATA: Only the first time? What have you been doing?

NARRATOR: Well, well—

ANATA: Are you coming here to live?

NARRATOR: No.

ANATA: I've heard many things about America.

NARRATOR: Would you like to live in America?

ANATA: No—this is my country. I was born here.

NARRATOR: You see, Anata, America is my country. I was born there.

ANATA: Well, perhaps one day I shall come to visit you.

NARRATOR:	That would be a pleasure.
ANATA:	But it will be a long time before I can go. I have much to do in Israel. We all have much to do.
NARRATOR:	Much to do. Everywhere you go you hear the same litany—"much to do." In the Galilee where they are reclaiming marshlands and turning them into sweeping fields of cotton—in Beersheba where the ground, once brown, now yields to immense carpets of green. Beersheba—in 1948 a Bedouin trading post of twenty-five hundred persons and now a metropolis of forty-five thousand. Beersheba—with the look of a Texas oil town—white and green and shiny—the heart of the Negev —and surrounding it, deposits of manganese, phosphate, iron ore, gypsum, copper, salt, granite and potash. But—like everywhere else in Israel—the most valuable resource is in the will of the people. You are all familiar with the old argument as to which came first—the chicken or the egg. I wonder if there isn't a like argument to be posed in connection with people and cities. Does the character of the city make the people—or do the characters of the people make the city? Let us take a look at some Israeli cities as seen by the people. We begin the roll call near the Sea of Galilee.
A MAN: (Thin, and with a small goatee and moustache)	I live in Safed. I'm an artist. Safed is a city built on hills. It is old—its streets worn with the footfalls of centuries. It is cool in Safed. An easy hour's ride from Safed is Tiberias, built by an ancient Ro-

man emperor who sought surcease from the ache in his bones in this lovely, warm spot on the Sea of Galilee. So the citizens of Safed and Tiberias have a pleasant working arrangement: in winter when it is cold in Safed we go to Tiberias. In summer when it is hot in Tiberias everyone comes to Safed. A working arrangement that makes sense economically. Both our cities are proud of their artists' colonies. We are proud, too, of the history that folds around us. We can see the Gilboa Hills. From these hills Goliath strode to meet an unglamorous end at the hands of a boy named David. From our mountains we can see the Huleh Basin, where the magic of newly reclaimed, fertile acres is taking place. And there are a lot of other things to see in the area where we live. Let a Christian friend speak for that.

(OVER THE NEXT SPEECH
THE ORCHESTRA PLAYS
A HYMN)

ANOTHER MAN: I traveled in Israel and spent time in the Galilee. I saw the Mount where Jesus preached His sermon. I stood by the waters where the Miracle of the Fishes and Loaves took place. I walked through Nazareth. I walked into the Franciscan Church on Mount Tabor—the scene of the Transfiguration. I stood outside the Church of the Annunciation and at Saint Mary's Well. I walked in the Jordan Valley and up the tan and violet hills of Galilee. I trod the Hattin Hills, where Crusaders died under the scimitars of the

Saracens. I was in Jerusalem, the City of
Peace. Part of Israel belongs to me. I
cherish it.

(THE MUSIC IS OUT)

NARRATOR: Let us move back to the coast for another
look at Haifa. This modern seaport, with
beautiful homes dotting the hills with
views that fill the eye everywhere you
turn—Haifa, the deep seaport that hums
with the traffic from many nations. Haifa
—with its views of Mount Carmel, the
vineyard of the Lord. And then from
Haifa, travel through the vale of Sharon
—past the ruins of Caesaria—past the
ma'abarot and *kibbutzim* that dot the
shoreline—past the new *kibbutz* at Ein
Hod—and then into the bustling, busy,
busy city of Tel Aviv, which is ever
building—ever fizzing. Tel Aviv, with its
Brooklyn coffee bars, its pizza stands,
expresso bars and German coffee houses.
Here you sense the twentieth century
urgency that pulses through this ancient
land. The traffic bustles through the
streets and new apartment houses deco-
rate the landscape. Neon signs mark the
night sky with green and yellow and red.
In Tel Aviv I met a teacher whom I
would like you to meet. He will convince
you in one easy lesson why you should
study Hebrew.

HEBREW TEACHER: Hebrew is a ridiculously easy language—
(A youngish man   you can learn it rapidly.
very breezy and   *"Lo"* is "no."
vibrant)   *"Ken"* is "yes."
                       "Shalom" is "hello." Also it is "Goodbye."

Also "peace." See how simple? There is
much Hebrew in English: shibboleth—
Sabbath — cherubic — bedlam — check-
mate—seraphim—abot. See what a headstart you have? And the speaking is
also so easy. You accent the last syllable
—you articulate each sound. Do not slur
the sounds and Hebrew comes like a
tide. Further, all Americans who wish to
speak have a headstart: Telephone—
aspirin — sandwich — banana — punc-
ture — okay — jeep — taxi — soda — cot-
tage. These mean the same in Israel as
they do in America. Do you know any
Yiddish? Then you have another headstart. Meshuga is Meshug*ah!* Balabass—
Balabeye-it! Neshumah — N'-sha-*mah!*
Some forty percent of Yiddish is Hebrew
—with a different accent, that's all.
Milchumah, Sheeva, Chalah, Chazan,
Kallah, Sechel, Mayvin, Cholem, Mazel-
tov, Kosher, Mishpocha, Bocher—where
do you think these words came from—
New Zealand? Hebrew! Believe me, it is
so simple— *Li* is me— *Me* is who— *Who*
is he— *He* is she—what could be clearer?

NARRATOR: I'm with you every step of the way—

HEBREW TEACHER: All you have to do is begin. Hebrew is a
living language. Does it have a literature?
The Bible! That's to begin with—and
whatever is in between is also excellent,
but also at the end—The Bible! Who has
written better? *Tov?*

NARRATOR: *Ken, Tov.* Good. I say, *tov m'od*—very
good. *Metzuyan! Meya Achooz! Batuach!*
Bi-vadai! Bomebah! B'seder! B'deeyuk!

HEBREW TEACHER: There, you see, there are so many Hebrew ways of expressing approval. Believe me, in twenty lessons you will be able to order breakfast.

NARRATOR: Thank you. My dear friends, what you have heard is *very* Israel. Is there a language to be learned; is there a bridge to be spanned; a city to be built; a marshland to be drained; a plain to be plowed; a desert to make bloom? All this can be done—is done—and you are sure you can do it with them. They have in Israel a contagious confidence. You soon become accustomed to the borders of hostile nations that ring the land island of Israel. Because there are things to be done—so very much, you can't think of hostility. And one task completed only means that work on the next one can begin.

(A MUEZZIN CALL IS HEARD)

That which you hear is what I heard as I stood on a balcony of the Hotel King David in Jerusalem. It comes over the narrow stretch of No Man's Land that separates the walled city from the new city. You will stand on the balcony and be told not to move—not to point. Because you are being watched by a man in Jordan who eyes you with the sight of his rifle. If you appear to him to be too curious (perhaps a military spotter), he will shoot.

THE
NEWSPAPERMAN: So, don't point.

NARRATOR: I won't.

THE
NEWSPAPERMAN: Are you frightened?

NARRATOR: Not really.

THE
NEWSPAPERMAN: Why not?

NARRATOR: It's so out of fashion in Israel.

THE
NEWSPAPERMAN: I'm delighted we meet again. Having a good time? Seeing the country?

NARRATOR: Yes—yes.

THE
NEWSPAPERMAN: Jerusalem is my city. It has a texture in the air. Come inside, so I can talk. When I talk I sometimes move my hands and I should not like to be shot in the middle of a pretty phrase.

NARRATOR: It would be a fatal wound for a poet.

THE
NEWSPAPERMAN: Indeed. Now about Jerusalem. Chaim Weizmann once said: "The air in Jerusalem is the clearest in the world. Through it you can see two thousand years." This is true. Everywhere you tour, history envelops you. This is the land of the prophets and the kings. But it saddens me to think that this city, whose name means City of Peace, has been the unhappy site of countless battles. This Holy Land, the fountainhead of three great religions that speak of peace, is surrounded by tortured earth and hills soaked with the blood of Arabs, Crusaders, Jews—with the blood of Allenby's Englishmen and Turks and fighters of the Haganah.

NARRATOR: On the way here, I saw the wreckage of
                        armored cars destroyed during the fight-
                        ing in 1948. They seemed freshly painted.

THE
NEWSPAPERMAN: Yes, we leave them where they fell as re-
                        minders. Keeping them painted is like
                        painting our minds to keep the images
                        fresh.

NARRATOR: Tell me, friend, when will this City of
                        Peace find peace?

THE
NEWSPAPERMAN: I am a reporter—not a prophet. Perhaps
                        the peace we seek will come when our
                        neighbors drive hate from their hearts. We
                        talk today as we have talked for years in
                        the United Nations about the Arab refu-
                        gees from Palestine—but our words fall
                        on ears plugged with prejudice.

A VOICE: (Hard and incisive)
                        I listen and my stomach turns. There is
                        only one thing the Arab understands—
                        force.

NARRATOR: Whose voice was that?

THE
NEWSPAPERMAN: The voice of some. But most pray that
                        we will not have to fight again. War
                        costs money and deprives us of tractors
                        and bricks and farms and of man hours
                        that are forever lost. And we pray that
                        the enemy does not pile death at our bor-
                        ders. Israel, you must understand, wishes
                        to remain free. We are a democracy.

NARRATOR: I know. You wear your freedom proudly.

THE
NEWSPAPERMAN: Why not? It is so new and shining. You

Americans must have worn it as proudly after your war of independence.

NARRATOR: Yes—I'm certain of that.

THE
NEWSPAPERMAN: Yes, we wear our freedom proudly—we Israelis—wear it as it must have been worn by George Washington and Patrick Henry and Thomas Jefferson and as it has been worn since by you Americans who have defended your freedom and fought for it ever since it was won at Yorktown. When a nation is born it is harrassed by the problems of living in a big world. It has growing pains and is often set upon by the bullies in the neighborhood. So every new nation learns to fight because it must fight—not because it wishes to. But do not be misled. There is in Israel poetry and music and painting and reflection and beauty.

NARRATOR: I'm aware of that. I have seen much of beauty—

THE
NEWSPAPERMAN: We'll meet again. *Shalom, shalom.*

NARRATOR: When I left Jerusalem I knew I would be forever conscious of its haunting beauty —and that it would be within me. The *n'shomah* of Israel—the soul of the nation —is in Jerusalem.

(THE SOUND OF THE HORRA IS HEARD AND THE VOICES CONTINUE WITH THE CLAPPING AND COMMANDS OF THE SONG)

That is some of the music of Israel. I

heard that one Sabbath night at the *kibbutz* of the Survivors of the Warsaw Ghetto Fighters. Before the Sabbath we had visited their museum. We saw the cakes of soap made of Jewish flesh, hair (for mattresses) taken from Jewish heads; we saw the yellow identification badges and the arm bands and the horror of the photographs taken from that bloody fight made us wince and then brought sudden tears. We walked out of the darkness of the museum into the light of the evening and the sun was still in the sky—and the green and the life of this *kibbutz* was a stunning contrast. An Israeli flag flew from a flagpole. This was a dramatic illustration of what Israel had done. It had taken the Star of David from a shameful arm band and placed it proudly on a flag of honor. We enjoyed that Sabbath night.

(THE MUSIC OF THE HORRA
DWINDLES AWAY)

We have spent some time hearing something of Israel, its cities and its people, but there is more—of places and people. May I introduce some of my friends to you? Our good friend Benny Budensky who—

WIFE'S VOICE: A moment please. You've forgotten to mention me.

NARRATOR: My dear, forgive me. My wife—

WIFE: Who hadn't wanted to go to Israel. But now I only ask, when do we go again? I don't want to live there—I want only to bring some of its energy and enthusiasm and excitement with me—like people bring back perfume and art and clothes and automobiles from Europe. Israel's chief exports now are rare commodities, cheap in price, but invaluable—they are spirit—dash—enthusiasm. I'm starting a collection.

NARRATOR: Thank you, my darling. May I continue, or would you like to carry out the introductions?

WIFE: I'd love to. First, our very dear friend and guide, Benny Budensky. He speaks seven languages but is self-conscious and apologizes for incorrectly pronouncing "euphemism." Mr. Budensky.

BUDENSKY: Thank you. You are too generous. What is it you would like me to say?

WIFE: I know you are by nature reticent, but what we would like to hear are some vital statistics.

BUDENSKY: Vital statistics? Well—I was born in Russia. I came to Palestine in 1938. I am married and have two children—*sabras.* In World War II, I was part of the Jewish Brigade that fought for the British. During 1947 I found myself fighting for Haganah against the British. In 1948 I fought as an Israeli against the Arabs. I will always remain here.
(HE PAUSES)
Is that vital enough?

WIFE: It isn't really—but that's all Mr. Budensky will tell you. The land of Israel is as familiar to him as his hands. He can speak to you articulately about archaeology, ancient history, contemporary art and philosophy. He also has a very nice singing voice. Now I should like you to meet Mr.

Allen Mayol. Mr. Mayol is a South African.

MR. MAYOL: (WHOSE VOICE IS QUITE
BRITISH)
I came to Israel in 1949. The reasons that impelled me here are, I am certain, familiar to all of you. Many of us from South Africa have interests in the Afridar Company, which is concerned with the building of the new city at Ashkelon. I, for one, would never think of living anywhere else but in Israel.

WIFE: Mr. Mayol should have included the fact that he is a consul from the State of Israel and that he has a daughter who is an expert radar technician in the army. May I now present Miss Kallarah, an artist from Safed.

MISS KALLARAH: I have studied and painted in France, in America, in Italy—but I have found in the air and in the color of Israel something that suits me quite well. Also in Safed, I must say, the noise of traffic is not a burden and the cost of living is quite in tune with what I earn.

WIFE: Miss Kallarah paints very well. If you are ever in Safed, I should remind you all her pictures are for sale. Another one of our friends is Mr. Jack Berlin, an architect.

JACK BERLIN: I am from Newark, New Jersey. I like being in Israel. While there is much of the old to see, there is so much room for the new to be built. Also, for reasons I do not know, my allergies have all left me. I plan to stay.

WIFE:

Thank you. Another friend whom we particularly want you to meet is Mr. Shlomo Rosen, the owner of a small hotel we visited.

SHLOMO ROSEN:

I was born here. I like the hotel business. It's the only business I have ever known and it is all I have done with the exception of some fighting I had to do in 1947 and then in 1948. I don't like fighting, but I had to do it—because they were shooting at my hotel—and I don't like people who destroy property. If you are ever in my neighborhood I'd love to be your host. We have nice rooms and very simple *hamish* —food.

NARRATOR:

It occurs to me that there are other places we visited that I must tell you of: an old folks' home—a refuge for the old and tired souls who, however, were still gainfully employed making dresses, suits, rag dolls and girdles. We heard from these people the same dreadful stories of abuse, torment and torture in Germany, Poland, Russia or Yemen—the same tragic tales of husbands and sons and brothers who fell in battle—of relatives drowned trying to break the blockade in 1947. But in this home was peace at last for their declining years. And then to the other end of the pole—the Youth Aliyah Settlement House. Here, hundreds of immigrant children from four to fourteen learn their Alephs, Bets, Gimmels, and from here they go to the *kibbutzim* to become farmers and engineers and students and factory workers. A word now about Israeli children: from one who should know—a schoolteacher.

A WOMAN
SCHOOLTEACHER:
(A dark-skinned
Yemenite)

A visitor to Israel once asked me, quite seriously: "Where do you hide your ugly children?" I understood what she meant because what impresses all visitors to Israel is our children. There is something about them that we personally do not give them—it is something they breathe in from the climate in which they live. We guard our children because they are, without a doubt, our most precious resource. And it is true that as a group they are happy, secure, healthy and beautiful. I explained this to our visitor, but she shook her head and again asked: "Where do you hide your ugly children?" So I did not try to answer her again.

NARRATOR:

Thank you.

(A LONG ROLL OF DRUMS AND
A BLARE OF TRUMPETS)

In 1897 Theodor Herzl wrote this in his diary: "At Basle I founded the Jewish State. If I were to say this today, I would be met by universal laughter. In five years, perhaps, and certainly in fifty, everyone will see it." Herzl was proved right—fifty-one years later the world saw the State of Israel—and now almost ten years since its birth it is a bouncing and muscular child in the family of nations. Travel if you will to the Port of Elath and see a new city building on the tip of the Negev. Return a week later and it has grown. Return a year later and your footsteps are covered by cement walks, buildings, docks and roads. Go over this new State, north to south, west to east, and fill your eyes with these wonders. The war took one university—they built another one—at Givat Ran. See Boystown with a Hebrew accent—the quarries at Castell, the Phoenica glass works, the Accadia Hotel, the ancient Philistine city of Ashkelon, the mosques at Acre—and the ever-present kerosene vendors with the peripatetic donkeys and "Shell" painted on the carts in Hebrew. Listen to the magnificent orchestra and see the paintings. And Israel has a peculiar, though not necessarily praiseworthy distinction—there is no Coca Cola. You drink Tempo—much like Seven Up.

A VOICE: You through talking?

NARRATOR: Not quite. Why?

A VOICE: When do you get to us?

NARRATOR: Right now. I was about to make my transition.

VOICE: I'll *shenk* you the transition. Come on, I'm in a hurry.

NARRATOR: Man in a hurry. One-phrase description of the gentleman who runs the Weizmann Institute in Rohovoth—Meyer Weisgal. We were Meyer Weisgal's guests at San Martin. This meant complete exposure to his dynamics. He is funny, kind, fractious, irritable, volatile and energetic. He swoons with fatigue and then is off like a whirlwind. He asks you to *kvetch* his arthritic finger and then slaps it on a desk as he bemoans the two-second delay of a phone call.

VOICE: Nu? I'm waiting.

NARRATOR: Very well. Ladies and Gentlemen—The Weizmann Institute! Come with me first to the tomb of this illustrious Jew and see the simple beauty of his final resting place, where he lies surrounded by all he loved so dearly. His orange groves—his stands of trees—his laboratories—his classrooms —his home and his land. The first President of Israel rests peacefully, and thousands each month come in a quiet pilgrimage to pay homage. It is only some hundreds of yards walk to the Institute itself, where the miracles of science are being forged by eager and brilliant minds.

1ST PROFESSOR: On behalf of my colleagues, thank you for the compliment.

NARRATOR: Would you be good enough to talk to us about one of your projects?

1ST PROFESSOR: We carry out research in over eighty projects in more than a dozen departments and sections in various fields of physics, chemistry and biology—about which one of these would you like to hear?

NARRATOR: Pick a number.

1ST PROFESSOR: Well, would you be interested in knowing that in the area of plastics, apart from industrial types, we are presently working with compounds that can contract and expand in a manner corresponding to the action of muscular tissue?

NARRATOR:	I'm interested, though I'm not sure I understand.
1ST PROFESSOR:	Or in the field of biophysics, you might care to hear of another scientist's work which taught us that anthrax, observed under a microscope, surrounded by white blood cells, actually engages in chemical warfare with these cells. This is leading into a new pharmacology which may be as revolutionary as Ehrlich's work—and perhaps will lead us to produce synthetically the very substances which the human body itself manufactures in combatting its disease-bearing invaders. Interesting?
NARRATOR:	Go on, Professor.
1ST PROFESSOR:	There is, of course, our work in cancer which deals with research into the causative mechanisms of cancer.
NARRATOR:	We pray that work goes well.
1ST PROFESSOR:	We are hopeful. Then—our Isotope Department has developed a process which makes it the world's only source of high quality heavy oxygen. Of this we are rather proud.
NARRATOR:	Professor—keep right on going.
1ST PROFESSOR:	Then, in atomic research, we have learned how to separate uranium from phosphates—so obtaining a stockpile of fissionable material for peaceful work in the atomic age.
NARRATOR:	Shall I say I'm overwhelmed?
1ST PROFESSOR:	Let me contribute to your state of being overwhelmed. Soon we will have, at the Weizmann Institute, an International Conference on Nuclear Structure, under

	the auspices of the United Nations and the International Union of Pure and Applied Physics. This means that our research in nuclear physics is being recognized.
NARRATOR:	Anything else?
VOICE:	Anything else? What do you want—more miracles?
NARRATOR:	I meant—anything else I didn't know.
2ND PROFESSOR:	What is it you do know, sir, about our work?
NARRATOR:	Well—I was told that—
2ND PROFESSOR:	Some of our work is top secret, remember.
NARRATOR:	May I say that the Institute has an electronic computer as fast as the one at Princeton University?
2ND PROFESSOR:	You may.
NARRATOR:	Can I say that at the time I was there the computer was engaged in a problem for the United States Navy and—
2ND PROFESSOR:	No. You can't say what the problem was.
NARRATOR:	How could I? I don't know what the problem was. I was going to say that when I was there the man engaged in feeding the machine was a young mathematician who was wearing a skull cap.
2ND PROFESSOR:	That's not top secret.
NARRATOR:	Thank you. Finally, they are completing their new physics building, which is the most modern one in the world.
2ND PROFESSOR:	Well, *one* of the most modern. Being a scientist, I deal only in the certainties.
NARRATOR:	Never—never—in the uncertainties?
2ND PROFESSOR:	Only if they can be proved to be certain. Is there something else you would like to say about the Institute—not top secret?

NARRATOR:	This I can say. It is not top secret. It is a certainty. The Institute is one of the finest research laboratories in the world; its staff is a collection of some of the most brilliant scientists in the world; it is a credit to Israel, to the world, to the human race.
2ND PROFESSOR:	I thank you. Perhaps you have overstated the case but—
VOICE:	Professor—please go back to your lab and let my friend and me do the talking.
NARRATOR: (To Voice)	All right?
VOICE:	You understand it—but it was okay. *Tov m'od*.
NARRATOR:	Not *bomebah?*
VOICE:	(reluctantly) All right, already. *Bomebah*.
NARRATOR:	(A ROLL OF DRUMS. IT CONTINUES SOFTLY) We must go now. It is *Yom Ha-atz-ma-oot!* The Day of Independence! We are in Tel Aviv. Israel, as you heard, has one million, eight hundred thousand people. In Tel Aviv this day, there are one million. The others guard the borders, tend the dynamos, run the railroads and water the fields. They have come here, this million, by bus, auto, truck, cart, donkey, horseback, bicycle and motorcycle—and by foot. They cram the streets and cheer each flight of jets that fly overhead. The flags dance in the breeze that blows in from the sea (the warm *chamseen* has fled into the Negev). The parade is scheduled to begin at ten-fifteen A.M. The parade is run by the Army which runs by a sec-

ond hand. I submit that any organization that can get a million Jews to start on time is quite an organization. But before the parade of troops and captured war booty sweeps by in shining and proud and straight ranks—a military band appears—

(The drums now change their beat. They move into a marching cadence. Then there is sudden silence.)

The conductor raises his baton. The streets are still.

(A pause)

Then the baton flashes the down beat.

(The band begins—a brass band arrangement, strong and vibrant of *Hatikvah*. They play one magnificent chorus.)

I had heard *Hatikvah* played many times here in America at Jewish affairs. That was the first time I heard it played in Israel. And for the first time I saw part of a million people who listened to it as a National Anthem. When it was over, everyone cheered—they had already cried.

(THE ORCHESTRA SOFTLY BEGINS "SENTIMENTAL JOURNEY")

The journey was at an end. We went to other places after Israel—to Greece, Italy, France and England. Much of what we saw we loved—but of all we saw we loved Israel the most, probably because it meant the most. Before we left I saw my newspaper friend at the airport.

NEWSPAPERMAN: Well, journey's end?

NARRATOR: Yes. It's been wonderful.

NEWSPAPERMAN: What about us? Do we have a chance?

NARRATOR: Good God, no one in Israel asked me that.

NEWSPAPERMAN: Some of us think it.

NARRATOR: (PAUSE)

You have a chance. If you fall—human society falls. In a world bursting with the emergence of new nations, your nation must have a chance or else they will all fall. Truly, if the bell ever tolls for thee—it shall toll for me.

NEWSPAPERMAN: Have a good trip home. Come back. *Shalom, shalom.*

(THE MUSIC IS OUT)

NARRATOR: And my wife said to me on the plane, "Write of what you have seen and felt and heard. Write it." One day, I promised her, I will; and now I have tried to do so. *Shalom,* my good friends—*L'hit-ra'ot!* To my friends in Israel: may God keep you well and strong and just, and patient and wise and brave. To all Israelis, young and old, *L'chaim—Bomebah!*

ALL THE VOICES: Bomebah! Bomebah! Bomebah!

(THE ORCHESTRA SOUNDS A LONG AND TRIUMPHANT CHORD)

CURTAIN

LIST OF CONTRIBUTORS

Moshe Davis—Provost and Professor of American Jewish History, The Jewish Theological Seminary of America; Visiting Director of The Institute of Contemporary Jewry, The Hebrew University (1959–61)

Mitchell Fields—Sculptor; Associate, National Academy of Design

Zino Francescatti—Concert Violinist

Waldo Frank—Author, Lecturer

Simon Greenberg—Vice Chancellor and Professor of Homiletics and Education, President of the University of Judaism, The Jewish Theological Seminary of America

Leon H. Keyserling—Former Chairman, President's Council of Economic Advisors; Consulting Economist and Attorney; President, The Conference on Economic Progress

Philip Klutznick—President, The American Friends of The Hebrew University; Honorary President, B'nai Brith

Walter Clay Lowdermilk—Pioneer Founder of the United States Soil Conservation Service; International Advisor on Soil Conservation and Land Development Problems

Bernard Mandelbaum—Provost and Associate Professor of Homiletics, The Jewish Theological Seminary of America

Samuel Lyman Atwood Marshall—Brigadier General, U.S. Army; Chief Editorial Writer and Military Analyst, The Detroit News

Theodore McKeldin—Former Governor of Maryland, Attorney at Law

Margaret Mead—Associate Curator of Ethnology, the American Museum of Natural History; Adjunct Professor of Anthropology, Columbia University

James A. Pike—Bishop of the Diocese of California of the Protestant Episcopal Church

JAMES S. PLAUT—Director Emeritus, Institute of Contemporary Art, Boston; Deputy U.S. Commissioner General, Brussels World Fair, 1958

DORE SCHARY—Producer, Writer

ROBERT ST. JOHN—Foreign Correspondent, Author, Lecturer

ANNA SOKOLOW—American Modern Dancer, Choreographer

GLOSSARY

(in addition to the footnotes accompanying each chapter, the terms which follow appear throughout the volume)

Halutz—pioneer settler of Israel
  Halutzim—plural of *halutz*
Hora—Israeli folk-dance, originating in the Balkans
Kibbutz—collective agricultural settlement
  Kibbutzim—plural of *kibbutz*
  "Kibbutznik"—member of a *kibbutz* (colloquial)
Kvutzah—now the same as *kibbutz;* originally, the *kvutzah* maintained a policy of limited maximum membership to ensure a sense of mutual participation
  Kvutzoth—plural of *kvutzah*
Mitzvah—commandment, precept
"Patch Tanz"—Jewish wedding dance (*patch*—clap, *tanz*—dance)
Sabra—native-born Israeli
Tallit—prayer-shawl
Tefillin—passages of Scripture in calfskin cases, which male worshippers place on the forehead and left arm for weekday morning prayers (usually translated: phylacteries)
Ulpan—a type of school in Israel, offering an intensive course in the Hebrew language

INDEX